251-

12/69

THE BRITISH BUDGETARY SYSTEM

SIR HERBERT BRITTAIN

KCB, KBE

The British
Budgetary System

Ruskin House

GEORGE ALLEN & UNWIN LTD

MUSEUM STREET LONDON

FIRST PUBLISHED IN 1959
SECOND IMPRESSION 1960

PRINTED IN GREAT BRITAIN
in 10 *on* 11 *pt Times type*
BY SIMSON SHAND LTD
LONDON, HERTFORD AND HARLOW

PREFACE

OTHERS besides myself have felt for some time that there is room for a new comprehensive account of our budgetary system and of the parliamentary and administrative arrangements that are part of it. For the last forty years *The System of National Finance* by Lord Kennet and Mr Norman Young has filled that role, and its three editions testified to the welcome it received and to its lasting qualities. It may seem rash to follow in its wake with a rather different volume on the same subject. But, while so much of the system has come unscathed through the test of time, some important aspects of it have greatly changed during and since the Second World War: for example, the wider economic significance now attached to the Budget; and the increasingly large part which the Exchequer plays in financing capital development in the country. Changes such as these are my reasons for offering this account of the budgetary system in its modern setting. Having worked within the system for nearly forty years, I cannot write with Lord Kennet's detachment; and I envy him the easy grace of his exposition. I shall be happy if this book is even partly as useful as his has been to legislators, administrators, students and the general public.

In so complicated a field—in which many strands of the subject are closely interwoven with each other—it has not been easy to design the best pattern of treatment. Should one start with the individual items and the procedure, departmental and parliamentary, by which they are prepared and built up together into the picture of the finished Budget? Or should one start with a broader picture of the final product of Budget Day and then break it down into detail? Chronologically the finished Budget follows consideration of the details; but its broad aim and direction are known all the time. On the whole, it seemed best to take something like the second of the above courses. If we have been forewarned of the broader considerations which may move a Chancellor of the Exchequer in deciding the general lines of his Budget, we shall be more able to appreciate the significance and relative importance of the individual items and the parts they can play in any given circumstances. It will be understood that the amounts of space devoted to the different aspects of the subject are not intended to signify relative importance: they mainly reflect complexities.

Another question has been how far, in a book which aims to describe a system, current figures should be quoted. Some use of figures has seemed necessary and useful to give the reader a due sense of proportion in considering the different items which enter into the Budget and into either side of the Exchequer account. In five or ten years' time the figures, and even the broad relations between some of them, will certainly be different. But, if anyone is reading this book then, it will be illuminating for him to note the difference and to discover why they have arisen.

This account is primarily descriptive and expository and it is written by an ex-administrator. There are no doubt many points in it that cry aloud for economists, politicians, City financial experts or others to pursue them further: for example, the pros and cons in given circumstances of this or that broad economic policy, which is here only noticed as one of the possibilities that any Chancellor may have to consider; or the economic or political theory of taxation and of the use that should be made of particular taxes. It is not for this book to offer guidance in such fields, which I leave to those I have just mentioned.

There are a number of points in the structure and administration of our budgetary system which have provoked, and will no doubt continue to provoke, criticism—though I think it is fair to say that such criticism has always been both spasmodic and sporadic. Where I have touched on such a point I have normally confined my comments to what I conceive to be the justification for existing practice. Apart from anything else, considerations of space have prevented me from dealing with such radical proposals as were contained in Professor J. R. Hicks's *The Problem of Budgetary Reform* (1948) or with some of the more restricted matters dealt with in the Report of the Committee on the Form of Government Accounts, 1950 (Cmd 7969).

Again, the Radcliffe Committee on the Monetary System is still sitting. Their field is a different one, though in many respects closely related. Quite apart from the recommendations they may make and the action which may be taken on them, the Committee's Report and the evidence to be published with it may well contain material, not at present publicly available, which will be very welcome to those interested in the subject of this book. But, while such material may supplement certain passages, I do not think it can invalidate anything I have written about current practice.

In conclusion, I must add two observations of a personal nature. First, having held a responsible position in Her Majesty's Treasury, I must make it clear that where I have strayed from pure description into interpretation or comment I do not purport to express what may at any time have been official views on the points under discussion. The interpretations and comments are put forward for myself alone.

Secondly, I should like to acknowledge a great debt to all those friends in the Civil Service and others who have helped me with facts—though only such as any member of the public can obtain—and with much useful advice. I must mention especially the tireless and generous help given to me by Sir Edmund Compton and several other ex-colleagues in the Treasury. Outside the Treasury I am indebted for much good advice given by Sir Henry Hancock and Sir James Crombie, the Chairmen respectively of the Board of Inland Revenue and the Board of Customs and Excise; the late Sir Frank Tribe, when Comptroller and Auditor-General; Mr P. J. Curtis, Secretary of the Exchequer and Audit Department; Sir Harry Campion, Director of the Central Statistical Office; some good friends at the Bank of England; and Mr Ralph Turvey, of the London School of Economics and Political Science. I must also thank the Controller of HM Stationery Office for permission to reproduce material from official publications. For the final shape and contents of the book, whether in fact or comment, the responsibility is of course mine alone.

H. B.

High Halden, Kent
September 1958

CONTENTS

INTRODUCTORY NOTE

The Exchequer and the Consolidated Fund

IT may be useful at the outset to explain two terms, one or other of which we shall meet at almost every turn, namely, 'The Exchequer' and the 'Consolidated Fund'.

THE EXCHEQUER

This dates from the time of King Henry I, when he collected around him a small group of administrators selected from the baronage and the clergy. When it sat for financial purposes this body constituted the Exchequer (*Scaccarium*). The name came from the chequered cloth which covered their table and which simplified the counting of money. In course of time the Exchequer separated into two parts with different functions—the Upper Exchequer (or Exchequer of Account), which sat as a Court of Law to hear cases relating to the royal revenues and also supervised the audit of the accounts of the revenues; and the Lower Exchequer (or Exchequer of Receipt) which was an administrative group of officials responsible for collecting the revenues and for making payments out of them for the King's purposes. The Court of the Exchequer maintained its separate existence until late in the nineteenth century when it became, in the first place, a Division of the High Court and finally, in 1880, lost its identity by being merged in the new Queen's Bench Division of the High Court.

The functions of the Exchequer naturally changed as the Crown relinquished to Parliament the right to impose taxation and the right to control expenditure out of the public revenues. From being a department wholly responsible to the Sovereign it gradually became, after 1688, responsible on its account side to Parliament, with the special function of ensuring that no payments were made out of public money without the express authority of Parliament. This function has since 1866 been exercised by the Comptroller and Auditor-General.[1] He is independent of the Government and is answerable only to the House of Commons. On this Exchequer side of his functions he succeeded to the duties of the 'Comptroller-General of the receipt and issue of the Exchequer'.

In the meantime the Treasury, developing out of the administrative functions of the Exchequer, had retained responsibility for the management of the public revenues and the charges on them, and in

[1] See page 257.

the course of time had built up for itself a position of considerable influence and control. As its full name ('Her Majesty's Treasury') implies, it remains responsible to the Crown; it is part of the executive Government and occupies a central and (in finance) a controlling position therein.[1] It is quite distinct from the Exchequer side of the Exchequer and Audit Department. The Treasury displays its ancestry in the fact that the revenues which it administers and which are the modern equivalent of the royal revenues administered by the old Exchequer, are received into 'Her Majesty's Exchequer'. But its use of these revenues is, as we shall see, subject to a check by the Comptroller and Auditor-General (through the Exchequer branch of his Department) to see that it conforms to the relevant parliamentary authorities.

THE CONSOLIDATED FUND

This has a much shorter history, for it was inaugurated in 1787. For a long time after Parliament secured the right to impose taxation the agreed taxes were earmarked to finance particular items of expenditure. Thus, until 1787, many different items of expenditure were charged directly on the Customs Revenue; the militia charges were paid from the Land Tax; certain hereditary annuities were met from the Post Office revenue. A Commission appointed in 1780 to review the general arrangements for the receipt and spending of public moneys—the 'Commissioners of Public Accounts'—drew attention to the disadvantages of such a system and recommended that there should be set up 'one fund into which shall flow every stream of public revenue and from which shall issue the supply for every service'. Effect was given to this recommendation over a large part of the field by the Customs and Excise Act, 1787, which provided that the several duties of Customs, Excise, Stamps and many more should be 'carried to, and constitute a Fund, to be called "The Consolidated Fund",' and which then directed that all public annuities should be payable out of the Consolidated Fund.

Subsequent Acts extended the process of concentrating the public revenues in this central fund and of charging payments on it. The Act of 1787 itself is no longer in force, having been repealed by the Statute Law Revision Act of 1871. The existing authority for the Consolidated Fund is, in fact, the Consolidated Fund Act, 1816, which, as part of the process of giving effect to the Union of Great Britain and Ireland, merged the parallel Consolidated Funds of the

---

[1] Parliament, in the interests of its own control, attaches great importance to Treasury control within the Executive. See page 214.

two countries into one 'Consolidated Fund of the United Kingdom'[1] which was to receive the revenues previously flowing into the two separate Funds and to meet the charges previously met from them.

As we shall see later, every item of expenditure out of the public revenues is now charged on the Consolidated Fund, either by special statute once and for all or through the 'Ways and Means' granted by Parliament in each year's Consolidated Fund Act and Appropriation Act to make good the Supply votes for the year.

THE RELATION BETWEEN THE TWO

The financial mechanism by which the principle of the Consolidated Fund is operated is now governed by the Exchequer and Audit Departments Act, 1866. Section 10 of this Act requires the gross revenues of the Customs and Excise, the Inland Revenue and the Post Office to be paid into accounts at the Bank of England and the Bank of Ireland to be called in each case 'The Account of Her Majesty's Exchequer',[2] as well as all other public moneys payable to the Exchequer. Section 11 requires the two Banks to consider all moneys paid to them on account of the Exchequer as forming one general fund in their books, out of which Treasury orders for payment shall be satisfied. When the Treasury desires to make a payment out of the Consolidated Fund—whether it is for a service charged once and for all on the Fund or whether it is an issue of the annual Supply which Parliament has voted for the spending departments— it must submit a requisition for credit for that amount to the Comptroller and Auditor-General, who, if satisfied that the charge has been authorized by Parliament, will then grant the Treasury a 'credit on the Exchequer Account' for the necessary amounts. The two Banks will require to know that such a credit has been granted before they will honour the Treasury's orders for payment. Thus, whenever any sum of money has been paid into the Exchequer it becomes part of the Consolidated Fund and can only be paid out of that Fund for

[1] That is still its title today. The funds of the Republic of Ireland, of course, no longer form part of it but it is the Consolidated Fund of the United Kingdom of Great Britain and Northern Ireland. Although Northern Ireland has its own Consolidated Fund, the United Kingdom Fund holds revenues and makes payments arising in Northern Ireland, subject to adjustments with the latter. See page 109.

[2] We shall notice later two exceptions to this requirement. The Revenue Departments can use revenue temporarily to meet their expenses. And many departments use incidental receipts, like fees, to help to meet their expenses, but only up to amounts authorized by Parliament.

some purpose which Parliament has expressly authorized to be charged on the Consolidated Fund.[1]

The word 'Exchequer' is thus still in active use in two contexts. In its less prominent use it means the department—or, rather, branch of a department—which controls on behalf of Parliament the purposes for which the Treasury seeks to spend the public revenues. The more frequent use of the word arises out of the fact that those revenues are paid into the Account of Her Majesty's Exchequer; and, since the Consolidated Fund is at any point of time the total amount standing to the credit of that Account,[2] there is good ground for the prevalent practice of treating 'Exchequer' and 'Consolidated Fund' as synonymous and interchangeable terms. In such phrases as 'charge on the Exchequer' and 'Exchequer advances' the references are strictly to 'charge on the Consolidated Fund' and 'Consolidated Fund advances'. No harm is done by this practice, which is often adopted in this book: but it is as well that we should understand how the two terms came to be at our disposal.

PUBLISHED ACCOUNTS, ETC., OF THE EXCHEQUER AND OF THE CONSOLIDATED FUND

This is a convenient place for a list of the published statements and accounts which give pictures of the state of the Exchequer or Consolidated Fund *as a whole*. We shall later have many occasions to refer to the contents of some of them in more detail. In chronological order of their appearance, the statements and accounts dealing with the finances of any particular financial year are:

(1) The *Financial Statement* (known as the 'Budget White Paper') is made available as soon as the Chancellor of the Exchequer has

[1] The phrasing of statutes varies over the years, but two examples illustrate the above general point. The Suez Canal (Shares) Act, 1876, said that certain receipts 'shall be paid into the receipt of Her Majesty's Exchequer and be carried to the Consolidated Fund of the United Kingdom'. Secondly, when Treasury advances under various parliamentary authorities are repaid with interest, the relevant statute nowadays provides that the receipts 'shall be paid into the Exchequer' and shall then 'be issued out of the Consolidated Fund' and applied (as to the principal) in redeeming debt and (as to the interest) towards meeting interest on the National Debt.

[2] Until 1954, statutes used to charge a particular service (say, National Debt interest) on the Consolidated Fund 'and the growing produce thereof', meaning by the latter phrase the accretions to the Fund resulting from all the revenues to be received in the future. But this practice was abolished by Section 34(3) of the Finance Act, 1954, which provided that 'any sum charged by any Act, whenever passed, on the Consolidated Fund shall be charged also on the growing produce of the Fund'.

finished his Budget speech and is published as a House of Commons Paper.[1] Its full title is: 'Statement of Revenue and Expenditure as laid before the House by the Chancellor of the Exchequer when opening the Budget.' Its final pages give a balanced statement of Exchequer Revenue and Expenditure as they will stand if all the proposals made in his speech are adopted. But this statement is preceded by a great deal of information about the out-turn of the past year, the National Debt, details of expenditure for the past and present year and the details of the taxation changes proposed in the Budget speech. No part of the Financial Statement is an account in the strict sense of the word. Its function is to bring together the essential figures of the Budget and of the previous year's accounts, together with other data which are relevant to discussion of the Budget.

(2) On Tuesdays during the financial year the Treasury publishes in the *London Gazette* the '*Weekly Exchequer Return*' showing the Exchequer Receipts and Issues during the year up to the previous Saturday. A similar return is issued to the Press on the evening of the last working day of each quarter (that is, at the end of June, September, December and March); and on these occasions the ordinary weekly issue for the Saturday nearer to that day is suppressed.[2]

(3) Within a month of the end of the financial year the Account of *Public Income and Expenditure* is published as a House of Commons Paper. This Account, which has to be certified by the Comptroller and Auditor-General, is prepared under the Sinking Fund Act, 1875, and is designed primarily to show, for the purpose of the 'Old Sinking Fund', the surplus, if any, of revenue available for the reduction of debt. (This matter is further discussed in Chapter IX, pages 202–204.)

(4) During the September or October after the end of the financial year the annual volume of *Finance Accounts of the United Kingdom* is published as a House of Commons Paper. This volume, which runs to over seventy pages, gives a wealth of additional detail about the different items of Exchequer Receipts and Issues, the National Debt and various other capital transactions of the State. These Accounts, which started in 1802, were the first to be systematically presented to Parliament. They are not certified by the Comptroller

---

[1] For the different types of official publications, see Appendix M.

[2] The weekly Returns and the first three quarterly Returns give only one total figure for Exchequer issues in respect of Supply Services. The Return for March 31st is accompanied by a supplement dividing the figure between the various Defence Departments and Civil Supply.

and Auditor-General but are issued on the sole authority of the Treasury.[1],[2]

[1] It should be noted that all the four publications here described are based on Exchequer Issues and not on the final, audited accounts of the expenditure of the spending departments: for the difference between the two sets of figures, see page 254. Similarly, they are based on the amounts of revenue paid into the Exchequer and not on the amounts received by the Revenue Departments: see page 63.

[2] The annual 'Consolidated Fund Abstract Account' does *not* cover receipts into, or even all issues out of, the Consolidated Fund: see page 105.

CHAPTER I

The Timing and Parliamentary Setting of the Budget

EVERYONE is familiar with the idea of a periodical budget. Most private households try to estimate for a period ahead—be it a week, a month or a year—what they intend or expect to spend and what funds are likely to be available to meet that expenditure. Most business enterprises do the same, usually for a year at a time. Only thus can they all avoid chaos or worse in their financial affairs. At intervals within the period, and at the end of it, the wise ones among them will look back and check the actual results against their earlier estimates—a proceeding from which there is always much to learn. And, of course, even if such prior estimates have not been made, most businesses must draw up and publish accounts showing, for a year at a time, the results of their financial transactions, not only for the guidance of the management but also for the information of the proprietors and others who have invested money in them. The Government adopts broadly similar practices. The annual Budget is an estimate, for a year ahead, of revenue and expenditure chargeable to revenue and of part[1] of its receipts and payments on capital account. This estimate is accompanied by figures of the out-turn for the past year, alongside which are set the estimates made for the corresponding items on the Budget of a year ago. The Budget is therefore an occasion not only for discussing policy and prospects for the year ahead (including the announcement of any changes in taxation) but also for reviewing what went right or wrong in the estimates for the year just ended.

THE PERIOD OF THE BUDGET

There have sometimes been discussions whether a year is the most satisfactory period for the Budget. On the one hand, it has been argued that if the level of taxation and Government expenditure were known for a longer period ahead—say three or even five years—a new, stabilizing element would be introduced into the economy

[1] See page 43.

which would, in particular, enable business to plan ahead with greater confidence. But any such idea is hopelessly Utopian. Budgetary policy must be settled in the light of current economic conditions both in this country and in the world at large and no one can predict what those conditions are going to be for several years ahead: it is already hard enough to take a view of them for even one year at a time. Quite apart from major changes of policy it would be impracticable to estimate most items of revenue and expenditure over a period of years with anything approaching the present degree of accuracy. And, of course, from the political point of view, no Government could bind itself not to make changes in taxation or in expenditure for a large part of its maximum life of five years. On the other hand, no one has seriously suggested regular Budgets for a period of less than a year: they would be too unsettling to trade and industry and would, in fact, be impracticable because the flow of revenue, and to some extent of expenditure, varies greatly between one part of the year and another. The present Budget period of one year seems to be about as satisfactory as one can devise.

THE FINANCIAL YEAR

The Budget statement (and all the accounts relating to the Exchequer and the Consolidated Fund) relate, not to the calendar year, but to a 'financial year' beginning on April 1st and ending on March 31st. From the times of the earliest financial records to 1751–2 each year's public accounts were made up to Michaelmas quarter-day, September 29th, and between that year and 1800 to October 10th ('New Style' for September 29th). For the Finance Accounts of 1800–1 the date was altered to January 5th, which was then the usual making-up day in commerce. In 1832 the Budget was presented for the year to April 5, 1833, and the annual Supply grants began to be voted for the year ending March 31st. But the Finance Accounts kept to January 5th until 1854 when the Public Revenue and Consolidated Fund Charges Act[1] of that year directed that they should in future be made up to March 31st each year, and the latter date has since been maintained as the end of the financial year.

'SUPPLEMENTARY' BUDGETS

There is, of course, no constitutional or other bar to Budgets at shorter intervals than one year and there are several examples of

[1] The primary object of this Act was to carry further the process of concentrating public income and expenditure in the Consolidated Fund. But the year of assessment for income tax and surtax still ends on April 5th.

'supplementary' Budgets. It is generally accepted that supplementary Budgets should only be resorted to in exceptional circumstances. During the Second World War there were such Budgets in September 1939 and July 1940. The first was necessary because the outbreak of war brought with it the need for increased taxation to curtail civilian demand, to release resources for war purposes, and to 'take the profit out of war'. Provision also had to be made for the greatly increased military expenditure due to the war. It was clearly necessary therefore to make drastic adjustments in the peacetime Budget of April 1939. The supplementary Budget of July 1940 followed the shocks to the Allies' fortunes in Europe, the change of Government in the United Kingdom and the general recognition that the war effort must be greatly intensified and financial policy tightened up. Again, the original Budget (that of April 1940) was greatly changed. A peace-time example of a supplementary Budget was that of October 1955, when the Government judged that its anti-inflationary policy must be intensified by increases of indirect taxation designed to damp down consumers' expenditure: there was also an increase of Profits Tax. From even these three examples it is evident that supplementary Budgets will vary much in their contents and in the degree to which they involve modification of the original Budget of the year. There is danger in the indiscriminate use of the word Budget to describe any and every change which may be made in taxation during the course of the year. The scope of the 1939 and 1940 autumn Budgets—both on the revenue side and in the increases of expenditure they provided for—fully justified the use of the term. The case of 1955 is more doubtful. The term was rightly avoided altogether when the petrol tax was increased in December 1956 at the time of the Suez crisis. It is desirable to avoid the use of the term supplementary Budget or autumn Budget if it would give an unfounded impression that the original basis of the finances of the year require significant adjustments.

THE COMMITTEE OF WAYS AND MEANS

The setting for Budget statements has its origin deep in our Parliamentary history. One of the Standing Orders of the House of Commons, which dates from 1707, formalized a long standing practice that the House would consider motions for granting money only 'in a committee of the whole House'. Until the eighteenth century was well advanced the Speaker was a nominee, and sometimes a Minister of the Crown; and the use of committees sprang from a desire to transact business under the Chairmanship of an independent member and (as it then was) in relative privacy. At the same time the Committee of the Whole House came to be regarded, early in the seventeenth century, as a reasonable medium of discussion of taxation and other important transactions. By Stuart times this had developed into a practice of having two Committees of the Whole House—one to consider Supply and one to consider Ways and Means for 'raising Supply' so granted. The functions of the two Committees—each of which was the whole house under another name—varied somewhat for the next century or so; but, by the end of the eighteenth century, two developments of importance had occurred—the Crown had gradually relinquished to Parliament the right to impose taxation on its own authority; and the proceeds of taxes, instead of being assigned to particular services, were paid into a general pool, the Consolidated Fund. After these changes the functions of the two Committees emerged more clearly. The Committee of Supply's function was to vote expenditure. The Committee of Ways and Means had a dual function—first to authorize the issue of money out of the Consolidated Fund to meet the voted expenditure, and, secondly, as a corollary of the first, to find ways of financing the issues from the Consolidated Fund. The first function is now a formal one. The second is primarily concerned with the imposition of the taxation necessary to cover the agreed expenditure; but it also involves the granting to the Treasury of power to borrow temporarily in anticipation of the revenue that will come in. Out of the taxing function it came about that any measure imposing taxation must be based on a resolution of the Committee of Ways and Means; and thus the practice arose that the Chancellor should make his Budget statement in that Committee.[1]

Every annual Budget—that is, one introduced near the beginning of the financial year—requires at least one resolution of the Committee, namely, a resolution to reimpose the income tax which is an annual tax requiring renewal from year to year. In order to ensure annual parliamentary discussions of the country's finances it was for a long time the practice that one important direct tax (the income tax) and one important indirect tax (the tea duty) should require renewal from year to year. But the tea duty, which had been abolished in 1929, was reimposed in 1932 as a permanent duty on the grounds that provision for its annual renewal was not really necessary to give Parliament control of the country's finances. The practice of annual renewal, therefore, now applies only to the income tax, and, as a corollary, to the surtax.

[1] The phrase 'opening the Budget' dates from the middle of the eighteenth century. The word 'budget', signifying a bag or wallet, in which papers might be carried, dates from the fifteenth century.

THE PROVISIONAL COLLECTION OF TAXES ACT

It was for a long time the unchallenged custom of the Government to put into operation changes of taxation on the day following the Budget statement, unless some other date was specifically mentioned. This was a necessary administrative action to prevent forestalments (e.g. Customs duty increases) and to safeguard other revenue (e.g. income tax deducted at source). In 1913 this custom, in its application to income tax, was successfully challenged in the courts and as a result Parliament passed the Provisional Collection of Taxes Act, 1913, which, subject to certain conditions, gave statutory effect to the aforesaid custom. As originally passed the Act applied only to income tax and customs and excise but it was extended to purchase tax in 1957. It applies only to the variation or renewal of an existing tax: that is, it does not apply to a tax newly imposed. The Act gives statutory force to a resolution of the Committee of Ways and Means for four months, and so enables the Government to put the resolution into force at once, provided *inter alia* that the resolution is agreed to by the House on Report within ten (sitting) days and that the Bill giving effect to the resolution is given a Second Reading within twenty (sitting) days from the Report stage. The Act also provides that the Government cannot continue to collect a temporary tax, such as the income tax, for more than one month after it is due to expire unless it is renewed within that period by a resolution of the House or of the Committee of Ways and Means.

DATE OF THE BUDGET

Up to 1913 there appears to have been no rule about any date by which the normal annual Budget statement must be made or any date by which the consequential Finance Bill must be passed. But the events of 1913 leading to the Provisional Collection of Taxes Act introduced a new limiting factor. The income tax year runs from April 6th in one year to April 5th in the next year and, under the last of the provisions of that Act mentioned above, if the Government is to continue to collect the tax after April 5th on which it is due to expire the necessary resolution renewing it must be passed within one month of that date, that is, by May 4th. This means, in practice, that the Budget statement must be made by May 4th. It is normally made in April, the precise date depending primarily on the incidence of Easter and the date of the parliamentary recess around Easter. There is nothing to prevent a Budget being presented before the beginning of the financial year to which it relates if for any reason, of urgency or otherwise, the Government so desire. But there are obvious inconveniences in such a course, since the Budget statement can then only contain forecasts, and not final figures, for the out-turn of the year just closing. (In 1952 the Budget was introduced on March 11th because the Government wished, in conjunction with the Budget, to press on with measures to counteract the heavy drain on the gold reserves.)

GENERAL DEBATE ON THE BUDGET

As soon as the Chancellor has made his Budget statement the Committee of Ways and Means votes at once, and without debate,[1] on the resolutions necessary for continuing existing taxes, increasing them or imposing new ones, and on any resolutions relating to reductions of taxes.[2] In addition a general resolution is proposed to the effect, normally, that 'it is expedient to amend the law with respect to the national debt and the public revenue and to make further provision in connection with finance'. This general resolution is necessary because the Finance Bill, which gives statutory force, where necessary, to the Budget proposals, may cover other matters besides taxation and it is a rule of the House of Commons that nothing may be included in a Finance Bill which is not covered by a previous resolution. This general resolution is not voted on at once but is used as the peg on which the general debate on the Budget is carried on.

Resolutions passed by the Committee of Ways and Means have to be reported to, and agreed by, the House itself. The Report stage used to be an occasion for debates on the individual resolutions, but in 1947 a Standing Order (now No. 86(2)) was passed under which the resolutions are now put to the vote, one by one, without debate.[3] The reason for this change was a feeling that there was a good deal of duplication of debate: even now the merits of any change of taxation can be discussed in the general debate on the Budget and on the various stages of the Finance Bill, particularly its Committee

---

[1] Under Standing Order 86 (1): see note 3 below.

[2] If it is proposed to reduce a tax, it is not strictly necessary to base the reduction on a Ways and Means resolution. But on occasions such a resolution has been taken in order to take advantage of the Provisional Collection of Taxes Act and allow the reduction to operate at once—provided, of course, the tax in question is one to which the Act applies. (Resolutions were so taken in 1958.)

[3] In view of this change, paragraph (1) of Standing Order No. 86 was passed at the same time. This made formal the long-standing informal arrangement by which the Budget resolutions had been voted on without debate when introduced in Committee of Ways and Means.

stage when the Clause relating to the change can be debated and voted on separately.

NATURE OF THE FINANCE BILL

As soon as the House has agreed to the Ways and Means resolutions, the Government formally brings in the Finance Bill in the same sitting. (The first name on the back of the Bill—before the Chancellor of the Exchequer—is the Chairman of Ways and Means, which signifies that the introduction of the Bill has the authority of the Committee of Ways and Means.) The Bill is at once 'read a first time' and ordered to be printed. It will normally be printed and published within a week or two afterwards, the precise date depending on the parliamentary time-table and the incidence of Easter (if that is late in the year) or of Whitsuntide.

Until 1894 the taxation proposals of the Government were embodied in 'Customs and Revenue Bills'; but in that year, owing to the introduction of the Death Duties, the short title clearly had to be widened and that of 'Finance Bill' was used for the first time. The title has been retained ever since, though the scope of the Bill has been gradually broadened. The scope of the Bill is clearly defined by its 'Long Title', which has now been established for many years and which describes the Bill as being one 'to grant certain duties, to alter other duties, and to amend the law relating to the National Debt and the Public Revenue, and to make further provision in connection with Finance'. Both the Government (in the interests of its control over Budget finance) and the authorities of the House (in the interests of the orderly conduct of business) interpret the Long Title very strictly in deciding what provisions may be included in the Bill. Its precise contents will, of course, vary from year to year, but it may include any or all of the following: changes in the rates of Customs and Excise duties, in their scope and in their administration; similar changes in the various Inland Revenue duties; changes in motor taxation and other licence duties; any necessary changes in the provisions about the National Debt, such as those relating to Sinking Funds, debt redemption and any new authorities required for borrowing; and special items from time to time which affect the Exchequer below-the-line,[1] such as the establishment of the Exchange Equalization Account (1932), the establishment of the National Land Fund (1946), and the reduction of the latter Fund (1957). 'Provisions authorizing expenditure not essentially connected with national

[1] On 'below-the line', see page 42.

finance, or not incidental to the taxing or administrative provisions of a Finance Bill, are outside the scope of a Finance Bill.'[1]

Every provision in the Bill for increasing a tax or renewing an annual tax must be covered by a corresponding resolution of the Committee of Ways and Means; and the Bill may not increase a tax above the level approved in such a resolution. Clauses reducing taxation or dealing with the National Debt are held to be covered by the general 'Amendment of the law' resolution already referred to on page 24.

Clauses which do not involve taxation but which involve charges on the Exchequer—such as those setting up the Exchange Equalization Account and National Land Fund, which the Exchequer financed—must be covered by another kind of resolution generally called a 'Money Resolution'. A Money Resolution is not peculiar to a Finance Bill, but is required whenever any provision in any Bill imposes a charge on public funds. Such a resolution must—by virtue of Standing Order No. 79, already referred to on page 21—originate in committee; but this time it is not the Committee of Ways and Means but a 'Committee of the Whole House'—again the House itself under another name, but with less restricted functions than the former Committee. Like Ways and Means resolutions, Money resolutions must be 'recommended from the Crown'; that is, they can only be moved by a Minister. Unlike Ways and Means resolutions, they need not be taken before the Finance Bill is introduced but can be taken at any time before the Clauses which they cover are taken in the Committee Stage of the Bill.

A further type of resolution is sometimes used—the 'Special Procedure Resolution'—when it is desired to include in a Finance Bill a provision which is strictly outside its scope. It is of the form: 'That, notwithstanding anything to the contrary in the practice of the House relating to matters which may be included in Finance Bills, provision may be made in any Finance Bill introduced in the present Session for . . . ' Such resolutions were passed in 1956 and 1958 to cover legislation in Finance Bills relating to the financing of the nationalized industries. They must be taken in the House itself before the Finance Bill is introduced.

THE FINANCE BILL IN THE COMMONS

Debate on the Finance Bill starts with the Second Reading, when one of the junior Ministers at the Treasury usually opens the debate with a survey of its contents and such supporting argument for them

[1] Erskine May, *Parliamentary Practice*, 16th Edition, page 800.

and for the general policy of the Budget as he likes to offer. This debate can range over the whole of that policy and indeed can include any subject which can have any conceivable relation to any aspect of Central Government finance. If the Opposition put down a 'reasoned' amendment for the rejection of the Bill, that will indicate the main topic or topics on which their speeches will concentrate and may decide the line, at least in part, of the final Government reply to the debate, which is usually made by the Chancellor of the Exchequer.

The Committee Stage is, in practice, always taken on the floor of the House and not in Standing Committee, and the debates in Committee Stage (and all subsequent stages) are exempt from the Standing Orders under which business is adjourned at ten o'clock (four o'clock on Fridays). In Committee, the clauses of the Bill are taken one by one. The more controversial of them always attract a host of amendments proposed by the Opposition and by private members generally; and there are usually in addition very many 'new clauses', similarly proposed, relating to taxation matters which are not being dealt with in the Government's Bill. The clauses of the Bill and amendments proposed thereto are discussed first, and new clauses taken afterwards. Sometimes such amendments or new clauses will be ruled out of order because they involve, or might involve, an increase of taxation for someone; but the great majority, of course, seek reductions of taxation in one direction or another. Very often many amendments will be proposed to a particular clause of the same general nature. In such cases the Chairman, in the exercise of his discretion, may allow a debate on one amendment selected by him, subsequently allowing, or not, divisions on the other amendments without debate. If the Government agree to make a concession on any point and the precise terms of the relevant amendment cannot be accepted on the spot, they will normally promise to propose an amendment of their own on the next (the Report) stage. If they do that, they must take care that the new amendment conforms to any Ways and Means resolution covering the matter in question. If it does not, the Committee of Ways and Means must be asked to pass an amended resolution, to be reported to and agreed by the House, and the clause must be taken in Committee again before the Government can introduce their promised amendment on the Report stage of the Bill.

On the Report stage, new clauses are discussed first and the clauses of the Bill and amendments thereto are taken afterwards. The Speaker (since the Bill is now in the House itself) exercises the same discretion about selecting new clauses and amendments as the

Chairman exercised in Committee. The most important rule affecting the Report stage is that no new clause or amendment may be proposed which extends a tax to persons who were not subject to it when the Bill was in Committee or which imposes a new charge. If the Government wish to do either of these things the relevant part of the Bill must be recommitted; that is, it must be taken again in Committee and any necessary prior resolutions of the Committee of Ways and Means must also be obtained.

The debate on the Third Reading of the Bill should strictly be confined to matters which make up the contents of the Bill; but it frequently widens into a general discussion on the Budget proposals. No amendments can be made at this stage.

THE FINANCE BILL IN THE LORDS

In the House of Lords there is usually only one debate on the Bill, that on the Second Reading, which ranges over the general policy of the Budget and any economic and financial matters which members like to raise. Their Lordships usually make no attempt to vote on the Bill or to amend individual clauses. Behind this restraint lies the fact that the Finance Bill is, normally, outstanding among Bills receiving the protection of the Parliament Act, 1911, which limits the powers of the House of Lords in relation to Bills passed by the House of Commons and, in particular, to 'Money Bills'. This Act was passed after the House of Lords had rejected the Budget of 1909 and two elections in 1910 had supported the then Government's proposals, which were subsequently embodied in the Act. It provides that if a Money Bill, having been passed by the House of Commons and sent up to the House of Lords at least one month before the end of the Session, is not passed by the House of Lords without amendment within one month, the Bill shall, unless the House of Commons direct to the contrary, be presented for Royal Assent and become an Act of Parliament on Royal Assent being signified. A 'Money Bill' for this purpose means a Public Bill which, in the opinion of the Speaker of the House of Commons, contains only provisions which, put shortly, deal with taxation, charges on the Consolidated Fund or moneys provided by Parliament, the appropriation of public money, audit, the raising or guarantee or repayment of any loan, and matters incidental thereto. Every such Bill must be endorsed with the certificate of the Speaker of the House of Commons that it is a Money Bill.

There have been a number of occasions on which Finance Bills have not qualified for the Speaker's certificates that they were Money

Bills. The reason for this is that they included some matters which, although quite properly included in a Finance Bill, did not fall strictly within the above list of subjects. When a Finance Bill is not certified, the actions of the House of Lords or any member of it will be governed by the ordinary understandings as to House of Commons privilege. This question of privilege has a very long history.[1] A landmark in that history was the passing by the House of Commons in 1860 of a series of formal resolutions averring that 'the right of granting aids and supplies to the Crown is in the Commons alone', and that any exercise by the Lords of their power to reject taxation Bills 'is justly regarded by this House with particular jealously, as affecting the right of the Commons to grant the supplies and to provide the ways and means for the service of the year'. Writing just after the turn of the century, Anson said that 'there can be no doubt that the principle of these resolutions has been expanded and that the Commons now regard as a breach of privilege not merely the imposition by the Lords of any charge by way of rates or taxes, but any dealing with the regulation or administration of such a charge'. The culmination of all this is to be seen in the Parliament Act, 1911, and in the definition of a 'Money Bill' in that Act. Even when the Finance Bill, or other Bill, is not formally certified as a Money Bill, that definition is a fairly clear guide to the extent of the Commons' privilege. In the Manual of Procedure of the House of Commons, issued under the authority of the Speaker,[2] it is summed up in one short sentence: 'The right of granting money in Parliament belongs exclusively to the House of Commons.'

[1] Cf. Anson, *Law and Custom of the Constitution*, Vol. I, Chapter VI, Section III (i).

[2] Published by HM Stationery Office (1951 edition).

CHAPTER II

The Economic Background to the Budget

IT is a commonplace today that the modern Budget is very different from the Budgets of a hundred, or even twenty, years ago. The old-style Budget is often dismissed as a mere matter of arithmetic or book-keeping. It is true that the main preoccupation of Chancellors was to show that their revenue was covering their expenditure, with, they would hope, something to spare; and it is also true that this some-times led them to take liberties with what financial purists would regard as the sacred principles of good accounting. Yet the dismissal was not fully justified. When he presented his first Budget in 1853, Mr Gladstone spoke for five hours and proposed changes, many of them of much importance, over practically the whole field of taxa-tion. There was clearly much more than arithmetic behind most of this: and in the intervening century there have been few Budgets in which fiscal and social justice, as interpreted by the Chancellor of the day, has not claimed as much of the limelight as pure arithmetic. But change there has been, and of a less disputable kind. In that Budget of 1853, Mr Gladstone had practically nothing to say about the general economic condition of the country or the state of its overseas balance. Compare this with the structure of the Chancellor of the Exchequer's Budget speech in 1957, which lasted for only one and three-quarter hours. Successive sections of his speech dealt with the balance of payments, the internal economy generally, the Exche-quer outturn for 1956–7 and prospects for 1957–8, the economic prospects for 1957–8, monetary policy and Budget objectives. He then considered 'to what extent and in what directions he could properly reduce taxation, having regard to the state of the economy'. It was only after all that, that the Chancellor proposed fiscal changes of a very modest kind.

This reorientation of the Budget into a wider economic setting may be said to date from 1941. Financial policy then had to be de-signed to support a fully-stretched war economy. Its primary objec-tive had to be to hold inflation in check by maintaining reasonably stable prices and by finding the right balance between taxation and borrowing for the financing of the war effort.[1] The sheer pressure of circumstances made it necessary for financial policy to be closely geared to economic policy and for both to be accepted as just and efficient auxiliaries to the country's military effort. The Budget was harnessed to the economy in a way that had never been known before. This is not the place to describe all the new administrative machinery and statistical equipment that made that possible: it has been done in great detail in various volumes of the official history of the Second World War. But mention must be made of the first attempt to provide estimates of the national income and national expenditure which were published in the first White Paper on the subject when the Chancellor opened his Budget in April 1941.[2] Statistical knowledge of what was happening in the economy, in the form of spendable incomes and the demands made on them, was essential if the financial defences against inflation were to be intelligently designed and resolutely held. As the war developed and the physical productive effort of the country became more intense the statistical equipment of Government expanded in all sorts of ways. But, for the purposes of financial policy, the comprehensive estimates of national income and expenditure, which greatly improved as the years went by, remained of fundamental importance.

The degree of direct intervention in the economy by the Government has greatly diminished since the war. Nevertheless, although the problems to be faced have changed from year to year, the reorientation of financial policy, and of the Budget in particular, that served us so well during the war, has in principle persisted ever since. In the formulation of financial policy, Governments do now, as then, seek to match that policy to the economic condition of the country and to the main economic objectives to which the national effort has, for the time being, to be directed.

MEASURING ECONOMIC ACTIVITY

Let us therefore, as a first step, see how we can from time to time obtain an overall picture of the economic condition of the country and, within that picture, information about the trends which are currently developing.

A great variety of economic statistics is published regularly: about, for example, the production of particular goods; employment and unemployment; financial transactions of different kinds;

[1] See R. S. Sayers, *Financial Policy*, 1939–45 (1956), Chapters I and III.
[2] Its full title was 'An Analysis of the Sources of War Finance and an Estimate of the National Income and Expenditure in 1938 and 1940' (Cmd 6261).

the balance of trade and of overseas payments. But it is impossible from them alone to obtain a clear picture of the totality of the economy. For one thing, there is no one physical unit which will enable us to show the total national resources available from the production of so much textiles, so much steel goods, so much chemicals, not to mention the financial gains from such items as shipping, overseas investment and international banking. We are in fact forced to reduce all these items to the common basis of money values. On that basis we can now obtain periodically a clear and useful picture of the economy as a whole and of the broad elements within it. This is done in the estimates of 'National Income and Expenditure' compiled by the Central Statistical Office. In April each year, just before the Budget, that office publishes as a White Paper *'Preliminary Estimates of National Income and Expenditure'* for the previous calendar year, which are set alongside the figures for the five preceding years. These estimates, which consist of about half-a-dozen summary tables, are later revised and expanded in much detail (in some sixty tables) in August, being then published as a Blue Book entitled *National Income and Expenditure*. In this Blue Book the comparison with earlier years is carried rather further back and figures for a pre-war year (1938) are added, though these last are necessarily subject to much more uncertainty than those for the post-war years. In addition to these annual publications, the Central Statistical Office has since 1947 published quarterly figures for the table on consumers' expenditure, and it has recently extended quarterly publication to several of the other tables, the figures being given in the Office's two monthly publications, the *Monthly Digest of Statistics* and *Economic Trends*.

The completion of these statistics is necessarily a highly technical task. Those who wish to study in detail how it is done and what precisely the figures mean should read the volume issued by the Central Statistical Office on the subject.[1] For the purposes of the present book we must, in more summary and less expert fashion, attempt to bring out those aspects of the statistics which are of primary significance for Budget purposes: but we shall draw heavily on the volume just mentioned.

THE NATIONAL INCOME

The basic concepts are the totals of the national income and national expenditure, since approach to economic problems of the kind which

[1] *National Income Statistics: Sources and Methods*, published by HM Stationery Office, 1956.

affect the Budget must, at some stage or other, involve consideration on the one hand of the trend of the national income and where it arises and on the other hand of the trend of the national expenditure and how it is spent. The income is a measure of the money value of goods and services becoming available to the nation from economic activity. It is in the main the total of the incomes which residents in the United Kingdom derive from the current production of goods and services in this country: that is, the wages and salaries of people in employment; the income of professional persons, farmers and others in self-employment; the trading profits or surpluses of companies, public corporations and other public enterprises; and rent.[1] To the total of these items is then added a relatively small amount (1 per cent of the total) for the net income received from abroad in the form of interest, dividends and profits on overseas trading.

Looked at in another way the total of the incomes derived from economic activity in this country can be described as the domestic product, that is the sum of the products of industries or productive enterprises within the nation, as represented by the values added at each stage of production in this country. After adding the net income received from abroad the final total may be described either as the national income or the national product. In this book we shall henceforth use only the term national income.[2]

THE NATIONAL EXPENDITURE

Against estimates of the national income built up in this way we have to set estimates of the national expenditure which may be regarded as comprising the nation's consumption and its investment. This expenditure is calculated in three stages. First, there is the group of domestic expenditures represented by consumers' expenditure and public authorities' current expenditure on goods and services; 'gross fixed capital formation at home'—that is, expenditure by individuals, companies, public corporations and Central and Local Governments on fixed capital assets like buildings, vehicles, plant and machinery, all of which is conveniently covered by the term 'investment'; and the cost of the physical increase in the stocks and work-in-progress of trading enterprises. Secondly, allowance must be made for the

---

[1] All items are gross before payment of taxes and rates; and the profits, etc., of companies, etc., are gross before providing for depreciation.

[2] We here ignore the point that, strictly speaking, the national income should represent the national product *less* what is required to provide for 'capital consumption' in the shape of physical assets (plant and buildings) used up in the course of production. This matter is highly technical and full of difficulty. The amount involved is about a tenth of the national product.

B

effect of the balance of our overseas trade and payments. The figures of expenditure include that on goods and services imported from abroad and this part of the expenditure must therefore be deducted to make the total expenditure comparable with the national income or product. Conversely, that part of the national product which is sold to foreigners in the form of goods exported or services rendered must be added back. Looking at it in another way, the more domestic products we export the less of our national resources are available for consumption or investment at home; the more we import, the more resources are available. We must, therefore, allow for this when we seek to compare the total of the national income with that of the national expenditure. Thirdly, certain adjustments must be made to the figures of domestic expenditure under the first heading above. This expenditure is calculated at market prices. But these prices may include indirect taxes paid by the producers or merchants or may exclude subsidies paid by the Government; and neither the taxes nor the subsidies will have entered into the figures which have made up the income side of the national account. Hence, to arrive at a total of expenditure comparable with that of income, we must deduct the taxes and add in the subsidies.

We now have two sets of statistics to measure the country's economic activity. On the one side—the national income side—we see where the incomes created by the activity arise and, therefore, where the spending power of the country lies. On the other side—the national expenditure side—we see how that spending power has, in fact, been used. The totals on both sides must necessarily be the same. The preliminary estimates for 1957 are given in Appendix A.

'SECTORS' OF THE NATIONAL ECONOMY

The figures so far discussed relate to the country as a whole. It is, however, essential for the purpose of economic and financial policy, and particularly of Budget policy, to break down the figures between what are known as the different 'sectors' of the national economy. A 'sector' is officially defined as 'a group of entities similar to one another in general characteristics affecting economic behaviour'. There must obviously be border-line cases the classification of which between the sectors is arguable; in some of these cases sheer statistical necessity may require them to be classed one way or another. These border-line cases are not, however, anything like important enough to affect the significance of the figures for any sector. For statistical purposes, then, the national economy is divided into a number of sectors:

Persons—this sector consists primarily of households and individuals, including self-employed individuals (such as farmers,
professional people and individual traders and partnerships).
Corporate enterprises: companies and public corporations.
Public Authorities: the Central Government and Local Authorities.

Transactions with the rest of the world.

For each of these sectors figures are published to show the amount
and type of income and current expenditure. Details are given of their
capital expenditure, together with information about the sources
from which they are financed—though in the case of companies and
the personal sector this latter information is unavoidably incomplete.

The details for any of these sectors may be very relevant when this
or that economic problem is under discussion; and the relative part
played by any one sector in the total economy will often be of the
greatest importance. We shall be closely concerned in this book with
the part played by the Central Government. But before commenting
further on that, we must refer to the 'public corporations' sector,
which covers what are known as the nationalized industries (e.g.
Coal, Transport, Electricity, Gas, Civil Aviation) and a number of
other public trading bodies which have a substantial degree of independence of management from the Central Government. The
direct contribution of these bodies to the total of the national income
is relatively small, being less than a tenth, Indirectly, of course, it is
much greater because, between them, they provide services which
are essential to the whole industrial life of the country. Of more
direct concern for our purposes is the fact that the investment programmes of practically all of these bodies are subject to control by
the Government and, as we shall see later, the outside finance they
require for those programmes is now borrowed from the Treasury.
The size of their programmes, and of the finance they require, must
therefore be closely bound up with the Government's economic and
financial policy from time to time. The importance of this may be
gathered from the fact that their investment programmes amount
annually to about a fifth of the total fixed investment of the country.

THE CENTRAL GOVERNMENT SECTOR

The Central Government naturally contributes only a small proportion of the national income: its contribution is confined, for practical
purposes, to the pay of the Forces and the salaries and wages of

Civil Servants. Together those items amounted in 1956[1] to about 8 per cent of the national income. On the national expenditure side the Central Government's share is larger—in 1956 and 1957 it was about 15 per cent: this covers all its current expenditure on goods and services and its investment in new buildings and equipment for the Post Office and the Defence Services and other departments. By themselves these figures do not give a proper indication of the importance of the Central Government's transactions. The reason is, of course, that when it lays out money in acquiring goods and services and in new investment it is not using income which it has itself generated but is using money which has been generated by others. The Central Government is for the most part financed by 'transfers' of income by the earners thereof—compulsory transfers in the shape of taxes, and voluntary transfers in the shape of National Savings and subscriptions to other Government loans. Such transfers make no difference to the total resources available in the country, which, as will be remembered, is what the figure for the total national income sets out to measure. Similarly (in addition to its expenditure on goods and services and investment) the Central Government makes large transfer payments the other way. When it pays retirement pensions or sickness benefits it is not thereby creating any new resources; nor is it using up national resources in the same way as it does when it buys paper or employs a man or builds a new office. It is simply transferring to the new beneficiary income which has been earned (or resources which have been created) by someone else. Thus neither sums transferred to the Government in the shape of taxes or savings nor sums transferred by the Government in the shape of social-service and other grants and subsidies appear in the totals of the national income and expenditure. That is not to say that these transfers are of no significance for our purpose: transfer payments by the Government in respect of the social services are now, clearly, an important factor in determining the level of taxation.

The transfer payments to and from the Government are set out in great detail in the statistical Blue Book. As we shall see below, they appear in the tables of Personal Income and Expenditure. They are also set out in the tables showing the Revenue Account and the Capital Account of the Central Government.

The two Central Government accounts just mentioned are not further referred to in this book for the following reason. Accounts are published weekly of the transactions of the Exchequer, in a form

[1] The 1958 Blue Book giving this detail for 1957 is not available at the time of writing.

which follows that used by the Chancellor of the Exchequer when he opens his Budget. This form is familiar to Parliament, people and Press and must certainly be taken as the basis for our subsequent discussions in this book. Unfortunately certain adjustments have to be made to the Exchequer Account figures in order to bring them into line with the basis adopted in the national income and expenditure tables. Thus: both receipts and payments have to be reclassified to distinguish between items which figure in the total of national income and national expenditure and transfer items of the kind just discussed on page 36. Again, the distinction between revenue and capital items must be more rigid in the national income tables than in the Exchequer accounts where a number of capital items (e.g. buildings and aerodromes) are, for good and sufficient reasons, charged to annual revenue. Finally, a number of items are classified under 'Central Government' in the Blue Book accounts which, although administered by the Central Government, do not pass through the Exchequer. Of these, the most important are the payments into and out of the National Insurance Funds, the Exchange Equalization Account and the sales and purchases of securities by the Issue Department of the Bank of England. It is unnecessary to elaborate here the reasons for these adjustments: they are obviously required if a clear and comprehensive picture is to be given of all the transactions of the Central Government in the same form as the transactions of the other sectors of the economy.[1] Nevertheless for the purposes of the present book it seems best to base our discussions on the more familiar Exchequer Account if only because that is the account on which is based the administrative and parliamentary machinery with which we shall have to deal.

After the accounts of the Central Government, come those of Local Authorities. We need not here stay to consider the details of their accounts; but perhaps it is worth while, in passing, to note that in recent years the current grants by the Central Government to Local Authorities have so increased that, excluding housing subsidies,[2] they are almost as big as the yield from rates and, if housing subsidies are included, they exceed that yield.

[1] For a full treatment of the relation between the Blue Book figures and the published accounts of the Central Government, see *National Income Statistics: Sources and Methods*, pages 179–230.

It should also be noted that the national income statistics cover Northern Ireland and that the accounts of the Government of Northern Ireland are therefore combined with those of the United Kingdom Government.

[2] In the tables of national income and expenditure, housing subsidies are accounted for separately from the current grants to Local Authorities.

SOME IMPORTANT TABLES

The subsidiary tables in the White Paper and Blue Book dealing with the income and expenditure of particular sectors of the economy are, if anything, of greater interest than the main tables which are on a national basis. They give a lot of information, for instance, about the transfer of spending power from one sector to another. Thus they show the proportion of income paid in taxes and rates to enable the Central Government and Local Authorities to meet the expenditure which these incur; and they show the income saved by individuals and (in the form of undistributed profits) by companies and used, directly and indirectly, to finance the increase in the country's capital wealth in such forms as houses, plant and machinery. Three points among these subsidiary tables are worth attention.

First, there is a very important table of 'Personal Income and Expenditure'. This collects together the incomes of private individuals from all sources, before tax, and shows how much has been spent, how much paid in taxes and how much saved. The incomes include not only the wages and salaries earned by the individuals themselves but also what they receive in interest and dividends, which are earned by the activities of others, and in national insurance benefits and other grants by public authorities, which are financed from taxes and rates paid by the community at large. The importance of this table arises from the relevance of private spending and saving to the economic condition of the country and particularly to the financing of capital investment. Also, any Chancellor will be concerned to watch the proportion of personal income which is taken by taxes and rates. The preliminary estimates of Personal Income and Expenditure for 1957 are given in Appendix B.

Secondly, another important table shows the distribution of Personal Income according to the range of the individual incomes, before and after tax. It is clearly of fundamental importance in the consideration of income tax and surtax policy to know how much of the total income of private individuals lies in the particular ranges of incomes. Equally, it is important to know how the total income left to be spent after tax is similarly divided. Thus, the 1957 Blue Book shows that in 1956 incomes under £600 a year before tax accounted for 65 per cent of the number of incomes, 40 per cent of the total of the incomes, 13 per cent of the income tax and surtax paid and 43 per cent of the income after tax.

Thirdly, there is much interesting information about the sources of the savings which are necessary to finance the country's invest-ment. Such 'savings' include not only the savings of private individuals[1] but the undistributed profits of companies and the revenue surpluses of the Central and Local Governments. Here, obviously, is much food for thought by a Chancellor considering the size of his Budget surplus. It is not yet possible to show in detail the uses to which the savings from each of these sources are put; but the broad picture is that persons, companies and (through the Budget surplus) the Central Government have savings available which are more than sufficient to meet their respective investment programmes and that their surplus savings are used (directly or indirectly) to help to finance the investment programmes of public corporations (that is, mainly, the nationalized industries) and Local Authorities.

Before leaving these figures (for the country as a whole) one word of warning about their use is desirable. Covering as they do the complex activities of a highly industrialized trading nation they have to be built up, and checked, from a great variety of statistical sources. The reliability of those sources, and therefore of the final figures for the different items, necessarily varies. Even so, the broad pictures they give of the economic life of the country are sufficiently reliable to be used as material factors in formulating economic and financial policy. Possibly more important, they can confidently be used to indicate and interpret trends in this or that economic factor from year to year. It is here, however, that caution is needed on one point. The statistics are collected, and the main tables are expressed, in terms of current money. This means that if, say, consumers' expenditure or capital investment has, between two years, changed from £X million to £Y million, part of the change may be due to a change in the price level. It is obviously important to be clear how much each of these two factors has contributed to the change, in money terms, which is being considered. Over a large part of the field the Blue Book helps us to do this by revaluing the figures 'at constant prices': it does this by eliminating changes due to movements of prices and so shows what changes have occurred in physical volume or (to use the technical phrase) 'in real terms'.

BUDGET USES

Here then is a wealth of basic statistical material at the disposal of a Chancellor of the Exchequer as Budget Day approaches. It is, of

---

[1] 'Personal savings' in the national income accounts represent the difference between personal incomes (after tax) and expenditure on consumers' goods and services. They may be used for investment in houses, business equipment, etc., or to increase financial assets like life insurance policies, investments in building societies or bank balances or 'National Savings' (National Savings Certificates, Defence Bonds, etc). Thus, 'National Savings' represent only one channel in which personal savings can be invested.

course, by no means the whole of the information, statistical and otherwise, about the country's economy which he will need and which will be available to him. He will go elsewhere for information—sometimes more up to date—about employment, production, changes in business firms' stocks[1] and investment plans,[1] overseas trade and payments and so on; and, as we shall see in the next chapter, he will have to take account of factors which may not be expressible in figures. Nevertheless, the statistics of the national income and expenditure will be of fundamental importance. The main table will show him whether the total value of national production is rising or falling in money terms and he will have available price indices which will tell him how far the rise or fall is due to price changes and how much to a change in volume. On the expenditure side, he will see how consumers' expenditure and investment are changing, and again, in each case, how far the change is due to prices or volume. With the help of the subsidiary tables about personal income and expenditure he can see whether saving is increasing or decreasing and, for example, what the relation of the change is to changes in consumers' expenditure. When he studies the make-up of the national expenditure on investment and the way it has been financed, he will look here also for any significant change. He will be particularly interested to see how far companies are maintaining the level of their savings in the form of undistributed profits and the relation between such savings and their investment. He will, of course, already have available from his own sources full information about trends in the revenue and expenditure of the Central Government and can collate these with what the statistics show him about the rest of the economy. When he has formed his impressions of what has been happening in the economy his view will have to contract from these wider horizons to the narrower problem of what implications those impressions have for his forthcoming Budget.

It would not be unnatural or illogical if, when he comes to present his Budget, the Chancellor gave a fairly full review and interpretation of the statistical evidence about the state of the economy, by way of preface to, and in part justification of, his proposals. But that would be an altogether too tedious proceeding for the House of Commons and the matter is more satisfactorily arranged in another way. Each year, just before the Budget, the Chancellor publishes a White Paper entitled '*Economic Survey*'. This consists in the main of a review of economic developments abroad and in the United Kingdom during the calendar year just ended. The review is largely based on the main

[1] Statistics for both these items are collected periodically by the Board of Trade.

statistical tables in the 'Preliminary Estimate of National Income and Expenditure'. Supplementary information is given about costs and prices, developments abroad and our overseas trade, and there are surveys of the state of particular industries. At the end of the Survey there is a short appreciation of the economic prospects of the United Kingdom in the year ahead. In his Budget speech the Chancellor may well give some of the salient points from the Survey, but the full paper should certainly be read by all serious students and critics of the Budget.

CHAPTER III

The General Design of the Budget

WE must now look broadly at the contents[1] of the Budget and at some of the problems which a Chancellor may have to face when he makes his speech explaining it. But we had better first look at the relation between the Financial Statement which is published on Budget Day and the weekly Exchequer Return. All the items which appear in the Financial Statement also appear, in due course, in the Exchequer Return; but, as we shall see, not all the items in the latter appear in the Financial Statement.

THE EXCHEQUER—ABOVE- AND BELOW-THE-LINE

The weekly Exchequer Returns show first the revenue of the Central Government from taxes and other sources of current income and the current expenditure to be met out of that revenue. Next they give receipts and payments on what is, broadly, capital account. These two sets of transactions are not, however, formally described as a 'revenue account' and a 'capital account'. Certain payments of a capital character are, in fact, charged against revenue; and some items are met out of borrowed moneys which are not strictly capital payments. The traditional practice is to draw a line across the middle of the Exchequer accounts and to put 'above-the-line' the Budget revenue and all expenditure charged to it and to put 'below-the-line' all receipts applicable to debt redemption[2] and all expenditure which the Government has power to finance by borrowing. On the other hand, there is nothing to prevent expenditure of any kind whatever being charged to revenue (instead of borrowing for it) if it is so desired and if Parliament either authorizes it as a Consolidated Fund service or votes it as a Supply service.

The possibility that capital payments may be charged either above- or below-the-line may seem strange when compared with the rigorous line drawn between the income and capital accounts of the

---

[1] They are described in much more detail in Chapters IV, V and VI.
[2] See also page 106 on certain interest receipts.

commercial world. But there is a quite logical and practical basis for the present system.[1] Take first the practice of charging certain capital costs to revenue—as is done with the costs of such buildings as Government offices or military barracks. Such costs are not only small in relation to the Budget total; but, more important, they occur every year in broadly the same total amount. Now, if any business undertaking is faced with capital expenditure which is specially large in one year or which is very large compared with the undertaking's annual profits, it is reasonable enough to charge it to capital account and borrow for it, which is a means of spreading the cost over a period of years. But the same considerations do not apply if the capital expenditure is relatively small and if it recurs year after year: there is no case for spreading it over a period, and to borrow every year would only increase the cost over the years by unnecessary payments of interest. Another type of capital payment may arise when the Government has agreed to make a loan to some party at a low or nominal rate of interest or even free of interest. If the Government borrowed in order to do this it would in effect be paying a continuing subsidy to the party concerned which ought to be charged to revenue. While the point is not pressed to the extent of annually voting such a subsidy to enable the borrower to pay the full interest to the Government, it is recognized by charging the loan to revenue once and for all.

THE FINANCIAL STATEMENT

This Statement brings together all the figures which the Chancellor uses in his Budget Speech or which help to explain those which he so uses. The final table in the Statement sets out what may be called the Budget proper, that is, the estimate of revenue for the financial year just commencing on the basis of such changes in taxation and other policies as the Chancellor may propose in his Statement. This table corresponds with the receipts and payments which will, during the year, appear in the Exchequer Return above-the-line. It is, however, immediately preceded by another table which gives, in addition to the same estimates above-the-line, estimates for most of the items below-the-line. Two groups of figures which may subsequently appear in the Exchequer Return below-the-line are omitted from these estimates. First, they do not include any repayments of existing Government stocks or other debt, even if it is known that such repayments

---

[1] This practice was generally approved by the Committee on the Form of Government Accounts, 1950 (Cmd 7969), subject to the proviso, which is duly observed, that capital items should be shown separately in the Estimates.

will have to be made during the year. The reason for this is that (as we shall see in Chapter VIII) the precise method by which any such maturing debt will be provided for will depend on a very complicated set of factors arising out of the day-to-day financing of the Exchequer and cannot always be foreseen at the time of the Budget. But the Chancellor will certainly have these maturities in mind throughout his planning of the Budget. It follows from this omission that no estimates are given of the amounts likely to be raised by borrowing during the year. Secondly, the below-the-line estimates also exclude any provision for certain other possibilities, such as capital which may be required by the Exchange Equalization Account[1] or the Civil Contingencies Fund.[2] These items are excluded because it is impossible to estimate for them in advance and because they are, in any case, in the nature of internal accounting transactions.[3]

In this chapter we shall follow the Budget estimates in the form and order in which they appear in the tables in the Financial Statement.

REVENUE

In the 'above-the-line' account the revenue from taxation falls mainly under two heads. The first is the Inland Revenue, which consists of income tax, surtax, death duties, stamp duties, profits tax, excess profits tax and a few minor other taxes. The second head is that of the Customs and Excise duties which are levied on goods and commodities (e.g. spirits, beer, wines, sugar, tobacco, oil and the goods subject to purchase tax) or particular services or transactions (e.g. entertainment and betting). The Customs duties fall on goods and commodities imported from abroad; the Excise duties fall on similar things produced at home (e.g. British wines and home-grown beet-sugar) or on transactions, like admissions to entertainments and betting, which have no imported counterpart. There is one further and separate item of tax revenue, namely the taxes on motor vehicles.

The two main heads—Inland Revenue and Customs and Excise—represent broadly the common distinction between 'direct' and 'indirect' taxes. Direct taxes are those which are finally borne by the person who pays them and are not normally passed on by the tax-

---

[1] See Chapter VII.

[2] See page 242.

[3] As from June 30, 1958, the form of the published Exchequer Returns was rearranged below-the-line to show, on each side, first (with a subsidiary total) the items covered by the estimates in the Financial Statement and then, below, the items omitted from those estimates.

payer in a charge to any other person. Indirect taxes, on the other hand, are normally expected to be so passed on by the person paying them (e.g. the merchant who imports sugar; or the manufacturer who imports tobacco; or the proprietor of a cinema) in the price he demands from the final consumer of the goods or the services concerned. Prior to the Second World War the proportion in which total taxation was divided between direct and indirect taxes was often a matter of much political argument. Those who were concerned to keep the weight of indirect taxes as low as possible represented that whereas the direct taxes, and particularly the income tax, fell in the main on those taxpayers who were better off, indirect taxes fell on necessaries of life (e.g. sugar) or articles of popular consumption (e.g. beer and tobacco) and so were borne by practically every household, including those with very small incomes. Since the war the controversy has rarely been pursued in that generalized form because sheer necessity has required the income tax to be levied over a much wider proportion of the population than previously.

In addition to the above receipts from taxation, the Budget revenue includes some relatively minor further items: the net receipt from the Post Office; broadcast licences; receipts in connection with 'sundry loans' (such as the dividends on the Government's shares in the Suez Canal Company and the British Petroleum Company, and repayments of loans made to other governments); and a very varied 'miscellaneous' group of receipts, including the surpluses on various trading services carried out by Government departments.

The relative importance of these different sources of revenue can be seen from the following Budget estimates of the revenue for 1958–9:

	£ million	£ million	%
Inland Revenue: Income Tax	2,312		(42·5)
Other	658		54·6
	—	2,970	
Customs	1,257		
Excise	932		
	—	2,189	40·2
Motor Vehicles Duties		104	1·9
Post Office (net receipt)		2	—
Broadcast Receiving Licenses		34	0·6
Receipts from Sundry Loans		30	0·6
Miscellaneous		110	2·0
TOTAL REVENUE		5,439	100·0

EXPENDITURE ABOVE-THE-LINE

Against this revenue, the Budget, above-the-line, sets the current expenditure of the Central Government. First are the 'Consolidated Fund Services', which are exempt from any need to be voted annually by Parliament because Parliament has, by statute, authorized the payments once and for all. They are of many different types and the details are given in Chapter V. But they have this one feature in common, that, by reason of such once-for-all authority, those interested in receiving them know that the payments are not subject to any risk that the House of Commons might, in one year or another, refuse to provide the funds to meet them. This is an essential assurance, for instance, in the case of the payments which represent interest and management charges on the National Debt.[1] But the main bulk of our annual expenditure is the 'Supply' voted annually by Parliament on the basis of Estimates submitted to it by the Government; and the amount which the Budget provides for this expenditure is the total of the Estimates presented to Parliament at the beginning of the financial year.[2] We shall look more closely later on at this 'Supply' procedure and at the expenditure which it covers. At this stage it is sufficient to note that roughly one-third of the expenditure is on Defence, and two-thirds on Civil services. The Defence total is built up from the separate requirements of the Army, the Navy, the Air Force, the defence activities of the Ministry of Supply and the expenses of the Ministry of Defence. The Civil total similarly represents the amount required for a very great variety of services, for which it will suffice here to give headings under which they are classified in the Estimates: Central Government and Finance; Commonwealth and Foreign; Home Department, Law and Justice; Education and Broadcasting; Health, Housing and Local Government; Trade, Labour and Supply; Common Services (Works, Stationery, etc.); Agriculture and Food; Transport, Power and Industrial Research; Pensions, National Insurance and National Assistance; and Tax Collection.

In the Budget estimate for 1958–9, the figures for expenditure chargeable against revenue were:

[1] The interest charged to revenue 'above-the-line' does not represent the whole of the interest on the national debt. As we shall see on page 106 a portion of the latter is charged below the line and balanced by interest received on loans made by the Exchequer out of money it has borrowed.

[2] Sometimes a Budget has made provision, in addition, for a round sum to cover Supplementary Estimates which may be presented during the year. This, however, is not normal. In every year there should be savings on the original Estimates which can be set off against part, at least, of the Supplementaries.

	£ million	%
Consolidated Fund Services:		
Debt Interest and Management	695	13·7
Other	121	2·4
Supply:		
Defence	1,418	27·9
Civil	2,841	56·0
	5,075	100·0

It will be seen that expenditure was expected to be £364 million less than revenue so that over the year as a whole the Budget would provide a surplus of that amount. We shall see in a moment how the surplus was to be used.

BELOW-THE-LINE

Now let us look at the estimates 'below-the-line', and let us start this time on the payments side. Apart from the item of debt-interest, balanced by interest receipts, which is referred to on page 46 (footnote), the payments are either of a purely capital nature which Parliament has expressly authorized to be met by borrowing if necessary; or, if not strictly of a capital nature, they are payments which Parliament has nevertheless authorized to be met by borrowing for some special reason. The purely capital payments consist in the main of loans to Local Authorities, loans to the nationalized industries (Coal, Gas, Electricity, Transport and Civil Aviation), loans to the Post Office for its capital expenditure and loans for New Towns and for colonial development and war damage payments. The payments which are not strictly of a capital nature are a legacy from the Second World War, namely income tax post-war credits. Parliament authorized these to be met by borrowing because, if and when the credits repaid in any one year are of much greater volume than at present, it might unduly distort the Budget revenue accounts if they had to be charged to revenue. (Also, it is not altogether irrelevant that when, during the war, the taxpayers paid the tax which these credits represent, the Budget was heavily in deficit and the amount which the Government had then to borrow for war purposes was correspondingly reduced.)

Estimated receipts below-the-line fall into two groups. First, there is the interest which is received by the Exchequer on loans made under a number of individual statutes and which, as we have just seen, balances an equivalent amount of National Debt interest charged below-the-line. Secondly, repayments of principal are received in respect of the Exchequer loans just referred to. To meet his total outgoings below-the-line the Chancellor will use any surplus of revenue over expenditure above-the-line and the below-the-line receipts just mentioned; and, in so far as all these together are not sufficient, he will raise the necessary balance by borrowing.

The Budget estimate below-the-line for 1958–9 was made up as follows:

RECEIPTS			PAYMENTS		
		£ million			£ million
Interest outside Budget	..	205	Interest outside Budget	..	205
Repayments of past advances:			Post-war credits	.. ..	18
Local Authorities ..	52		War Damage ..	.. ..	20
Nationalized Industries	29		Advances to:		
Others	.. ..	37		Local Authorities ..	65	
	—	118	New Towns	..	31	
			Post Office ..	..	38	
			Colonial Development	12	
			Nationalized Industries	507	
			Others	.. ..	27	
				—	680
		323			
Net sum to be borrowed or met from surplus above-the-line	.. ..	.. 600			
		923			923

Thus, given a net sum of £600 million required to balance this account in 1958–9, the Chancellor estimated that he would derive £364 million from his surplus above-the-line and would have to borrow £236 million.[1]

THE CHANCELLOR'S PROBLEMS

The figures which have just been quoted from the Budget of 1958–9 have been given only to indicate broadly the relative importance of the various items. They will vary from year to year—possibly, in some cases, significantly. Let us now therefore forget the figures and consider in general terms the kinds of problems which may face any

---

[1] This way of putting the matter conveniently short-circuits the process by which the above-the-line surplus is in fact used (as the Old Sinking Fund) to redeem debt and therefore to reduce the increase in the total of the National Debt which would otherwise result from the borrowings necessary to meet the below-the-line issues. (See page 204.)

Chancellor when he is preparing his Budget. They can be conveniently discussed under three headings—prudent finance; social and political commitments and claims; and broad economic and financial policy.

PRUDENT FINANCE

The Chancellor of the Exchequer is the steward of the nation's purse. Quite apart from any wider responsibilities, his first duty is to see that the national finances are conducted prudently and efficiently, both above-the-line and below-the-line. As we shall see later, that does not necessarily mean, even above-the-line, that revenue ought in each and every year to balance expenditure. It does mean that the state finances must not be allowed to drift, that not only the current position but future trends are clearly seen, and that all the necessary provisions are made with eyes open. This is not a duty which appears only with the Budget: it is with the Chancellor all the year round. But it is specially prominent at Budget time because if major decisions have to be taken they must normally be implemented then, or at least explained, and also because they may affect, or be affected by, other aspects of Budget policy. Take the question of the level of current expenditure. This will have been pre-occupying the Chancellor all through the year. Final decisions may have to depend on whether broad economic conditions make it desirable for the Government to spend less or more: but as a prerequisite even to such decisions the level of expenditure must be considered in its own right, so to speak. What is the trend in that level, not only in the immediate future but in the longer-term? Is there a risk that it will outstrip the revenue available to meet it, even at the high levels of taxation associated with inflationary conditions? If so, what is to be done about it? If taxation cannot be, or ought not to be, increased, where shall any necessary reductions in expenditure be made, bearing in mind that significant reductions of expenditure must involve changes of policy that are bound to be challenged in one quarter or another? Can Defence expenditure be reduced either because of changes in international political and strategic conditions or by finding ways of meeting current policies more economically? Is there any practicable way of damping down the rate at which the cost of the social services continues to increase? Should the scope of the services be reduced or can their cost to the Exchequer be lessened by requiring higher contributions or other payments by the beneficiaries for the services they receive? And so on. All these questions, and many others, will have been surrounding the Chancellor privately throughout the year: but they will inexorably demand his attention in public at Budget time because it is then that he must disclose in terms of policy and actual figures what he proposes to do about them.

On the revenue side also, questions of prudence and efficiency arise. The structure of a given tax may have been reasonable and tolerable at any one point of time. But over the years conditions change: anomalies or injustices may arise; or a tax may become patiently too burdensome. The spending habits of people may change; and the yield of a particular tax may show signs of falling as a consequence. And there is always the need to catch up with ingenious people who manage to find ever new ways of legally avoiding this or that tax or part of it. Such matters crowd in upon a Chancellor every year and must at least be considered, even if he decides, in any particular case, to take no action.

In addition, the Chancellor may have to deal with purely management questions below-the-line in order to see that the large capital payments which appear there are efficiently organized and provided for. A notable addition to his responsibilities in this respect was made in 1956 when Parliament provided that those nationalized industries which had previously borrowed on the market to meet their capital expenditure could, for the next two years,[1] be financed direct from the Exchequer. The purpose of this change was to streamline the total demands on the market. Instead of a number of borrowers being forced to go to the market when they needed money, whatever the state of the market, the Treasury would provide them with funds whenever they needed them and—having facilities for financing itself in the meantime—would itself go to the market (in so far as it needed to borrow at all) at the times most suitable and convenient in the light of market conditions and other factors.

SOCIAL AND POLITICAL QUESTIONS

This book is not the place to assess party political programmes, even though they may have such serious consequences for the nation's finances. (It used to be said that, whichever party won an election, the loser was always the Treasury.) Every Chancellor no doubt starts with certain commitments or aims or predictions which he shares with the rest of his party; but he, unlike his party friends, has the unenviable responsibility of advising the Cabinet how quickly they can be implemented or realized having regard to current economic and financial conditions. Further, and quite apart from party considerations, every Government has to act from time to time as a

[1] Later extended, see page 131.

result of the march of domestic events or the development of social and political ideas, and he is a very fortunate Chancellor indeed who does not have to face the consequences, large or small, in the shape of increased expenditure or reduced revenue. And these consequences very often come upon him with such force that not even the most compelling arguments the other way, based on unimpeachable economic or financial grounds, can withstand them.

BROAD ECONOMIC AND FINANCIAL POLICY

A Chancellor is probably more master in his own house—in the sense of being freer to assess needs and devise policies to meet them—in dealing with his third group of problems, those relating to broad economic and financial policy. The very size of the Budget figures makes it clear that Budget policy cannot properly be decided without reference to prevailing economic conditions in the country and to any corrective measures which may be required from time to time. That is not to say that any Government can, through the Budget or otherwise, provide all the correctives that may be required. The process of correction must depend very largely on the judgments and actions of the community generally, that is to say of individuals, business undertakings and organized parties in industry. Still, whatever the conditions, the Government will have much to decide and to do.

(i) If conditions are inflationary, because total demand for goods and services is excessive in relation to the national productive power available to meet it, then, clearly, the Chancellor must consider at least whether the Government's own current demands for goods and services can be reduced: this, as we have already seen, will almost certainly involve looking at important aspects of Government policies which involve expenditure. His review must also extend to the capital expenditure of the Government and of the public undertakings whose capital programmes it controls, because these also mean calls on the productive power of the country. Taxation policy must be looked at to decide, in the first place, whether anything should be done by increases in taxation to curtail demand by consumers; though it will, on the other hand, have to be considered whether increases in direct taxation may not reduce the existing level of saving or whether increases in indirect taxation, by encouraging wage claims, may be positively inflationary. (Parallel to the question of increasing taxation, although outside the Budget, is that of increasing the charges of nationalized industries: but this is a matter for Government influence or 'gentleman's agreement' rather than for unilateral action by the Government.)

On the other hand, taxation must also be considered with another, and more positive, object in view, namely whether anything can be done to encourage an expansion of the nation's productive power, either over a wide industrial field or over some specially important narrower one. But if action of this kind is to be taken it must be remembered that while increased investment in plant and machinery and buildings should increase productive power eventually, its immediate effect is to increase the demand on resources which is already, in total, excessive. It may be that the need to curtail present demand is so pressing that the Chancellor will feel not merely that he cannot encourage any increase in investment but that he must actually reduce such encouragement as taxation already gives it.[1] The need, in this field, to balance short-term and long-term advantages may be the most difficult problem the Chancellor will have in deciding the final shape of his Budget. In doing so he will naturally give great weight to the size of the revenue surplus he will almost certainly want to produce above-the-line. Such a surplus has both negative and positive aspects. Negatively, it is a means of reducing the incomes which give rise to consumers' demand. Positively, it is a means of saving, as a result of which, over the nation as a whole, more resources are left free for other purposes, notably for investment in the expansion and modernization of the nationalized industries, which are basic to industry as a whole. The Chancellor may have to decide whether, or to what degree, it is better to raise revenue for that purpose or to remit it as an encouragement to private investment.

(ii) The economic conditions of the country may at some time be of a quite opposite kind: the problem may be one of counteracting deflation. Total demand may be insufficient to employ all the available national resources of man-power and material, some of which, in consequence, may be standing idle. All the converse questions then arise. Should the Government increase its demand for goods and services, whether on current account or for capital purposes? In the conditions assumed it would be terribly easy for the Government to find new ways of spending more money. It would be all the more necessary to watch for waste and extravagance and to be sure that the favoured plans were really the best ways of employing the man-power and materials involved. Should consumers' expenditure be stimulated by reductions of taxation? It may be that reductions in taxation will stimulate demand more quickly than an increase in Government expenditure. If, at one and the same time, expenditure

[1] Cf. the abolition of the income-tax 'investment allowance', save for certain special cases, in 1956. On the other hand, note the increase in the 'initial allowances' in 1958.

is to be increased and taxation reduced, a Chancellor might have deliberately to plan for a deficit on his Budget above-the-line. That will depend on the state of his Budget—that is, the size of any surplus above-the-line—before his anti-deflationary programme is put into operation. It may well be that the shrinkage of income due to the deflation will already have reduced any such surplus.

What attitude should be taken towards the principle of deliberately budgeting for a deficit? In the first place, and in the interests of maintaining adequate control, any deficit must clearly be kept to the lowest figure which will meet the circumstances of the time. Secondly, regard must be had to the fact that any deficit inevitably means an increase in the national debt: the Chancellor will have to borrow to meet some of his expenditure above-the-line, and, having no surplus to carry down, he will have to borrow more to meet capital expenditure below-the-line. A good deal of his borrowing below-the-line may be offset by productive assets and to that extent— provided the relevant projects are wisely conceived and efficiently carried out—the increase in the national debt on this account need not cause undue alarm. But matters are different with an increase in the national debt incurred to balance revenue and expenditure above-the-line. This will normally provide no corresponding new productive assets. Its aim is to give work to idle existing capacity, and in so far as it does this there will be an increase in production which will justify some increase in consumption. Nevertheless these results will be achieved only at a certain price, namely that in future years, whatever the then state of the economy, the general taxpayer will have to find the interest which has to be paid to the holders of the newly-created debt. The balance of advantage and disadvantage may make a policy of budgeting for a deficit worthwhile for a given year or even for two or three years—but only on two conditions. First the deficits must be kept as low as possible. Secondly, the policy must not be accepted as one of indefinite duration. Over a period of years the Budget should certainly be balanced above-the-line; otherwise that part of the debt which is not covered by new assets will increase indefinitely.

Arguments have been put forward for a less restrictive view of the acceptability of a policy of budgeting for a deficit. It is said, for instance, that an indefinite increase in the national debt does not matter so long as the rate of increase is less than the rate of increase in the national income.[1] The logic of this particular limitation is not obvious: why should the amount of the national debt charge, which

[1] This argument received some countenance in the White Paper on 'Employment Policy', 1944, paragraph 78 (Cmd 6527).

is one particular transfer within the country, be related only to the total production of the country irrespective of what is happening to other such transfers? Again, if the argument is that a rising national income means rising Budget revenue and that the latter can support a higher debt charge, it may be dangerous to mortgage in advance any given part of the increase in revenue for the debt charge, irrespective of other possible claims. Finally, the argument would seem to imply that if, in a period of acute deflation, the national income falls or ceases to rise, the debt should not be increased at all. All told, there would seem to be a strong case for a more cautious approach to the question on the lines suggested above.

(iii) So far, in this part of our discussion, we have proceeded as though the Chancellor could operate in a 'closed economy': that is, without any reference to the fact that this country depends for its livelihood on its vast two-way trade with the rest of the world. Yet every aspect of its domestic economy is affected by movements and trends in its mercantile and financial relations with other countries. Conversely the state of its domestic economy can have profound effects on its balance of trade and payments. We are both traders with, and bankers for, a large part of the rest of the world. Since nearly half the world's trade is carried on in sterling, and the whole world is therefore vitally interested in the worth of our currency, the eyes of the world are continuously on our domestic economy as an indicator of the soundness of sterling. For the Commonwealth we are not only bankers but the expected source of much of the finance they need for their development, and, over a period, we can only provide them with that finance if we have ourselves first earned it by a surplus of exports over imports. For our present purposes it is not necessary to try to look at all the problems raised by these overseas relations. Some matters which may cause difficulty—like the movement of capital funds over the exchanges, or the extent of foreign borrowing in London—do not, in any case, lend themselves to treatment by Budgetary measures. On the other hand, some points are very relevant to any discussion of Budget policy.

A first and general point is that foreign confidence in sterling will always depend on the view which overseas observers take of the state of our domestic economy and on their assessment of the adequacy of the steps which the Government are taking to correct any dangerous trends in that economy. The Budget is, *par excellence*, the occasion when the Government's plans in this respect are made known and justified. It is not in the Chancellor's power to command the confidence of such observers in his policies: but he should certainly be the first to appreciate what the consequences for this country will be if that confidence is not forthcoming.

Secondly, this country depends on imports for a large proportion of its food and other necessaries of life, and for much of the raw materials on which its industries depend. Imports therefore increase if consumers' expenditure increases or if the general productive activity of the country increases. So if, as a means of combating inflation, the Chancellor takes measures to curtail consumers' expenditure he will, other things being equal, help to reduce the deficit on our visible balance of trade; but if, despite the increased demand it entails, he seeks to encourage increased production he must accept some increase of imports and some worsening of that balance in the first instance. He will, of course, hope that in either case the measures he is taking will at the same time encourage an increase of exports: more productive capacity should be available to feed the export market. His hope, however, will only be realized if the price and quality of our goods are competitive in foreign markets—which emphasizes the importance of his whole anti-inflationary policy—and our manufacturers go all out to seize the new opportunities of export which are being provided. If the conditions in which the Chancellor has to draw up his Budget are, on the contrary, deflationary and he adopts policies designed to increase demand of all kinds—consumers' expenditure, Government expenditure, public and private investment —he will have to watch just as carefully, if not more so, for the effects on our balance of trade and payments. That will depend on what state the balance is in. But such increase of demand will certainly mean a noticeable increase of imports. How far there will be any compensating increase of exports is problematical: the very deflationary conditions the Chancellor is trying to cure may be due largely to a falling off of production for export because, for example, of a trade recession in the rest of the world. It is possible, therefore, that reflationary policies may have serious results for the balance of payments and for the country's foreign exchange reserves.[1]

(iv) Broad questions of economic policy may not always present themselves in the clear-cut form—as between inflation and deflation —which the preceding paragraphs may have suggested. The Chancellor's hardest task may well arise when inflationary conditions have not merely become less so but may possibly be giving way to an incipient deflation, and vice versa. There will always be room for difference of opinions on these questions even when the situation is

---

[1] 'It is altogether too comforting to suppose that this country, with its tiny reserves, can spend its way out of a world recession' (*The Times*, January 23, 1958).

fairly clear-cut, and still more so when economic forces, as yet possibly half-hidden, are making for a change. But one thing is clear. The inevitable uncertainty of economic developments makes it essential that the Government should have prompt and adequate knowledge of changes in the economic situation of the country so that necessary measures, whether anti-inflationary or anti-deflationary, can be introduced at the earliest possible moment. Only then can the inflation or deflation be prevented from proceeding so far that it has dangerous results not only from the human and social points of view but also from the point of view of confidence in the public finances and in the country's balance of payments.[1]

FINDING THE SOLUTIONS

When the Chancellor has, in the light of current conditions, studied such questions as we have just been posing and has decided broadly the direction in which his Budget ought to go, he then has to decide what particular steps he shall take. These will depend first on such quantitative estimates as he can make of the likely changes in the economy. For the year just closing the figures of national income and expenditure discussed in Chapter II will give a picture of the balance between expenditure of various kinds (including, for this purpose, exports) and the total supplies available in the country (including imports). The figures will show, for example, how far any change in the total national product for the year has been due to change in consumers' expenditure or Government expenditure on goods and services or investment or exports. Estimates must then be made of the likely changes in such factors during the coming year. Obviously the making of such estimates is a risky undertaking: nevertheless it is well worthwhile to try to get some idea of the order of magnitude of the changes as a guide to the answer to the Chancellor's problem. The argument runs like this. During the year just closing, when the Budget showed a certain surplus or a certain deficit, such extra supplies as became available went in this or that direction, desirable or undesirable. What was desirable or undesirable would depend on the circumstances; more exports will nearly always be desirable; in

---

[1] See the White Paper on 'Employment Policy' (Cmd 6527), published in May 1944 and written when there was some anxiety about maintaining full employment after the war. Most of this paper—and certainly the passage dealing with Central Finance (paragraphs 74–9)—has stood up to the test of post-war expenditure remarkably well. But see also the sequel to it, 'The Economic Implications of Full Employment' (Cmd 9725), published in March 1956 and written in the full glare of the rising prices which had accompanied full employment.

time of inflation consumers' expenditure and Government expenditure on goods and services would no doubt be undesirable. Whatever the recent pattern, it happened partly because of, or despite, the current Budget surplus or deficit. A Budget surplus above-the-line means that so much net purchasing power has been extracted from the private sector and (probably) used to finance public investment, while a deficit means that so much has been injected into that sector to be spent as the sector wishes. According as the trends in national expenditure in the past year are judged to have been satisfactory or otherwise, there is ground or not for supposing that the size of the actual Budget surplus or deficit was broadly reasonable. From this starting point it is possible to go on to decide broad aims for the coming year. Given the estimated trends under the various heads of national expenditure it can be judged whether the Budget should show a bigger surplus or deficit than in the year just closing and, very roughly, how much the difference should be. The Chancellor, having decided on a figure for this difference, then has to give effect to it by adjustments of either Budget expenditure or Budget revenue. He will probably settle first the possibilities on the expenditure side and in the light of them turn to action on the revenue. And on the revenue side he will have to decide what particular taxes can best be adjusted to meet the needs of the situation. Will those needs best be met by changes in direct taxation (income tax or the profits tax on companies) or in the indirect taxation on particular goods or commodities (such as the purchase tax)?[1] Such questions can only be answered in the light of the circumstances of the time.

The Budget surplus or deficit we have just been discussing is that above-the-line. If there is a deficit above-the-line—which implies deflationary conditions—the whole of the net expenditure below-the-line must, of course, be met by borrowing; and the amount of such borrowing will depend primarily on the total of the capital investment which the Government judge they should finance to help to offset the deflation. In times of inflation, which will be the occasion for any substantial surplus above-the-line, the net balance of the Budget 'overall'—that is, taking above-the-line and below-the-line together—will be of some importance. It may be assumed that, as his

[1] In considering possible adjustments of a surplus or deficit, whether through expenditure or taxation, it may be necessary to consider not only the amounts involved but also the degrees to which those adjustments would in fact be inflationary or deflationary. The economic effects of increasing (or reducing) the surplus or deficit may, if taxation is the medium of the change, vary as between taxes (e.g. the income tax and estate duty). They may also vary as between increasing (or reducing) a tax by a given amount and reducing (or increasing) a particular form of expenditure by a like amount.

contribution towards limiting total demand, the Chancellor will be keeping to the minimum the capital expenditure which he has to finance below-the-line. The important question is how far, if at all, he should let that expenditure exceed his surplus above-the-line. It is doubtful whether there is a case, even in times of inflation, for insisting that he should avoid such excess altogether: that is, that he should balance his Budget overall. If he feels confident that real savings are going to flow into the Exchequer in a certain amount during the coming year, he will be justified in arranging for at least that amount of capital expenditure to be met by borrowing. Even in time of inflation, essential capital development must go on and if it is made possible by real voluntary saving that is a wholly desirable result.

Two points must now be mentioned which, although not as closely connected as the above problems with the actual Budget figures, may well play a part in the Budget statement. The first is that financial policy in its broadest sense goes wider than adjustments of Budget revenue and expenditure and may include measures designed to support the policy underlying such adjustments: the obvious measures are those affecting interest rates and credit policy. Both these matters lie primarily within the technical responsibility of the Bank of England; but they must clearly form an integral part of the general economic and financial policy of the Government. There is therefore the closest consultation and collaboration between the Bank on the one hand and the Chancellor and Treasury officials on the other, not only about these two matters but over the whole policy field. It is not necessary for us to pursue here the economic implications of movements in the Bank Rate or of measures to secure, for example, the tightening or relaxing of credit by the commercial banks. They are only mentioned here for the sake of completeness because, in his Budget statement, the Chancellor may have to explain and justify measures which, although they form part of his general policy, are for the Bank of England to carry out or supervize.

The second point is that, in speaking of conditions in times of inflation, we have assumed that the inflation arose from an excess of total demand over total resources available to meet it—what is known as 'demand inflation'. There is another type of inflation, known as 'cost inflation', which forces up prices and which will most commonly be due to rises in wage rates which are not balanced by rises in productivity. Cost-inflation may well lead to a state of excess demand which must be dealt with by Budgetary measures of the type we have been discussing above. But it is very unlikely that any Chancellor will seek by such measures to deal directly with any unbalanced increases in wage rates. Governments may seek to educate workers and employers about the economic and social consequences of such increases; but no Government has yet interfered with the general run of wage settlements arrives at through the use of the normal negotiating machinery. Exceptions to this general rule might arise if there were a risk that the Government might be called upon to finance increases being negotiated by others (e.g. by a nationalized undertaking). And, of course, the Government must be responsible for granting or refusing increases to employees, civil or military, of the Crown.

PUBLICATIONS

These, then, are the problems which may face any Chancellor as he builds up the proposals which he will make when he 'opens his Budget' in the House of Commons. What those proposals will be will depend on the precise circumstances of the time and on the views which he takes of them. And the method and mode of the presentation of the Budget will depend not only on those circumstances but on the Chancellor's own personal habits of thought and speech. So we cannot carry further our study of the possible general designs of future Budgets.

But it should be added that, as the background to the Chancellor's personal Budget statement, Parliament and the country are presented, before or on Budget Day every year, with a wealth of statistical evidence and official comment on the economic condition of the country and cognate matters. All this is contained in no less than seven White Papers. We have already referred to the *Preliminary Estimate of National Income and Expenditure* for the calendar year just ended and previous years (page 32), and to the *Economic Survey* (page 40). In addition there is a very full paper on the *United Kingdom Balance of Payments* during the past calendar year and previous years; and a paper on *Defence Policy* which explains the policy underlying the Defence Estimates for the coming year, the figures of which are set out in a separate White Paper, *Defence Statistics*. The Civil *Vote on Account*[1] will have given the estimated total of Civil Supply expenditure. Finally, as soon as the Chancellor has sat down after his Budget speech, the *Financial Statement* is issued.

THE POLITICAL SIGNIFICANCE OF THE BUDGET

To conclude this chapter we must notice, though there is little need to emphasize, the importance of a Budget to the political prestige

[1] See page 221.

and stability of the Government whose Chancellor presents it. The Budget cannot fail to signalize the Government's policies in three main directions, in each of which they may arouse controversy. First, the Estimates of expenditure for which the Budget seeks to provide must embody the Government's policies in such vital fields as Defence, the Social Services and Agriculture. Secondly, its taxation proposals actively display, or at least imply, the Government's policy on the distribution of taxation. Thirdly, both sides of the Budget must reflect the Government's approach to the broader economic problems of the moment.

If the Government were to be defeated in the House of Commons by an attack on the whole Budget from any of these angles, it could hardly fail either to resign or to seek a dissolution with a view to an appeal to the country. How far the same would apply to a defeat on one particular element in the revenue or expenditure would no doubt depend partly on the intrinsic importance of that element and partly on the extent to which the critics themselves had made it the occasion for a general display of lack of confidence. It might be that pressure to amend or abandon a particular proposal could be met, satisfactorily to both sides, by the withdrawal of the proposal either temporarily, pending the introduction of revised proposals, or permanently.

CHAPTER IV

The Budget in Detail—(1) Revenue

(A) INTRODUCTORY

IN this and the next two chapters we propose to give a short guide to the contents of each head of the Budget, starting in this chapter with the Revenue. We shall take the Revenue items in the order in which they appear both in the Budget White Paper (the 'Financial Statement') and in the weekly Exchequer Return. Although we shall endeavour to notice all but the very smallest items, we must necessarily be very selective in giving details from the vast amount of information available on the subject.

ESTIMATING THE REVENUE

The revenue figures given in any Budget are, of course, estimates of what the different heads of the revenue are expected to yield during the coming year, and, before describing the individual items, it may be as well to notice how those estimates are framed in some of the important cases. The Income Tax alone is estimated to yield £2,312 million in 1958–9, and the Customs and Excise £2,189 million. Where such large sums are concerned everything that is humanly possible must be done to avoid in the estimates larger margins of error which might invalidate the general basis on which the Budget is framed. The estimating procedure must differ from case to case. That for the income tax is the most difficult of all. The gross income of all kinds to be assessed is of the order of £20,000 million a year. It is derived from all sorts of occupations and other sources. By far the largest element, about two-thirds of the whole, is made up of salaries and wages, from the great bulk of which tax is deducted currently under 'Pay-As-You-Earn'. The total of this may be affected greatly by future economic developments which may have their origins either in this country or abroad—such as the course of trade and industry and therefore of employment, and changes in the levels of prices and wages. In this field, therefore, the Inland Revenue Department enlist the help of the Economic Section of the Treasury and, between them, they endeavour to form the most informed and intelligent estimate possible of the total of salaries and wages in the coming year. It will then be for the Inland Revenue Department, on the basis of their long experience of the working of the complicated system of reliefs and allowances, to estimate how much tax is likely to be paid on that total. But, however much care is taken by everyone concerned, it is clear that they are subject to all the limitations that attach to human efforts to forecast economic conditions for twelve months or more ahead. Another group of incomes—much smaller in total than salaries and wages, but still large, comprising nearly a quarter of the whole—consists of the profits from businesses. These are normally taxed on the 'previous year' basis, and the estimating problem is therefore a different one. In this case, the business world lends its help. A large number of firms, who together form a fair sample of the whole, give the Department, in February, advance information of the profits likely to be assessed to tax in the coming year and from this information the Department can exercise a check on its own provisional estimates.

For the Customs and Excise, estimating must take a rather different form. The Department will certainly use whatever information and advice is available about general trends, such as the likely course of overseas trade affecting the Customs or of personal expenditure on goods subject to Excise duties and the Purchase Tax. But all this will have to be set alongside their knowledge or forecasts of special factors affecting individual commodities, e.g. any noticeable or expected trends in the consumption of tobacco or beer or other alcoholic drinks or in the number of new motor-cars on which Purchase Tax will be paid.

The estimates to which we have been referring are, of course, estimates of the yield of the various taxes as they exist just before the Budget. When the Chancellor of the Exchequer proposes changes in those taxes he normally states what difference they are expected to make in the revenue figures. In some cases the forecasting of such differences may be fairly straightforward, as for example, for a change in the standard rate of income tax or in the child allowance. In the case of the Profits Tax, the new universal flat rate of tax removes some of the difficulties of estimating the effects of changes in the former differential rates. In the Customs and Excise the effects of changes in rates of duty on consumption may in some cases be of the essence in estimating their financial effects. Changes, for instance, in the beer duty or in the Purchase Tax on motor-cars, may have quite important effects on the future level of consumption. Demand in the two cases just mentioned is, in varying degrees, fairly 'elastic';

while in the important cases of the tobacco and petrol duties, as well as in some of the less important cases like the duties on sugar and other imported commodities, it is probably very much less so.

In accouncing changes in taxation, the Chancellor of the Exchequer normally gives two estimates of the financial effect of each change—first, one for the Budget year and, secondly, one for 'a full year'. The 'full year' figure will normally be the greater. The reason for the difference between the two varies from tax to tax.

In the field of Inland Revenue the reason is that not all the tax charged for a year of assessment (say, 1958-9) is collected in that year. Some of it will not reach the Exchequer until 1959-60 or even 1960-1. In the case of tax deducted from earnings under PAYE the employer usually pays over the tax at monthly intervals in arrear, so tax deducted during the last month of 1958-9 will not appear in the accounts of the Inland Revenue Department until the beginning of 1959-60. Individual traders who are assessed under Schedule D pay tax in two instalments, one due in the January of the year of assessment and one in the following July; so that only half the tax assessed for 1958-9 is due in that year, the other half being due in July of the year 1959-60. Again, although companies should pay all the tax assessed for 1958-9 in January 1959, they may not for various reasons—such as delays in agreeing the amount of taxable profits—settle their full liability until the following year. Generally, the proportion of a full year's effect of a change of income tax which falls in the year in which the change is first made is higher in the case of a change in the standard rate than in the case of most other changes in the tax: this is because a high proportion of standard rate tax is paid by companies, while changes in reliefs and allowances involve adjustments of tax liabilities which will not be fully effected until the following year.

A change in a Customs or Excise duty will always take effect from a specified date and, except in the unusual case of a Budget being opened on April 1st, the change will operate for less than a complete year in the Budget year. In addition, the persons responsible for paying in the proceeds of a Customs or Excise duty often do so at agreed intervals on the basis of periodical accounts of their liabilities; and the incidence of the paying-in date may delay the effects on the revenue of a change in a duty, because some duty at the old rate may be paid in during the current year.

It should be noted that the total of Inland Revenue or Customs and Excise revenue actually transferred to the Exchequer during any financial year is unlikely to be the precise amount actually received in the year by the department concerned. It may be either larger or smaller, though the difference is always relatively small—a fraction of 1 per cent of the revenue. The reasons for this difference will vary from case to case but it may be due to changes in working balances or in the amount of revenue in transit at the beginning or end of the year or to the procedure (as described below) by which some revenue is temporarily retained to meet outgoings.

COSTS OF COLLECTION

The annual cost of collecting the two main groups of revenue—the Inland Revenue and the Customs and Excise[1]—is, relative to the revenue collected, extremely small. In the case of the Inland Revenue it is about 1·3 per cent (about threepence in the pound) of the gross revenue collected. In the case of the Customs and Excise the corresponding figure is 0·8 per cent (just under twopence in the pound).[2] The Inland Revenue requires a staff of about 53,000, whereas the Customs and Excise, yielding three-quarters of the amount of the Inland Revenue, requires a staff of only about 15,000. The difference is due primarily, of course, to the greater complexity and wider incidence of most of the Inland Revenue duties. The Customs and Excise have their difficult problems, but they are not so intricate or ubiquitous as the questions of assessment and valuation arising under the complicated legislation governing the income tax, surtax, death duties and profits tax.

Finally, where such large revenues are being collected at so many points of the country, it is essential that there should be adequate checks and audits. The checks are provided in the first place within each department under the directions of the Accountant and Comptroller-General. After that, the accounts are audited by the Comptroller and Auditor-General.[3] By Section 2 of the Exchequer and Audit Departments Act, 1921, the accounts of the receipt of revenue by the Department of the Inland Revenue, the Customs and Excise and the Post Office are to be 'examined by the Comptroller and Auditor-General on behalf of the House of Commons in order to ascertain that adequate regulations and procedure have been framed to secure an effective check on the assessment, collection and proper allocation of revenue' and he is to 'satisfy himself that any such regulations and procedure are being duly carried out'. He is to

[1] On the expenses of the Post Office, see page 97.

[2] The figures for both departments exclude the cost of non-revenue work and of services rendered to other departments but include charges met out of the Votes of other departments on the revenue departments' behalf.

[3] On this official's status and duties, see Chapter XIII.

'make such examination as he thinks fit with respect to the correctness of the sum brought to account in respect of such revenue' and report to the House of Commons thereon when he reports on the departments' Appropriation Accounts. The Permanent Head of each revenue department is examined on his revenue accounts, along with his Appropriation Accounts, by the Public Accounts Committee of the House of Commons.

(B) THE INLAND REVENUE

GENERAL

For the year 1958–9 the Inland Revenue duties in force and their estimated yields to the Exchequer are as follows:

	£ million
Income Tax	2,312
Surtax	163
Death Duties	163
Stamps	56
Profits Tax (and late settlements of Excess Profits Tax and Excess Profits Levy)	275
Other duties	Less than 1
	2,970

The total accounts for 55 per cent of the estimated Budget revenue, and the income tax alone for 43 per cent. At these figures, the total shows an increase of about 55 per cent, and the income tax an increase of 77 per cent, over the corresponding estimates for ten years previously (1948–9). The cause of this great increase in the yield of the income tax is, of course, the increase in salaries, wages and profits. In the ten years salaries and wages have roughly doubled, and so have company profits, while the trading profits of individuals and partnerships have increased by nearly 50 per cent. Against this must be set the fact that the standard rate of tax has been reduced by 6d and every tax relief and allowance has been increased; with the result that the average effective rate of tax levied on each pound of actual income has fallen from 3s in 1948–9 to something under 2s 10d in 1958–9. Surtax tells a different story. Although the number of surtax payers and their total income have increased by more than half, the increases have been almost wholly in the lower and middle ranges of income: the general increase in all personal incomes has pushed new

C

taxpayers into the surtax field and increased the incomes of those who were already in its lower ranges. In the result, while the average income assessed to surtax has steadily fallen, the estimated yield of tax in 1958–9 is 81 per cent above what it was ten years previously. (The only important changes in the tax made in those ten years were the reduction of the highest rate from 10s 6d to 10s in the £ in 1951, and the reduction from taxable income of certain personal allowances in 1957.) The Death Duties, of which the yield fluctuates from year to year, do not lend themselves to such comparisons or show any steady trends. The case of the Stamp Duties is very similar—a fluctuating revenue dependent on, among other things, the current general level of property values including those of stocks and shares. It is not possible to give any brief account of trends in the course of the profits tax, for a number of reasons. There have been frequent changes of the rates; prior to 1958 the rate on distributed profits was steadily made more severe relative to that on undistributed profits; an important change was made in 1952 when the existing rates were much reduced but the amount paid in profits tax ceased to be allowed as a deduction for income tax purposes; and finally, in 1958, a universal flat rate of tax was substituted for the then existing differential rates on distributed and undistributed profits.

Anyone who wishes to examine the yields of particular taxes in detail should study the Annual Reports of the Commonwealth of Inland Revenue. These Reports contain a great wealth of statistical matter—notably in relation to the different type of income and of their owners—which is of the greatest value not only to the student of public finance but to all interested in the wider aspects, including the sociological aspects, of the distribution of incomes and capital wealth and in the profits (and their distribution) of individual trades and industries. Most of this material appears, with up-to-date additions, in each Report; but occasionally the Commissioners include special items, like the results of the special survey of the distribution of incomes in 1954–5 which appeared partly in the Ninety-ninth Report (for 1955–6) and partly in the Hundredth Report (for 1956–7).[1] The latter Report included fairly full outlines of the structure of the various Inland Revenue duties, which have been freely used in the short accounts of the various duties given below.

ADMINISTRATION

The Inland Revenue duties are all administered by the Commissioners of Inland Revenue, who together constitute the Board of Inland

[1] Cmnd 54 and Cmnd 341 respectively.

Revenue and who are now appointed under the Inland Revenue Regulation Act, 1890. But the Board's origins lie much farther back in the distant past. Curiously enough, the earliest duties in the Inland Revenue field were the Excise duties, which since 1909 have been administered by the Board of Customs and Excise. The Excise originated in the seventeenth century when an Excise Board was appointed. In 1694, stamp duties were imposed and a Board of Stamps set up, and in 1718 a Board of Taxes was appointed to administer the land tax and other small inland taxes. By the end of the eighteenth century there were six separate Boards of such kinds; but Stamps and Taxes were amalgamated in 1834, and in 1849 the first Board of Inland Revenue was set up to cover Excise, Stamps and Taxes.

The Board now consists of seven senior permanent Civil Servants— a Chairman, who ranks with the Heads of major Departments, two Deputy Chairmen and four other Commissioners. Under the Board the Department is organized in the following branches with the duties shown: the Secretaries' Office (general administration and management of the Inland Revenue duties, staff management, statistics and intelligence and the collection of arrears of tax which cannot be collected locally); the Office of the Chief Inspector of Taxes (executive application of the law relating to income tax and profits tax, with over 650 local Tax Offices throughout the United Kingdom, each under one of HM Inspectors of Taxes, in addition to staffs in London and certain provincial centres); the Office of the Accountant and Comptroller-General of Inland Revenue (primarily responsible for the collection of income tax, land tax and profits tax in England and Wales and Northern Ireland[1]—the first two taxes being collected at about 250 local offices each under a 'Collector in Charge'; the receiving, controlling and bringing to account of all Inland Revenue duties; controlling and accounting for expenditure out of the Inland Revenue Vote); the Office of the Special Commissioners of Income Tax (assessment and collection of surtax and certain income tax assessments); the Estate Duty Offices in London and Edinburgh (assessment and collection of estate duty and some old death duties); the Office of the Controller of Stamps (assessment of stamp duties at headquarters and local offices in England and Wales); the Office of the Director of Stamping (mechanical work at headquarters and local offices in connection with the collection of stamp duty); Solicitors' offices in London and Edinburgh (advice on legal questions and representation of the Department in legal proceedings); the Comptroller of Stamps and Taxes, with headquarters in Edinburgh (exer-

[1] On taxation generally in Northern Ireland, see page 109.

cising for Scotland many functions which for the rest of the United Kingdom are performed by other branches of the Department) and local Collection and Stamp Offices; two Valuation Offices with headquarters respectively in London and Edinburgh and each with separate local and regional organizations (capital valuation of property in connection with Inland Revenue taxation and a variety of work for other Government departments, notably in England and Wales, the preparation and maintenance of rating valuation lists); and a Head Office Typing Branch.

Two general points about this organization must be noticed. First, although the Commissioners of Inland Revenue are responsible for the general management of the Inland Revenue duties they are not the statutory assessing authority for all the duties collected. Originally, the greater part of the administration of the income tax was exercised by local unpaid bodies called General Commissioners of Income Tax, and although the tax is now largely calculated by local Inspectors of Taxes, acting under the directions of the Board, the said General Commissioners still appoint Additional Commissioners to sign and allow assessments under Schedules A and B, and also under Schedule D except where the taxpayer opts to be assessed by the Special Commissioners. The local Inspector of Taxes is now the statutory assessing authority for tax under 'Pay-As-You-Earn'. There are special arrangements for assessments on the Bank of England, and in Northern Ireland and on interest and dividends under Schedules C and D.[1] All assessments to surtax are made by the Special Commissioners; those to profits tax by the Commissioners of Inland Revenue on calculations made by the local Inspectors of Taxes.

The second point is that the process of collections is throughout kept separate from that of assessment. In England and Wales, when the appropriate assessing authority has assessed a person to income tax or land tax, for instance, that person pays his tax, not to that authority, but to the office of the local collector if the assessment was made locally or direct to the Accountant and Comptroller-General if it was made by the Special Commissioners. (An employer deducting tax under the PAYE system usually pays it over at regular intervals to the local collection office.) All other Inland Revenue duties, except stamp duties, are paid direct to the Accountant and Comptroller-General. In Scotland, payments not made locally are made to the Comptroller of Stamps and Taxes, Edinburgh. The accounting authorities of the Department are thus able to check that an assessment to tax and the tax actually paid in respect thereof—coming to them from two independent sources—agree.

[1] On these 'Schedules', see page 71 below.

REMITTANCE OF THE REVENUE TO THE EXCHEQUER

In England and Wales, each Collection Office and Stamp Office lodges its receipts daily in an account with a local branch of a Clearing Bank in the name of the Commissioners of Inland Revenue. At weekly intervals—or, in the case of some collections, twice a week or even daily—the Head Office of the Bank transfers the amounts of these lodgments to the General Account of the Commissioners of Inland Revenue at the Bank of England. The balance on the General Account—after providing for authorized outgoings and for an agreed permanent balance—is then transferred daily to the Account of HM Exchequer at the Bank of England, each day's transfer being allocated to the respective duties by the Accountant and Comptroller-General, who notifies the Treasury and the Comptroller and Auditor-General accordingly.

The above arrangements are designed primarily to give effect to Section 10 of the Exchequer and Audit Department Act, 1866, which, as we have already seen,[1] concentrated all revenue receipts in one account (that of the Exchequer) and required the Commissioners of Inland Revenue, with others, to pay the revenues they receive into that account.[2] In fact, the Act also allowed the diversion of some of the revenues in two directions. First, the Commissioners (like the other Revenue Departments) are allowed to set off repayments and discounts against receipts. Secondly, a rather cumbrous proviso says that collectors of the revenues shall not be prevented 'from cashing, as heretofore, under the authority of any Act or regulation, orders issued for naval, military, air force, revenue, civil or other services, repayable to the revenue departments out of the Consolidated Fund, or out of moneys provided by Parliament'. This proviso allows the Department, as necessary, to finance temporarily out of revenue in its hands, work it may have undertaken for other departments, subject to repayment by the latter. More important for our purpose, it allows the Department to retain revenue temporarily to meet its own expenses for staff and other administrative outgoings. The machinery for this latter purpose is as follows. The head office and local offices of the Department make payments continuously of salaries and wages and other outgoings chargeable to the Supply Vote for the Inland Revenue. Each local office makes such payments from an official Drawing Account at a local Bank

---

[1] Page 15.

[2] In the case of the Inland Revenue, the regulated remission of revenue to the Exchequer is also required by Section I of the Public Accounts and Charges Act 1891.

which is kept in funds by advances from the Accountant and Comptroller-General (or, in Scotland, by the Comptroller of Stamps and Taxes, Edinburgh) who records these advances as if they were outgoings from the Commissioners' General Account in respect of income tax; that is, he temporarily diverts income tax revenue for the purpose. He also uses income tax revenue to meet head office expenses chargeable to the Inland Revenue Vote. To put matters right the Treasury credits the Commissioners' General Account each month with an advance in respect of the Vote and that amount is immediately returned to the Exchequer as income tax revenue. Over the year these credits received from the Treasury are sufficient to cover the expenditure of the year within the amount voted by Parliament. By this procedure we have got to the required accounting position in which the Exchequer has, on the one hand, received the revenue in full and has, on the other hand, itself met the Department's expenses as Parliament intended.

THE INLAND REVENUE DUTIES

Income Tax

From at least the fourteenth century many direct taxes—such as property and land taxes, and even poll taxes—were graduated in some degree according to the incomes of those on whom they were levied. And in 1797—the year before he introduced his income tax—William Pitt the Younger had himself proposed to rely, to help finance the war with France, on additions, regulated according to income, to a medley of the old direct taxes known as 'assessed taxes'.[1] But he quickly realized the imperfections of such a patchwork system and in 1798 replaced the war additions by the tax which has always since been known as the income tax and which was levied on annual incomes exceeding £60 and at graduated rates rising to 2s in the £ on incomes of £200 and upwards. Except for the year of delusive peace, 1802–3, for which it was repealed, this tax, with modifications, lasted until 1816 when, after the end of the Napoleonic Wars, public opinion secured its repeal. It was revived in 1842 by Sir Robert Peel in order to enable him to abolish a very large number of indirect taxes on articles of trade, and it has been operative ever since. In its origins, therefore, it was a wartime tax—an elastic and productive source of emergency finance, of which Mr Gladstone said in 1853 that was was the very time when it was 'desirable that you should have the power of renewed and free resort to this mighty

[1] E.g. taxes on inhabited houses, land and tenements, servants, carriages, riding horses, etc.

engine, to make it again available for the defence and salvation of the country'. And so it has been. Although enduring through times of peace at rates not dreamt of a hundred years ago, the income tax was, in a crescendo of increasing effect, a relatively 'mighty engine' in the Boer War (raised from 8d to 1s 3d), the First World War (raised from 1s 3d to 6s, together with an increase from 1s 4d to 4s 6d in the top rate of super tax) and in the Second World War (raised from 5s 6d to 10s, with a top rate of surtax throughout at 9s 6d). We need not speculate on the question whether taxation policy would have any practical meaning in any future total nuclear war; but, short of such a catastrophe, the income tax must continue to be regarded as the first available source of increased taxation to raise finance in war or other emergency and, in particular, to counter the inevitably inflationary effects of war expenditure.

As everyone knows, the tax is a highly complicated one. The last consolidation of the law about it was the Income Tax Act, 1952, which ran to 532 clauses and 25 schedules. The complications are not the result of any perverse desire of bureaucrats to make things deliberately difficult for the taxpayer. They are the inevitable result of a search for fairness (as in the many varied personal reliefs and allowances), of deliberate policy in encouraging certain forms of expenditure (as in the investment allowances to certain industries) and of closing loopholes by which the more ingenious taxpayers seek legally to avoid taxation which they were intended to bear.

The tax applies to all income which has its origin in the United Kingdom, and to all income, wherever originating, which accrues to a person residing in the United Kingdom. The Income Tax Act does not attempt a general definition of income as such; and indeed no such general definition has ever been laid down by the Courts in interpreting the Act. On the other hand, the Act specifies income which falls under each of five classes or 'Schedules', A, B, C, D and E. These Schedules cover the following sources of income:

Schedule A: Income from the ownership of land, buildings and other hereditaments. (This does not necessarily mean cash income from the property. Tax is charged on its net annual value; that is, on its gross annual value—the annual rent at which it was let or worth to be let in 1936—less a deduction for repairs, etc.)

Schedule B: Income from the occupation of lands. (This is now confined to amenity lands and woodlands. The profits of farmers and others occupying land for business purposes are assessable under Schedule D.)

Schedule C: Interest on certain British Government Securities and certain securities of governments and public authorities outside the

United Kingdom. (Except in certain special cases the tax is deducted at the source by the authority paying the interest who then accounts to the Inland Revenue Department for the tax.)

Schedule D: Profits and income arising under six heads or 'Cases'; namely, I. Profits of a trade; II. Profits of a profession or vocation, not dealt with elsewhere; III. Interest (except that charged under C) and similar receipts; IV. Income (except that charged under C) from securities (e.g. debentures) out of the United Kingdom; V. Income (e.g. dividends) from other possessions outside the United Kingdom; and VI. Income not charged elsewhere. (Under Cases I, and II there is a system of allowances for capital expenditure, normally spread over the lives of the assets concerned, and, in a few special cases, additional 'investment allowances'.)

Schedule E: Income from an office, employment or pension including emoluments for duties performed overseas by a person resident in the United Kingdom. (For the great bulk of this income tax is deducted by employers under the PAYE scheme. The employers make the deductions by reference to code numbers and tax tables supplied by the Inland Revenue Department and reflecting the entitlements of the employee to various tax allowances.)

In the case of the individual taxpayer (as distinct from e.g. a company) the tax payable is graduated by means of various reliefs and allowances. For example, there are reliefs for earned income (as distinct from investment income), life insurance premiums, age (up to a certain limit of income) and small incomes; and there are allowances to each single and married taxpayer, and for children, dependent relatives and others. These reliefs and allowances are in effect subtracted from the total income to arrive at the taxable income; and the first £360 of taxable income is taxable at reduced rates. The result of all these reliefs and allowances is that very many people with small incomes pay no tax at all and that, for those who do, the 'effective' rate of income tax payable by any individual over his whole income is always less, and generally very much less, than the 'standard 'rate' Thus, in 1956–7, out of 20,900,000 individuals with total incomes above the exemption limit, 3,500,000 were entirely relieved from tax by the operation of allowances. A married couple entitled to allowance for three children could have an income of about £700 a year before they were called upon to pay tax at all. If their income was £2,000 a year the effective rate of tax on the whole of their income was 3s 8½d as compared with the standard rate of 8s 6d. Over the whole field of actual income under all Schedules the net produce of the tax for 1955–6 represented an average effective rate of 2s 8d in the £.

Companies are not entitled to the personal reliefs and allowances but are liable to tax at the standard rate on their total income irrespective of its amount—after, of course, deducting the appropriate allowances for capital expenditure on plant and machinery, etc. When they distribute interest or dividends they in effect pass on the tax they have paid by deducting tax at the standard rate from the gross amounts they distribute. (The gross amounts distributed are treated as incomes of the recipients who can then claim their appropriate reliefs and allowances against those incomes.) The undistributed income of a company remains liable at the full standard rate in the hands of the company.

To show the relative importance of the different Schedules under which income tax is collected, the following table gives the net produce of tax[1] for 1955–6:

	£ million	%
Schedule A	92·0	5
„ B	0·1	—
„ C	97·0	5
„ D	1058·0	55
„ E	680·0	35
Total	1927·1	100

Wherever possible, income tax is deducted from income at its source. This applies notably to salaries, wages and pensions under the PAYE system already referred to; and to other cases like rents, royalties, mortgage interest, other periodical interest payments (as on British Government securities) and dividends paid by companies. The chief classes of income on which tax is collected direct from the taxpayer are the trading profits of individuals and partners, the undistributed profits of companies, and the income from professions assessable under Schedule D.

The income tax is obviously a very flexible instrument, adaptable both to the needs of broad economic policy and to finer adjustments, as between individuals, of the necessary level of total taxation. A change of 6d in the standard rate of tax can, at a stroke, reduce or increase Budget revenue—and therefore increase or reduce spendable incomes in the private sector of the country's economy—by something around £120 million a year, of which rather more than half will relate to companies and other business undertakings. On the

[1] The 'net produce of tax' is the estimated ultimate yield from the tax assessed in the year, whether actually collected in that year or later, after deducting all discharges and remissions and setting off all repayments.

other hand, for a seventh of that sum significant increases have been made in some recent years in the allowances for children; while sums much smaller still can provide worthwhile easements for special cases like old people with small incomes.

Over such a vast taxable field, change in rates and conditions of tax, if they are to be handled and directed effectively, must be based on adequate statistical information. Some extensive examples of the profuse information available to the Inland Revenue Department are given in its Annual Report and will amply repay careful study. Notable tables among those provided in the Hundredth Report (published in January 1958) are:

Schedule D:

Table 30—Classification of assessment made in 1955–6 on trading profits by range of profits and status of concern (individuals, partnerships, companies, etc.).

Tables 32–50—Analysis of trading profits by trade groups.

Schedule E:

Table 55—Classification of Schedule E income (principal source) by sex and range.

All Schedules:

Tables 56–8—Classification of personal incomes by range of income and family circumstances.

Tables 59–155—Classification of personal incomes by range of income for each county (based on a sample survey of incomes for the year 1954–5).

Surtax

The surtax (which replaced the old super-tax in 1927) is essentially an extension of the income tax by graduated additions to the standard rate of income tax for the higher incomes. It is charged in the case of any individual whose total income from all sources, after making certain deductions,[1] exceeds £2,000. It is not payable by companies except where they are caught by certain statutory provisions designed to prevent avoidance of surtax by means of companies which are under the control of not more than five persons, in which the public are not substantially interested and which fail to distribute a reasonable part of their income to their members.

The surtax additions to the standard rate of income tax increase

---

[1] The deductions are, first, mortgage interest, annuity payments, etc., from which the payee is entitled to deduct income tax and, secondly, the amount by which the taxpayer's income-tax allowances (single or married, children, housekeeper, dependent relative) exceed the single personal allowance.

for successive slices of income. Thus, on the income for 1957–8, the addition was 2s for the slice £2,000–£2,500, 2s 6d for £2,500–£3,000, and then increased by 1s for each further specified slice to a rate of 9s 6d for £12,000–£15,000 and a rate of 10s for all incomes over £15,000.

Surtax is payable as a deferred instalment of income tax on or before January 1st following the year of assessment. For example, surtax for the year 1957–8 is payable on January 1, 1959. The reason for this delay is that, whereas income tax can be deducted from or collected on individual sources of income, surtax is essentially a tax on a person's total income from all sources, and it takes some time after the end of the income tax year before his total income can be established and assessed to surtax. In the result, for any given year's income, Parliament normally settles the rate of surtax a year later than it settles the standard rate and other conditions of the income tax. Thus, the Finance Act, 1958, Section 12, provided that 'Income tax for the year 1958–9 shall be charged at the standard rate of eight shillings and sixpence in the pound, and, in the case of an individual whose total income exceeds two thousand pounds, at such higher rates in respect of the excess as Parliament may thereafter determine'. But Section 13 then fixed the rate of surtax for 1957–8 (payable on January 1, 1959) by saying that 'Income tax for the year 1957–8 shall be charged, in the case of an individual whose total income exceeded two thousand pounds, at the same higher rates in respect of the excess as were charged for the year 1956–7'.

Tables in the Hundredth Report on the Inland Revenue classify by range of total income the incomes on which surtax has been payable in recent years and also (Tables 169–71) show how the incomes in the different ranges were made up of earned income and investment income respectively.

Death Duties

The title 'Death Duties' is used to cover seven duties still on the Statute Book, of which only estate duty is payable in connection with deaths occurring at the present time.

Estate duty was first imposed by the Finance Act, 1894. It is a graduated *ad valorem* tax chargeable broadly on all property situate in Great Britain,[1] movable or immovable and settled or not settled, which passes or is deemed to pass on death, and is charged irrespective of the domicile of the deceased. It is also charged on movable property situate abroad if the owner on whose death it passes was domiciled in Great Britain or if the property passes under a dis-

[1] Northern Ireland imposes its own death duties: see page 109.

position governed by the laws of Great Britain. The legislation which gives effect to these broad principles is necessarily complicated: it defines, for example, the many varied types of properties, and interests in property, which fall within the scope of the duty, and also the types which are exempt from duty. We need not pursue the details, save to note that estates not exceeding £3,000 are exempt from duty altogether.

Estate duty is payable on a graduated scale according to the value of the estate at death. The rate payable depends on the scale in force at the date when death occurred; but for deaths occurring after July 29, 1954, the scale rises from 1 per cent of estates between £3,000 and £4,000 by over twenty steps to 80 per cent of estates exceeding £1,000,000.

Tables in the Inland Revenue Annual Reports show the numbers and estates within various ranges, on which duty was first paid in each of the last ten years. There is a detailed analysis of the types of personal and real estate comprising the estates on which duty was paid in the year reported on, both by total and, in rather less detail, for the different ranges of estates. There are also classifications by range of estate and by age and sex of the deceased.

Forecasting the yield of estate duty for the purposes of the Budget is subject to some special difficulties. First, the number of deaths fluctuates considerably from year to year—over a period of years the number in any particular year may easily be 10 per cent above or below the average. Again, a large part of the total property attracting duty in any year consists of Government and municipal securities (18 per cent in 1956–7) and stocks, shares, etc., of companies (29 per cent in 1956–7): the market value of such securities can vary considerably from year to year and between the time the Budget estimates are prepared and the end of the financial year concerned. Such variations will be reflected in the duty leviable on the securities.

The six 'death duties' other than estate duty, which are referred to at the beginning of this note, brought in only some £700,000 in 1956–7, as compared with £167 million from estate duty. They are: legacy and succession duty, which were levied at rates dependent on the relationship of the beneficiary to the deceased, but which are now only collected in connection with deaths arising before July 30, 1949, when the duties were terminated; corporation duty, which was imposed in 1885 by way of compensation to the Revenue for the non-liability to death duties of certain property belonging to or vested in corporate or unincorporate bodies; and a group of old duties which only apply to deaths in certain periods ending in 1914 and are now of very little importance—probate duty (in Scotland called inventory duty), account duty, temporary estate duty and settlement estate duty.

Stamp Duties

Under a variety of statutes many kinds of commercial and legal documents require to be stamped with stamps denoting the payment of duty. The responsibility for stamping a document with the proper duty rests primarily with the taxpayer; and the main protection for the revenue lies in the fact that documents which are not duly stamped cannot (except in criminal proceedings) be given in evidence or be available for any purpose whatever. In 1956–7, when the yield of the stamp duties was £63 million, the main classes of documents contributing to that total were: conveyances on sales of land and houses (£11 million)[1]; transfer of stocks and shares on sale (£22 million); companies' share capital duty (£3 million); cheques (£7 million); receipts (£5 million); and marine insurance policies (£3 million).

In some cases the duty is a fixed duty; in others it is an *ad valorem* duty depending on factors such as the value of the property transferred, the amount of the consideration, the amount secured and so on. Stamps are of two kinds, impressed and adhesive. Adhesive stamps are compulsory for some documents and permissive for others; except in those cases, impressed stamps must be used.[2]

Profits Tax

The profits tax is charged on the profits or trades or businesses carried on in the United Kingdom by bodies corporate, unincorporated societies or other bodies, or carried on abroad by bodies ordinarily resident in the United Kingdom. It is thus payable by companies but not by individuals or partnership of individuals.

Prior to April 1, 1958, if distributions were less than the chargeable profits, 'non-distribution relief' was given to the difference so that, in effect, distributions attracted a higher rate of tax—indeed, a very much higher rate—than indistributed profits put to reserve and similar uses. (The definition of 'distributions' for the purposes of the tax was of some importance in that it excluded, in general, interest paid on debentures. This exclusion was a major point of criticism of the tax on the grounds that the incidence of the tax thereby varied

---

[1] Relatively important reductions were made in 1958 in the duty on conveyances of property other than stocks and marketable securities, costing £5½ million in a full year.

[2] The Inland Revenue Department also collects fees and patent charges by means of stamps for other departments but these are not Inland Revenue duties. (Examples of the fee stamps are those for the Supreme Court of Judicature, the Land Registry and Companies' Registration.)

according to the proportions in which companies had raised capital by debentures and shares—which should be no concern of the State—and that it acted as a deterrent to the raising of equity capital.) From April 1, 1956, to March 31, 1958, the rates of tax were 30 per cent on profits distributed and 3 per cent on profits not distributed. In 1955–6, of the chargeable profits roughly a quarter was distributed and three-quarters undistributed. But since the former were charged at a much higher rate the proportion was reversed in the yield of the tax, rather more than three-quarters of which came from distributed profits.

As from April 1, 1958, the basis of the tax was radically altered and the two different rates for distributed and undistributed profits were replaced by a single rate to be levied on the whole of a company's profits. The single rate was fixed at 10 per cent—a round figure rather less than the $10\frac{1}{2}$ per cent which would have been necessary to maintain the yield of the tax (£275 million) on the old basis. The object of the change, which had been recommended in 1955 by the Royal Commission on Taxation, was to help to remove the distortions of company capital finance which the old system had encouraged.

Closely related to the administration of the profits tax are some settlements of outstanding assessments of profits to two taxes now repealed—the excess profits tax, which was in force in April 1939 to December 1946; and the excess profits levy, which was in force only from January 1952 to December 1953. The amounts involved annually in these two cases are now relatively small.

Other Inland Revenue Duties

Apart from very small remnants of the excess profits duty (imposed during the First World War) and the war damage contribution (levied from 1941 to 1945,) the other Inland Revenue duties, which bring in only about £500,000 a year altogether, are:

(a) Special Contribution: This 'once-and-for-all' tax was imposed by the Finance Act, 1948, on all individuals whose total income for 1947–8 exceeded £2,000 and whose investment income exceeded £250. It was charged according to a scale which increased from 2s in the £ on the first £250 investment income above £250—to 10s on the top slice of that income above £5,000.

(b) Land Tax: This very old tax was first imposed in broadly its present form towards the end of the seventeenth century. In 1798 quotas were fixed for each parish in England and Wales and for counties and burghs in Scotland, where the quotas were distributed according to the annual values of the available properties. There were provisions for voluntary redemption. In 1949 unredeemed charges below 10s were extinguished and the remainder were stabilized at the 1948–9 level and required compulsorily to be redeemed (at twenty-five times the annual charge) over a period of years. About half the charges stabilized in 1949 have been redeemed.

(c) Mineral Rights Duty: This duty, first imposed in 1910, is an annual tax of 1s in the £ on the rental value of all right to work minerals (excluding certain substances like clay, sand, chalk, limestone, gravel) and of all mineral wayleaves.

(C) CUSTOMS AND EXCISE

GENERAL

First the Customs (which originated in Anglo-Saxon times) and then the Customs and Excise together were for centuries the mainstay of the Royal revenues. They did not yield first place to the Inland Revenue until just before the First World War—a transformation due, of course, to the development of the income tax and super tax. Since the end of that war, the Customs and Excise has accounted for some 30–40 per cent of the total tax revenue, that is, of the total of Inland Revenue, Customs and Excise and the motor vehicle duties. The broad tendency was for the percentage to rise but between 1947–8 and 1957–8 it varied only between 41 and 44 per cent. In those last ten years the total Customs and Excise revenue rose by some 50 per cent, from £1,426 million to £2,150 million. As would be expected in a revenue covering so many dutiable articles, there is no one general explanation of this increase. Over a third of it arose on one item, hydrocarbon oils, on which the rate of duty was increased by more than threefold and of which consumption increased by more than half. The yield from purchase tax exactly doubled, partly due to an extension of the field of the tax, partly to increased volume of consumption of the taxed goods and partly (because this tax is *ad valorem* and not specific) to increase in prices. The yield of tobacco duty increased by a quarter, partly due to an increase in the level of the duty but partly to an increase in consumption. Having regard to the variety of goods taxed, to the graduation of the tariffs and to the changes therein over the ten years, it would require a very laborious calculation—if indeed it were possible at all—to estimate the extent to which the total increase over the ten years was due to rates of duty, to changes in the volume of consumption and to changes in prices respectively. However that may be, the Customs and Excise revenue as a whole must always be very responsive to changes in consumer demand and could hardly

fail to show an appreciable increase over a period in which consumers' expenditure, excluding price changes, increased by some
17 per cent and including price changes by some 78 per cent.

The broad distinction between the field of Customs duties and that
of Excise duties is that the former are imposed on goods imported
from abroad and the latter on those produced in the United Kingdom.[1] Certain duties levied on services arising in this country are
classed as Excise duties—namely, the entertainment duty and the
pool betting duty. The purchase tax (which is payable both on home-
produced and imported goods), although not in law an Excise
duty, is accounted for to the Exchequer as part of the Excise
revenue.

Some classes of goods appear under both the Customs and the
Excise tariffs. This arises out of the distinction between 'revenue
duties' and 'protective duties'. Revenue duties, as their name implies,
are imposed primarily to raise revenue for Budget purposes. They are
levied because it is considered reasonable that consumers of the
goods concerned should contribute to the revenue irrespective of
where the goods originally came from. Spirits, for instance, bear
revenue duties whether they are imported brandy and rum or home-
made whisky and gin. Beer and sugar are other cases. But it is im-
plicit in such a policy that the Customs duty on the imported article
and the Excise duty on the article made at home should be broadly
the same. Protective duties, on the other hand, are Customs duties
which are primarily designed to protect home manufacturers against
the full force of foreign competition; and in such cases there are
naturally no countervailing Excise duties. They will be pointed out
in the detailed list of duties below; but in fact they account for a
relatively small amount of the total Customs and Excise revenue—
only some 4 per cent. The distinction between revenue and protective
duties is of great importance in negotiations about international trade.
When the United Kingdom sets out to bargain with a foreign country
for some mutual reductions in tariffs, the revenue duties are almost
always excluded by us from the negotiations and, except in one or
two exceptional cases, this is accepted abroad.

Both revenue and protective duties enable this country to give a
preference to Commonwealth goods over their foreign counterparts.
This is done by providing that goods grown, produced or manu-
factured in the Commonwealth and consigned therefrom shall be

---

[1] Originally, in 1643, Excise duties were payable on both home-produced and
imported goods, and were in addition to any Customs duties on the latter. It
was not until the early part of the nineteenth century that the Excise duties were
confined to home-produced goods.

relieved of part or all of the duties levied on the foreign goods.[1] The significance of this 'Commonwealth Preference'—its original statutory name was 'Imperial Preference'—naturally varies from case to case. Thus the proportion of imported goods admitted to preference runs down from practically 100 per cent in the case of rum, nine-tenths for tea and cocoa, two-thirds for coffee and nearly half for tobacco to nothing at all in cases where Commonwealth countries do not produce the goods concerned or do not export them to us.

All Customs and Excise duties are intended to be borne by consumers in the United Kingdom and not by consumers in other countries; and so there are provisions—mainly in connection with the revenue duties and purchase tax—by which dutiable *goods exported* from the United Kingdom may be relieved of duty. This is not only good sense but also good business, because it would not help our export trade to make it a means of requiring foreign purchasers of our goods to contribute to our domestic revenue. When imported goods are intended for re-exportation as they stand they need not pay Customs duty: they may be put into bond and exported from there or may be immediately transhipped to another port of shipment. Similarly, home-manufactured goods ordinarily subject to Excise duty are allowed to leave the place of manufacture and be exported without payment of duty. For certain goods which have paid Customs or Excise duty and which are either exported as they stand or are used in a manufacturing process of which the final product is exported, there are arrangements for the repayment of the duty, which is known as '*drawback*'.

Reference has already been made to the fact that some duties are '*ad valorem*' and some are 'specific'. *Ad valorem duties* are expressed as a percentage or other proportion of the values of the goods as defined by the statutes imposing them: for example, most protective duties are expressed as a percentage of the value of goods as imported; the purchase tax is one of several percentages of the wholesale value of the goods. *Specific duties*, on the other hand, are chargeable at a specified rate in terms of money on a specified unit of quantity or weight: for example, the Customs duty on imported hydrocarbon oils is 2s 6d a gallon, and that on tobacco is 61s 2d per lb. Which type of duty shall be used in any particular case is largely a matter of convenience. Where a common rate of duty applies to a very great number of different goods—as in the case of the purchase tax—it would be an impossibly laborious proceeding to calculate

---

[1] The benefits of this preference apply also to the goods of certain past members of the Commonwealth; e.g. Burma and the Irish Republic.

and maintain appropriate specific duties for every individual item. When a duty covers a wide field, the *ad valorem* basis ensures that its relative weight remains broadly the same over the whole field, whatever price changes take place. Also, the *ad valorem* duties are more convenient where goods enter into international trade, since they permit comparisons to be made more easily between the degrees of protection given to the same line of goods by different countries. On the other hand, most of the revenue duties cover limited and well-defined classes of goods and there is no difficulty in making them specific. There is also much to be said for a specific duty where a revenue duty is a high multiple of the price excluding duty: it would look rather ludicrous to express the duty on cigarettes as something like 270 per cent of the ex-duty price. Again, very high *ad valorem* rates magnify changes in the price excluding duty and tend to produce instability in the revenue yield.

In describing some of the revenue duties below, reference is made to the *basic duty* under a particular head of revenue. When a commodity is subject both to Customs and to Excise duty, the basic duty is that applicable to whichever of the two sources of supply, import or home-manufacture, is the more extensive. (Excise is basic for spirits; Customs for tobacco.) The basic duty having been settled, the other is calculated from it by making allowances for certain factors which must be brought into the reckoning if the burdens of the two duties are to be fairly balanced. Thus, a Customs duty may have to be made greater than a basic Excise duty, and an Excise duty made less than a basic Customs duty, by an amount representing such items as the costs which home manufacturers incur as a result of the revenue supervision of their factories or the losses, e.g. wastage, incurred through using duty-paid materials. Where any class of goods is subject to Commonwealth Preference, the Customs duty, whether basic or not, will have to consist of two rates, the 'full' and the 'preferential'. In some cases the preference amounts to complete freedom from duty.

For the details of the various Customs and Excise duties given below very free use has been made of the latest annual *Report of the Commissioners of Her Majesty's Customs and Excise*[1]. Apart from the Report itself, which deals mainly with recent and current developments, the volume contains nearly two hundred pages of statistics and explanatory notes about all the individual duties. These Annual Reports, like the corresponding Annual Reports on the Inland

[1] Report for 1956–7, Cmnd 344. This Report contains a short 'Retrospect' of the changes in the Customs and Excise since the first Reports were published a hundred years before.

Revenue, are a mine of essential information about many aspects of the public revenues.

ADMINISTRATION

The Customs and Excise duties are administered by the Customs and Excise Department, at the head of which is the Board of 'Commissioners of Her Majesty's Customs and Excise', consisting of six senior permanent Civil Servants—a Chairman, who ranks with the heads of major Government departments, a Deputy Chairman and four Commissioners. Historically, so far as the Customs duties are concerned, the collecting agency first took shape as a Board in 1671, when Commissioners appointed by Letters Patent took over the collection of Customs duties which had previously been 'farmed out' to private individuals. The Excise duties, first introduced in 1643, were collected by a separate Excise Department under Excise Commissioners. This department was later amalgamated with that of Stamps and Taxes to form the Inland Revenue Department. Later still, in 1909, it was amalgamated with the Customs Department which then became the Customs and Excise Department. Whatever the earlier case for regarding the Excise as a form of 'inland' revenue there is no doubt that the form and administration of the Excise duties are so much akin to those of the Customs duties as to make the present arrangement of departmental responsibility the right one.

At its headquarters the Board has the assistance of a Secretaries' Office, to oversee the administration of this revenue collection; an Intelligence Branch, which among other things, prepares estimates of the revenue and advises on changes in revenue duties; a Valuation Branch to deal with questions concerning the valuation of goods for duty and purchase tax purposes; a Chief Inspector, who is the head of the Outdoor Service, which is responsible for the assessment and collection of duties; an Inspector-General of Waterguard, who is the head of the Waterguard Service, which guards against smuggling; an Investigation Branch, which deals with cases of fraud and other evasions of the revenue law; and—all having tasks which their titles indicate—an Accountant and Comptroller-General's Office, a Solicitor's Office and a Statistical Office. Under the Board the Department necessarily has a complete network of local offices throughout the country, this network consisting of two separate services—the Outdoor Service and the Waterguard Service, with the respective functions just mentioned.

In the Outdor Service the whole country is divided into a number of Collections, each under a Collector; a Collection is divided into a number of Districts, each under a Surveyor; and a District is divided into Stations, which are staffed by Officers of Customs and Excise and which, according to the nature and volume of the work involved, may cover a wide area, part of a large town, part of a dock area, or a single building or warehouse. The Collector's office is the place of receipt of payment of duty and may cover Customs duties or Excise duties (including purchase tax) or both. As to the mechanics of charging and collecting duties, the master of every ship arriving in a British port or airport from overseas is required to present to the local Custom House a 'Report', which consists mainly of a list of the cargo carried. At the same time the importer (or his agent) of each individual consignment in the cargo must 'enter' the consignment with the Customs, by giving them the description, quantity and value of the goods, the amount of duty payable, and the country from which they have been imported. If the importer wishes to clear the goods at once for home consumption he is required to pay the duty at the Custom House when the 'entry' is checked. An officer at the ship's berth (or at the freight shed of an airport) will later scrutinize the entry and, after any necessary physical examination of the goods, will, if he is satisfied, authorize their release. The importer is, however, required to pay the duty to another and independent official. For each consignment, two reports then go independently to the Accountant and Comptroller-General—one from the officer who has cleared the goods, and who advises him of the amount of duty due, and one from the official who has taken payment and who advises him of the amount of duty actually received. The Accountant and Comptroller-General are thus enabled to check the duty actually paid and brought to account against the charge which has been raised and to see that they agree. When dutiable goods are exported from bond duty-free or on drawback, the goods must be entered in a 'Shipping Bill'; they are examined by an officer either in the bonded warehouse or at the premises where they are packed for shipment; and another officer at the dock verifies that they are duly shipped on board. Thereafter freedom from duty or payment of drawback finally requires evidence that the goods have in fact been taken out of the country.[1]

On the Excise side of the Outdoor Service's duties, there is no similar uniform machinery and the arrangements differ from case to case according to the nature of the goods and the manufacturing processes. Thus, in the case of the beer duty, which is charged on the quantity of beer made by a brewer, he must give notice of each

---

[1] These procedures have been slightly modified in the case of traffic across the Land Boundary between Northern Ireland and the Republic of Ireland.

occasion when he intends to brew and enter in a 'Brewing Book' the quantities of the various materials to be used and particulars of the beer produced. These details are subject to physical checks by an officer of Customs and Excise. On the other hand, the entertainment duty is collected by means of weekly certified returns of admission. But even here there are physical as well as accounting checks by the officer.

The structure of the Waterguard Service is very similar to that of the Outdoor Service. There are fifteen Divisions, each under a Waterguard Superintendent; a Division is divided into Districts, each under a Chief Preventive Officer; and a District is divided into Stations, each being operated by a Preventive Officer. This staff works at all seaports, harbours and creeks along the coast and at inland airports, and patrols the Irish Land Boundary. It also serves on Revenue protective vessels. In its defence of the revenue against smuggling it boards ships and aircraft on first arrival, and keeps ships under watch during their stay in port; controls the dutiable stores (e.g. tobacco and spirits) carried by ships; examines the baggage and personal effects of passengers and crews; searches for concealed contraband; and supervizes coastwise and fishery shipping.

REMITTANCE OF REVENUE TO THE EXCHEQUER

Like the Inland Revenue Department, the Customs and Excise Department is subject to the provisions of Section 10 of the Exchequer and Audit Department Act, 1866, requiring all revenues to be paid into the Exchequer account and allowing them to be retained temporarily for certain purposes, including its expenses for staff and other administrative outgoings. But the actual procedure in this case is slightly different. A Collector of Customs and Excise duties pays his daily receipts into his local bank account; but he draws on his balance in that account to meet payments of drawback, etc., payments on behalf of other departments and payments for his own expenses, and remits the resulting net balance (by means of four-day bills) to the account of the Commissioners of Customs and Excise at the Bank of England. At the same time he sends daily to the Accountant and Comptroller-General a statement showing his gross receipts, the sums paid therefrom under all the heads just mentioned and the net sum remitted to the Bank. The Bank also sends to the Accountant and Comptroller-General a daily list of the sums received from Collectors. The Headquarters of the Department also requires cash to meet administrative expenses and this, again, is provided temporarily out of revenue in the Department's hands: in this case the Commissioners themselves transfer the necessary sums out of their account at the Bank to a separate account also at the Bank in the name of the Accountant and Comptroller-General, from which he meets the expenses in question. Next, the Commissioners make daily transfers to the Exchequer of the available balance on their account. Once a month the Accountant and Comptroller-General sends to the Treasury a statement of the amount of revenue retained to meet the administrative expenses of Collectors and Headquarters. The Treasury then pays that amount to the Commissioners' account at the Bank from the Exchequer, debiting it to the parliamentary Vote for Customs and Excise. The Commissioners, having received this payment, immediately transfer it back to the Exchequer as revenue. Here again, therefore, the result is that the Exchequer has received the revenue in full and has itself met the departmental expenses out of the appropriate Vote. One small point in this procedure may be noticed. A local Collector will meet his administrative expenses, before remitting to the Commissioners' account at the Bank of England, by drawing on his balance at the local bank which may represent Customs, Excise and other receipts. In the daily transfers from the Commissioners' account to the Exchequer, however, the Excise revenue is transferred in full and all retentions to meet administrative expenses are consequently deducted from Customs revenue. When the Treasury credits the Commissioners' account with the monthly amount due from the parliamentary Vote that amount is transferred back to the Exchequer as Customs revenue, so that in the end the Exchequer has received that revenue in full. These arrangements, made for the sake of accounting convenience, do not in any way invalidate the final published details of Customs and Excise revenue respectively, because the latter are based on the figures of Collector's receipts before the temporary use of revenue to meet expenses.

THE CUSTOMS AND EXCISE DUTIES

A complete list of the heads under which the Department collects Customs and Excise duties is given in Appendix C, with the amounts expected to be received under each head in 1958–9. It will there be seen that tobacco is by far the biggest contributor to this revenue, accounting for 34 per cent; then come purchase tax (22 per cent) and alcoholic liquors (20 per cent, beer alone being 12 per cent); then oil at 16 per cent; with the rest very small individually. A great deal of information about each of the heads of revenue is given in the Annual Report of the Commissioners of Customs and Excise, which has already been referred to; but the following short comments on some of the heads—in the order in which they appear in the Appendix —may be of interest here. They are largely based on details given in the Report.

Spirits. Nearly 80 per cent of the revenue under this head is Excise on spirits made in this country, mainly whisky and gin. The Customs revenue comes mainly from imported rum and brandy. The United Kingdom spirits on which duty is payable are, in fact, only a small proportion of the total amount of spirits produced in the country. In 1956–7, for instance, some 54 per cent of production escaped duty by being used in art or manufacture or converted into methylated spirits; about 17 per cent was exported; less than 10 per cent was retained for consumption in this country and paid duty; and most of the balance was added to bonded stocks.

The basic duty is an Excise duty of £10 10s 10d per proof gallon[1] of spirit which has been warehoused for three years and represents 24s 7d in the price of a bottle of whisky selling retail at 37s 6d.

Beer. The basic duty is the Excise duty on beer brewed in the United Kingdom and is assessed on each 'bulk barrel' (36 gallons) of 'worts', that is, the liquid produced from the mash before fermentation has begun. The duty is 155s 4½d per barrel at 1,030 deg. gravity[2] plus 6s 7½d for each additional degree of gravity. For an average pint bottle of light or brown ale selling at 1s 8d the duty element in that price is 8½d. Since so many different kinds of beer are brewed, at varying degrees of gravity, comparison of one year's brewings and revenue with another's is best made by converting the 'bulk barrels' into 'standard barrels', that is, barrels of 36 gallons at a gravity of 1,055 deg.; this conversion is done in the annual Customs and Excise Reports. An interesting table in those Reports shows the quantities of the individual materials used in the brewings and the resulting barrelage of beer. More than once in the last ten years a decline in beer consumption, and therefore in revenue, has caused the Depart-

[1] A proof gallon contains that quantity of ethyl alcohol which, if made up with distilled water to a volume of one gallon at a temperature of 51 deg. F, would weigh twelve-thirteenths as much as a gallon of distilled water at the same temperature! At 60 deg. F proof spirit contains 49·28 per cent of alcohol by weight and 57·1 per cent by volume.

[2] 'Gravity' here means the gravity of the worts before fermentation commences. The gravity is expressed as a number of degrees, that number being the ratio of the weight of a volume of the worts at a temperature of 60 deg. F to the weight of an equal volume of distilled water at the same temperature, multiplied by 1,000.

ment some anxiety, especially as it was not clear whether this was due to a gradual change of taste, which might have serious results for the Exchequer. Happily for the latter, that trend seems to have changed.

Wine. There are two basic Customs rates for still wine imported otherwise than in bottles—a lower rate for light wines and a higher rate for heavy wines. Higher rates are charged on still wine imported in bottles and on sparkling wines. The basic duty at the lower rate is 13s a gallon and at the higher rate 38s a gallon. (On a bottle of the cheaper claret bottled in this country and selling at anything from 7s 4d to 14s 6d that lower rate works out at about 2s 2d.) Imports of still heavy wine have been fairly steady over the last ten years; but there has been an increasing demand for light wines.

Tea. The revenue from this is very small and is only mentioned here as a reminder that the once very controversial tea duty is no longer, for practical purposes, a burden on the housewife. When the basic Customs duty was reduced from 8d to 2d per lb. in 1949, the long-standing Imperial Preference of 2d per lb remained unaltered, which meant that thence forward Commonwealth tea was admitted free of duty. Of all tea now imported into this country, only some 7 per cent pays the duty of 2d per lb.

Sugar. There are separate scales of duty according to whether the sugar comes from foreign countries or the Commonwealth or (by production from sugar beet) from this country. The last of these duties is an Excise duty, the others being Customs duties. Each scale varies the duty according to the sugar content as shown by polarization. In each case the highest duty is on the greatest sugar content, that is, on fully-refined sugar, and this gives a measure of protection to refiners in this country. Of the total amount of sugar consumed in this country, roughly 5 per cent comes from foreign countries, 70 per cent from the Commonwealth and 25 per cent from home-grown beet. Sugars from all sources are well mixed for sale in this country. In the result, the duty element in a lb. of granulated sugar sold retail for 8½d per lb. is ½d.

Tobacco. The basic rate is the Customs duty of 61s 2d per lb. on unstripped leaf tobacco containing not less than 10 per cent of moisture. Similar tobacco of Commonwealth origin bears a preferential duty of 1s 6½d per lb. below the full rate. There are different rates on other kinds of imported tobacco; and an Excise duty (2d per lb. less than the preferential rate) which is largely inoperative as only trivial amounts of tobacco are grown in this country. In the result—after taking account of the blending of foreign and Commonwealth tobaccos in some brands—the duty element in the price of an ounce of pipe tobacco selling at 4s is about 3s 1d; and in the price of twenty cigarettes selling at 3s 11d it is 2s 10½d. This source of revenue—the most productive of all the Customs and Excise duties—has shown a remarkable resilience over recent years. Despite appreciable increases in the rate of duty up to and including 1947, the heavy overall cost to the regular smoker, the refusal of so many of the rising generation to have anything to do with tobacco in any shape or form, and the statements about a statistical connection between smoking and lung-cancer, the revenue (helped by only a slight increase in the rate of duty) was higher by a quarter in 1957–8 than in 1947–8.

Oil. The basic duty under this head is a Customs duty of 2s 6d a gallon on imported hydrocarbon oils. The latter term covers all petroleum (and some other) oils which are divided into two groups—light oils (mostly motor spirit) and heavy oils (kerosene or paraffin, lubricating oil, diesel or gas oil, and fuel oil). But heavy oils, unless intended for use as fuel in road vehicles, are entitled to a full or partial rebate, which means that they are in effect free of duty or (mainly in the case of lubricating oils) liable at a reduced rate of 1d a gallon. Most oil is nowadays imported in crude form and refined in bond, in which event the duty, instead of being charged on importation, is charged—and any rebate allowed—on the products delivered from the refinery for home use. Since 1950 an Excise duty has been charged on hydrocarbon oils produced in this country from materials other than imported hydrocarbon oils, e.g. from shale or as coal tar products, and certain other minor products. The rate of Excise duty is now 1s 3d; but it produces less than 3 per cent of the total revenue. Reference has already been made to the great increase in the consumption of hydrocarbon oils, which reflects the general expansion in economic activity and the increase in the number of private cars.

Entertainments.[1] In relation to the amount of revenue it has brought in, this duty has probably given more trouble to Ministers and the Department than any other items in the list, not excepting the purchase tax. Between 1952 and 1957 there were three scales of duty; the highest related to the cinemas, the intermediate one to racing,

[1] Earlier enactments on the Entertainments Duty, mostly spread over Finance Acts, were consolidated in February 1958, by the Entertainments Duty Act, 1958.

games and other sports, and the lowest to the living theatre, ballet, circuses and so on. Each of these forms of entertainment has had its sympathizers in the House of Commons, where they have vigorously campaigned for exemption for their particular protégés in Budget debates year after year. The most persistent claims for relief came from those affected by the middle and lowest scales. In 1957 the last two scales were abolished altogether and the duty was confined to entertainments consisting wholly or partly of a cinematograph or television show, for which the scale was remodelled. In 1958 this new scale was reduced and now imposes a duty equal to one-third of the amount (if any) by which the payment for admission, including duty, exceeds 1s 6d. Thus, for prices of admission, including duty, of 2s 6d and 6s 6d, the duty payable is 4d and 1s 8d respectively. Before the 1957 changes the revenue from the duty was about £40 million a year of which about £34 million came from the cinemas. The result of the 1957 and 1958 change is that the revenue, all coming from the cinemas, is expected to be about £10 million a year.

Television. This is, not unnaturally, the newest duty of all, having been first imposed in 1957. Classed as an Excise duty, it is charged at the yearly rate of £1 on television receiving licences. (There are appropriately different rates for licences of special types.) The proceeds of the duty go entirely to the Exchequer and remain there: it is quite distinct from the fee of £3, which is charged for the television licence and the bulk of which goes, via the Exchequer, to the British Broadcasting Corporation.[1]

Liquor Licences. Excise duties are paid on the licences issued to persons manufacturing, dealing in or retailing liquor and are at rates varying with the type, and sometimes volume, of the business carried on. In 1956–7 there were about 220,000 of such licences. In addition, some 23,000 registered clubs paid a 'Club Duty' of 3d in the £ on their purchases of intoxicating liquor. *Monopoly Value* is payable to the Exchequer, often by instalments, in respect of any new on-licence and represents the difference between the value of the premises concerned when licensed and when unlicensed.

Protective Duties. The form, but not the substance, of these duties is to change on January 1, 1959, as a result of the passing of the Import Duties Act, 1958. The object of that Act was twofold: first, to provide a new permanent procedure for the imposition of import

[1] See page 102.

duties in this country; and secondly, to consolidate the law relating to the protective duties and to authorize the making of such changes of nomenclature in the United Kingdom tariff as are necessary to conform to recent international agreements on the classification of imports.

As to procedure, the system before 1939 was that protective duties were imposed by Treasury order but only on the recommendation of an Import Duties Advisory Committee consisting of independent, non-official members. During the Second World War this system was put into abeyance by the Import Duties (Emergency Provisions) Act, 1939, which enabled the Treasury to make import duty orders on the recommendation of the Board of Trade. This latter procedure is now made permanent as from January 1, 1959; but the new Act sets out the considerations which the Treasury and Board of Trade shall take into account in deciding what import duties are to be charged. They are to have regard, among other things, to maintaining and promoting the external trade of the United Kingdom and efficiency of production and to the interests of consumers in the United Kingdom, as well as to international agreements to which this country is a party. Any Treasury order imposing or increasing any Customs duty will cease to be effective unless it is approved by a resolution of the House of Commons within twenty-eight 'sitting' days after it is made.

As to nomenclature, the new Act will enable this country to amend its tariff classifications so as to conform with an international Convention of 1950 on Nomenclature for the classification of goods in Customs tariffs, amended by Protocol in 1955.[1]

As a transitional measure the protective duties which will be in force immediately before January 1, 1959, will (subject to the approval of the House of Commons) be reimposed, with some adjustments, by a Treasury order under the Act. This order will also make the changes of classification necessary to conform with the Convention just mentioned.

When the new tariff of Customs duties under the Act of 1958 comes into force it will bring together under one head protective duties which have previously been shown in the accounts of Customs revenue under six separate headings, namely: dried or preserved fruits; silk and artificial silk (originally—in 1925—revenue duties but subsequent Finance Acts converted them to a protective basis);

[1] The Convention was drawn up by the Customs Co-operation Council on which some twenty countries (including the United Kingdom) are represented and which exists to facilitate the movement of trade by co-operation in Customs matters.

key industry duty (imposed under the Safeguarding of Industries Act, 1921,[1] to protect industries regarded as essential for national security); duties under the Import Duties Act, 1932[1] (this Act signalized the adoption by this country of a general policy of protection, imposed a general *ad valorem* duty of 10 per cent on goods not wholly chargeable under other Acts, and permitted the imposition of duties, either *ad valorem* or specific, 'additional' to the general duty); Ottawa duties (duties imposed by the Ottawa Agreements Act, 1932,[1] on imports from non-Commonwealth sources of a number of products—mostly food, but excluding meat—of kinds largely produced in the Commonwealth); and the beef and veal duties (imposed by the Beef and Veal Customs Duties Act, 1937,[1] on various forms of these meats imported from non-Commonwealth sources). In the cases of dried or preserved fruits, silk, the key industry duty and the duties under the Import Duties Act, 1932, Commonwealth goods have normally been admitted free or at preferential rates, and these arrangements will not be disturbed under the new system.

Purchase Tax. This tax was originally introduced as a war measure in 1940 with the twofold purpose of raising revenue and restraining consumption. Considered only in relation to the goods taxed, these two objects may have been logical alternatives; but in so far as the public went on consuming such goods the purchase tax they paid must have obliged them to restrict consumption in other directions. From the latter point of view the tax has always secured both its original objects.[2] Very few Budgets since then have not contained some modification, large or small, of the structure of the tax and it would be too tedious to attempt to give an account of all the changes. The tax is, and always has been, an *ad valorem* tax on the wholesale value of a wide range of specified goods and is imposed, in general, at the wholesale stage in the distribution of the goods. It also applies on the importation of like goods into the United Kingdom, unless the goods are going into a wholesaler's stock or are used as materials in manufacture, in which cases they are brought within the scope of the internal tax law. The very varied list of goods free from tax includes foodstuffs, fuel, books, cloth in the piece, young children's clothing and footwear, soft furnishings, office machinery, most industrial and building materials and appliances and most articles

---

[1] These four Acts are repealed by the Import Duties Act, 1958, except for certain parts of the Ottawa Agreements Act, 1932.

[2] R. S. Sayers, *op. cit.*, gives a full account of the origins of the tax and of its development during the war.

subject to other indirect taxation. From 1942 to 1953 there were generally three rates of tax, but by 1957 the number had increased to seven. In 1958, however, a considerable measure of simplification was introduced (at the cost of some £40 million of annual revenue) by reducing the number of rates to four—60 per cent, 30 per cent, 15 per cent and 5 per cent. The goods chargeable at any particular rate are many and varied and it is not easy to provide generalized descriptions of them. Moreover, any detailed list of goods and the taxes they bear might well soon be out of date. A broad indication is, however, given by the words of the Chancellor of the Exchequer in introducing the 1958 changes: 'With these changes the structure of the tax will be, effectively, a standard rate of 30 per cent on a wide range of goods; a higher rate of 60 per cent on a few big revenue producers, notably cars, wireless and television, gramophones and records and cosmetics; and lower rates of 15 per cent and 5 per cent broadly as at present on the more essential domestic and personal articles.'[1]

Parliamentary proposals, repeated year after year, for a reduction of tax on this or that class of goods have been legion and have taken up a great deal of parliamentary time. So much so, that in recent years the Chancellor of the Exchequer, with an eye on the parliamentary time-table for his Budget, has secured that the 'amendment of the law' Resolution[2] should practically rule out discussion of individual items. Thus, in 1957, the Resolution explicitly ruled out all relieving amendments to the purchase tax except those applying to all chargeable goods (that is, those about the administration of the tax) or those reducing a particular rate of tax for all goods to which that rate applies. This course was not followed, however, in 1958, in view of the extensive changes which the Chancellor was himself then proposing.

It should be noted that changes in the incidence of the purchase tax have not necessarily to be made by statute. Under the Finance Act, 1948 (Section 21), as amended by the Finance Act, 1953 (Section 11), the Treasury may by order make any change in the classes of goods chargeable to the tax or may substitue any existing statutory rate of tax for any other rate in respect of goods of any class or may reduce the rate to a rate which is not an existing statutory rate. But if such an order extends the incidence of the tax or increase the rate of tax it must be approved by resolution of the House of Commons within twenty-eight days; and any other order is subject to annulment by such a resolution.

[1] Hansard, April 15, 1958, col. 73.
[2] See page 24.

Betting. Pool betting duty has been levied since 1948 on the stake money paid on all pool betting except betting through a totalizator on an approved horse racecourse. There are now two rates of duty: 10 per cent of the stake money at totalizators on dog racecourses; and 30 per cent of the stake money in football and other similar pools. Of the total receipts from this duty in 1957–8 (about £29 million), £6 million came from the 10 per cent rate and about £23 million from the 30 per cent rate. In addition, Bookmakers' Licence Duty is payable by bookmakers operating at dog race meetings on tracks at which a totalizator is operated. A licence is issued for a meeting and the rate of duty depends on the particular enclosure in which the bookmaker operates, the number of enclosures at the track and the number of races at the meeting. In 1957–8 some 150,000 such licences were issued and produced altogether £1·6 million in licence duty.

(D) MOTOR VEHICLE DUTIES

SCOPE OF THE DUTIES

These duties are estimated to produce £104 million of revenue in 1958–9.[1] They are levied under the Vehicles (Excise) Act, 1949—a consolidating Act—as subsequently amended. They are charged in respect of mechanically propelled vehicles used on public roads in Great Britain and take the form of annual payments on licences to be taken out by the persons keeping the vehicles. The vehicles taxed fall into five broad categories—certain vehicles not exceeding 8 cwt. in weight unladen (e.g. bicycles and tricycles, for which the duty varies with the cylinder capacity of the engine in cubic centimetres); hackney carriages, that is, vehicles standing or plying for hire (for which, in cases other than tramcars, the duty varies according to seating capacity); tractors, etc., including agricultural tractors and earth-moving equipment, not used on public roads except for certain specified uses (the duties mostly depend on weight unladen); goods vehicles of many different forms and sizes (the duties again depending mostly on weight unladen); and 'other vehicles', which consist almost entirely of private motor-cars, the main duty on the latter being at the flat rate of £12 10s per vehicle.

The relative importance, from the revenue point of view, of the different classes of vehicles is shown by the following figures for the make-up of the total revenue derived from the duties in the year

---

[1] Including nearly £4 million from fees for driving licences.

ended November 30, 1957:

	£ million
Vehicles under 8 cwt.	3·1
Hackney carriages	5·7
Tractors, etc.	1·0
Goods vehicles	30·4
Cars, etc.	50·3
Miscellaneous	0·6
	91·0[1]

COLLECTION OF THE DUTIES

The Act of 1949 provides that the duties shall be levied by County Councils[2] in accordance with provisions to be made by Order in Council; and for this purpose the Act gave every County Council and its officers the same powers, duties and liabilities as the Commissioners of Customs and Excise and their officers with respect to Excise duties. The County Councils are reimbursed their expenses out of annual Supply Votes.[3] The Minister of Transport and Civil Aviation can give directions to the County Councils to secure uniformity of administration in the collection of the duties.

Each County Council pays the proceeds of the duties into a 'Motor Tax Account' at its local bank and from each of such accounts transfers are made, normally twice a month, to a central 'Motor Tax Account' at the Bank of England. Subject to repayments to meet refunds, etc., and to a minimum balance, the Bank of England transfers the amount standing to the credit of the central account to the Exchequer on the same day as it is received.

Licences are also issued, subject to certain limitations, at Post Offices and the duties received on these licences are paid periodically by the Postmaster-General direct to the 'Motor Tax Account' at the Bank of England.

[1] See *Road Motor Vehicles*, 1957, published for the Ministry of Transport and Civil Aviation by HM Stationery Office, 1958. The same return shows that in the ten years 1947–57, the proceeds of the motor Vehicle Duties increased by 87 per cent (goods vehicles by 84 per cent and cars by 97 per cent). The total number of vehicles licensed, and the number of cars, each increased by some 115 per cent and goods vehicles by rather more than 80 per cent.

[2] Including County Borough Councils in England and Wales and Large Burghs in Scotland.

[3] The expenses for the whole of Great Britain (estimated at £2,915,000 in 1958–9) are borne on the Vote for Roads, etc., England and Wales.

SOME PAST HISTORY

Brief reference may be made to two points which are now only of historical interest but which have figured prominently in past discussions of these duties.

First, the Roads Act, 1920, established the Road Fund, to which—subject to certain payments (since discontinued) to Local Authorities—the proceeds of the Motor Vehicle Duties were to be credited. After meeting the expenses of collecting the duties and other items, the balance on the Road Fund was to be used to meet the Central Government's expenditure on road development. The Fund had a chequered career, including four raids on its balances for the general purposes of the Exchequer. From 1937 the Motor Vehicles Duties ceased to be paid into the Fund and were paid instead into the Exchequer, and the Fund then became simply a channel for expenditure on roads out of annual Supply Votes. There was no particular need for any such channel, but it was not until 1956 that the Fund was wound up altogether, under the Miscellaneous Financial Provisions Act, 1955. That Act provided that all expenditure which would otherwise have been met out of the Fund Should be met out of annual Supply Votes; it is now borne on two Votes, Roads, etc., England and Wales, and Roads, etc., Scotland.

Secondly, the duty originally imposed on private motor-cars by the Roads Act, 1920, was £1 per horse-power. After much public discussion this basis of duty was changed in 1945 on technical grounds. It was accepted that, from the point of view of the most efficient design of motor-car engine, there was 'appreciable advantage in altering the basis of the calculation from the cross-section of the cylinders, as now, to their cubic capacity' and the rate was changed from 25s per horse-power (which it had by then become) to £1 per 100 c.c.[1] A more radical change was made as from January 1948 when, in order to 'divorce design from taxation' altogether, the duty became a flat rate of £10 for each car, except that the horse-power basis was retained for cars registered before January 1, 1947. As from January 1953 that remaining link with horse-power was abolished for all but the smallest cars: the main duty became £12 10s per car, with lower rates (£9 and £10 10s) for cars not exceeding 6 and 7 h.p. respectively which were registered before January 1, 1947.[2]

[1] The quotation is from the Budget speech of April 24, 1945 (*Hansard*, Cols. 698/9); but, owing to the election that year, the change was not made until the autumn Budget when it was embodied in the Finance (No. 2) Act, 1945. It was actually applied as from January 1, 1947.

[2] In the September quarter of 1957, about 1½ million out of just over 4 million cars were still classified by horse-power.

(E) POST OFFICE (NET RECEIPT)

The Post Office is the third of the 'Revenue Departments', but it is quite different in character from the Inland Revenue and the Customs and Excise Departments. Both the latter collect very large sums from the public in taxation at a cost, in the expenses of collection, equal to around 1 per cent of the total collected. The position of the Post Office is almost the reverse of that. It has to spend large sums on staff, stores and maintaining its equipment and the net yield of its operations—that is, the amount by which its revenue exceeds its expenses—is a very small percentage of those expenses. The reason for this is plain. The Post Office earns its revenue by rendering postal, telegraph and telephone services to the public; and all these require staff, stores and equipment, the cost of which is of the same order of magnitude as the revenue raised.

THE POST OFFICE ACCOUNTS

The principles now governing the relations between the Post Office and the Exchequer are set out below. But we had better first look at the rather complicated dual system under which the Post Office accounts are presented. One set of accounts shows its cash relations with the Exchequer. The other is a set of 'trading' accounts on a commercial basis.

As to the Exchequer accounts, the Post Office is like any other department in the sense that its revenue accounts, its Estimate, its Supply Vote and its statutory accounts of its expenditure out of that Vote are all on a cash basis—that is, they show the cash actually received or paid out during the year. Revenue received by the Post Office in cash, like that of the two other Revenue Departments, is— apart from sums due to other departments, telegraph companies and others—paid wholly into the Exchequer. On the expenditure side, the Post Office Vote for each year covers all current expenses (including the annuities by which it is repaying past capital borrowings) and such part of its capital expenditure as can be met out of the provision made during the year for the depreciation of its assets. Capital expenditure to be met out of borrowed moneys is met out of the Vote, but the borrowed moneys are appropriated in aid of the Vote, so that this part of the expenditure does not add to the net amount of the Vote and therefore is not a charge on the Budget above-the-line. (The arrangements for providing this loan capital are described in Chapter VI, page 129.) If the year's cash revenue

D

exceeds the net expenditure out of the Vote, the excess—and only the excess—is included as Budget revenue under the heading 'Post Office (Net Receipt)'. The rest of the revenue, being the amount required to balance the expenditure, is accounted for in the Exchequer account above-the-line, but outside the Budget proper, as 'Self-balancing Revenue—Post Office'. The expenditure, an equal sum, is charged to the Exchequer above-the-line, but again outside the Budget, as 'Self-balancing Expenditure—Post Office', and this is shown as a compensating item directly opposite the self-balancing revenue. If the cash revenue is less than the expenditure out of the Vote, there is no 'net receipt'. Instead, there is an item on the expenditure side of the Budget called 'Balance of Post Office Vote', that is, the part of the Vote expenditure not covered by cash revenue. The rest of the expenditure, being the amount covered by revenue, is charged as 'Self-balancing Expenditure' and the whole of the revenue is accounted for as 'Self-balancing Revenue'. Thus the Budget only takes account of the net difference, either way, between cash revenue and expenditure out of the Vote. Complicated as they may seem, these arrangements have the merit of avoiding the inflation of figures on both sides of the Budget which would occur if the full cash revenue and the full expenditure (each exceeding £350 million) were included within the Budget.

As to the second set of accounts, the Post Office, like other departments carrying on 'trading' services, publishes trading accounts which are called 'Commercial Accounts' and are designed to show its trading position in accordance with commercial practice. The very informative volume containing these accounts explains in detail how they differ from the cash account, that is, from the Appropriation Account of the expenditure out of the Post Office Vote, the account (appended to the Appropriation Accounts) of capital expenditure out of depreciation provisions and money borrowed from the Exchequer and the account of the cash revenue received by the Post Office and paid into the Exchequer. The Commercial Accounts, as the name implies, are designed to show the trading position of the Post Office in accordance with commercial practice. They are used to determine financial policy, including the fixing of charges to the public. Among the differences from the cash accounts they include for any year income earned irrespective of when it is received and expenditure incurred irrespective of when it is paid; they exclude all capital payments, but include depreciation and interest on capital; they include the value of all services rendered to and by other Government departments; and they are debited not merely with pensions paid in cash during the year but with all pension rights accruing to the staff within the year. The volume includes a detailed reconciliation between the cash and commercial accounts. At the same time, the parliamentary Estimate contains as an appendix an estimate of the year's out-turn on the commercial basis and a reconciliation between the cash provision in the parliamentary Estimate and the estimated expenditure on the commercial basis.

THE POST OFFICE AND THE EXCHEQUER

Returning now to the general principles governing the financial relations between the Post Office and the Exchequer, these were reviewed in 1955, when new arrangements were agreed for a period of five years beginning with 1956–7.[1] Broadly the arrangements provide that the Post Office will fix its charges at levels sufficient, taking one year with another, to cover its expenditure (including a contribution to the Exchequer); that it will pay a fixed annual contribution to the Exchequer of £5 million[2]; and that any surplus or deficiency after charging the Exchequer contribution shall, together with interest on it, be carried to the General Balance Sheet and be offset by an Exchequer liability to the Post Office in the case of a surplus and by a Post Office liability to the Exchequer in the case of a deficiency. In principle, though not in detail, these arrangements are similar to those which operated between 1933 and 1940. In return for the fixed contribution to the Exchequer the Post Office is subject to a less detailed control by the Treasury and has a freer hand in deciding how any commercial surplus on its operations shall be used: it could, for example, be used to reduce charges or to improve services, although an alteration of charges still requires Treasury approval. (The cost of any such concessions will, of course, recur year after year and the Post Office will have to see that its accumulated surplus, taken in conjunction with its future financial prospects, is sufficiently large to justify whatever recurrent concessions it wishes to make.) Generally, these measures give the Post Office increased incentives to enterprise and economy.

The calculations necessary to give general effect to the above arrangements, and those necessary in particular to decide the level of

[1] See Appendix 2 to the White Paper on Post Office Development and Finance (Cmnd 9576), 1955. This Appendix is also reproduced with the Commercial Accounts for 1956–7 (House of Commons Paper, No. 14, 1957–8).

[2] The general basis of this contribution has not been defined. The figure of £5 million is broadly in line with the amount which the Post Office would, but for its tax exemptions, have been paying in previous years by way of taxation, including income tax. It is, equally broadly, the average of the annual profit made by the Post Office in the years just before 1955.

Post Office charges, are based on income and expenditure as shown in the Commercial Accounts. This means that the calculations have to take account of factors which do not enter into the Exchequer accounts—such as services rendered without cash payment to and by other departments; and the difference between provision for accruing pension liabilities and actual current payments for pensions. The result is that the figures shown in the Budget for the cash surplus or deficit on the operations of the Post Office during any year are never any guide to the true commercial surplus or deficit for that year. For the same reason the Budget will never show directly the annual contribution of £5 million payable by the Post Office to the Exchequer: it will be masked by factors such as those just mentioned. And since the values of such factors will change from year to year it is not possible to give any general formula for the reconciliation of the cash and the commercial positions. Thus in 1956–7 there was a cash surplus, showing a 'net receipt' for the Budget, accompanied by a commercial deficit; conversely a cash deficit charged to the Budget may be accompanied by a commercial surplus. All that is clear is, of course, that when the Post Office reduces its charges or (in order to provide more services or increase wages) increases its expenditure, that will tend in future years to reduce any 'net receipt' in the Budget and any commercial surplus, or to increase any cash deficiency being charged to the Budget and any commercial deficit.

SOME RECENT CHANGES

A word or warning is necessary about an important change which was made on April 1, 1958, in the basis of the Post Office Vote and therefore in the relations between the cash accounts and the Commercial Accounts. The change was announced and explained in a Memorandum issued by the Postmaster-General in 1957 (Cmnd 318). It relates to the ways in which the provision for depreciation of assets is accounted for and used. Since the Post Office's charges for its services are based on expenditure including that provision, the revenue received includes the amount so provided; and the total amount is likely, for a long time to come, to be greater than the amounts being currently spent on renewals. Prior to April 1, 1958, a part of the depreciation equal to the expenditure on renewals was placed at the disposal of the Post Office through its Vote and the balance of the depreciation provision remained in the Exchequer, which advanced to the Post Office, below-the-line, the whole of the loan capital necessary to finance new development. Since April 1, 1958, the Post Office has been allowed to spend, through its Vote, the whole of the depreciation provision, the excess of that provision over the amount of the renewals being spent on new development. This means that the Exchequer has to provide less for the latter in the form of loans. The change was only one of accounting and form and had no effect on the physical programmes for renewals and developments. But since it meant that the net total of the Post Office Vote was appreciably increased above its former level, care is necessary in statistical comparisons of the cash accounts for periods before and after the date of change.

A further change was made at the same time. Previously, expenditure met out of borrowed moneys was excluded from both the gross and the net totals of the Post Office Vote. As from April 1, 1958, under the authority of the Post Office and Telegraph (Money) Act, 1958, such expenditure has been charged to the Vote in gross but has been balanced by equivalent amounts of the borrowed moneys, involving no addition to the net total of the Vote. This change affects comparisons of gross totals but not of net totals.

(F) BROADCAST RECEIVING LICENCES

Under the law anyone setting up a wireless telegraph station in this country as well as anyone using apparatus to receive wireless messages requires a licence from the Postmaster-General, who may attach conditions, financial or otherwise, to such licences as he grants. This legal framework is the setting for the financial arrangements between the Government, acting through the Postmaster-General, and the British Broadcasting Corporation. In order to conduct its broadcasting services the Corporation requires a licence for its transmitting stations. On the other hand, it cannot itself make any charge to those who receive its broadcasts in this country because only the Postmaster-General can license the receiving sets and collect any fee for such licences. The arrangement between the various parties is broadly, therefore, that the Corporation gets a licence to broadcast; members of the public get licences to receive, on payment of a fee to the Postmaster-General; and the latter pays over an agreed portion of the fees to the Corporation to enable it to finance its Home broadcasts. Since the Corporation was established there have been many successive agreements between it and the Postmaster-General on, amongst other things, the financial basis of these arrangements. The latest agreement is dated February 1, 1957, and was presented to Parliament as Cmnd 80. This Agreement provided that during the three financial years 1957–8, 1958–9 and 1959–60 the Postmaster-

General should pay the Corporation $87\frac{1}{2}$ per cent of the net revenue from broadcast receiving licences, that is of the licence fees less the costs of collection of the fees and other relevant expenses. There was provision for the Corporation to make representation at any time that these payments were insufficient for the adequate conduct of the Home Services and, if the Treasury was satisfied on the point, for the payments to be increased. The payments to be made after 1959–60 were left open. The balance of the net licence revenue, after these payments to the Corporation and after meeting expenses, is retained by the Exchequer and may be regarded either as a contribution to the public revenues by the Corporation in recognition of the special facilities it enjoys or as a contribution by the receiving public in respect of the entertainment they enjoy.

The gross receipts from the fees for receiving licences, being public moneys, are taken in full into the Exchequer as Budget revenue. For 1958–9 it was estimated that the amount to be so received by the Exchequer would be £34 million. Against this it was estimated that the Post Office would pay £27·8 million to the Corporation, as its $87\frac{1}{2}$ per cent share of the net revenue, through the Vote for Broadcasting (Class IV, Vote 13). Hence the Exchequer should retain, as its own share, about £4 million. The balance of the gross receipts of £34 million, namely about £2 million, covers the expenses of the Post Office in collection, which are charged to its own Vote.

It should be noted that the licence revenue in question above consists only of the basic fees of £1 for sound and £3 for sound and television combined. It does not include the additional duty of £1, first imposed in 1957, which is included under Excise revenue[1] and which goes wholly to the Exchequer.

Further, the above arrangements between the Corporation and the Exchequer relate entirely to the Home Services of the Corporation. Its overseas broadcasting and monitoring services are financed wholly by the Exchequer, the necessary provision being made under other subheads of the Vote for Broadcasting.

(G) RECEIPTS FROM SUNDRY LOANS

This is a mixed bag of receipts of interest, dividends and repayments of principal arising out of investments and loans made by the Government in past years. The dividends on the Government holdings of shares in the Suez Canal Company[2] and British Petroleum Ltd

[1] See page 90.
[2] See page 141.

(formerly the Anglo-Persian Oil Company) account for a large part of the item. So also do interest and instalments of principal on various loans to Colonial and other Governments, including advances to certain Allied Governments during the Second World War. Smaller items are interest on advances made by the Exchequer and adminis-tered by the Public Works Loans Board for Land Settlement between 1919 and 1927, and dividends on the Government holdings of shares in Cables and Wireless Ltd. Details of these receipts are given in the annual Finance Accounts.

(H) MISCELLANEOUS REVENUE

This is an even more mixed bag of well over a hundred items of all kinds and sizes, and the reader is again referred to the Finance Accounts, where the full details take up some half a dozen pages. The Financial Statement issued on Budget Day contains, below Table II, figures for the main items of Miscellaneous Revenue in the previous year. The biggest present source of this revenue, though a dying one, is the surpluses realized by two departments—the Ministry of Agriculture, Fisheries and Food and the Board of Trade—who are winding up the trading activities they conducted during and after the war or reducing strategic reserves of raw materials. Next in total size come receipts which departments expected to use as appropria-tion-in-aid of their parliamentary votes but which exceeded the amounts which Parliament authorized to be used that way and which are therefore paid direct into the Exchequer as 'Exchequer Extra Receipts'.[1] Other Exchequer Extra Receipts are a very varied collec-tion of receipts by departments which are not of the kinds to be used as appropriation-in-aid, such as the once-and-for-all proceeds of capital assets disposed of, and the interest on and repayments of loans made for various purposes by or through the departments. A varying, but usually a relatively small item, represents repayments of the amounts by which issues to departments from the Exchequer in respect of their Supply votes for the previous year eventually proved to exceed their expenditure in that year.[2] The surplus income from the Crown Estates, which used (as 'Crown Lands') to appear as a separate item in the Budget, is now included under this head of revenue. From such levels the orders of magnitude of the other items descend to £3,728 paid in by the Bank of England in 1956–7 for 'sums accrued from unpaid fractions of a penny on account of

[1] See page 228.
[2] See page 254.

dividends on National Debt, etc.' and £2,372 in 'money remitted to the Chancellor of the Exchequer by sundry persons for conscience' sake, etc.'

(I) SELF-BALANCING REVENUE

This heading is used in order to exclude from the 'Ordinary Revenue' included in the Budget proper two items which, as the title implies, are exactly balanced by corresponding items of expenditure. This procedure avoids the inflation of both sides of the Budget figures by a large sum. Practically the whole of this head represents Post Office Revenue and has already been discussed.[1]

The balance represents tax deducted from the relatively small remaining statutory refunds of part of the excess profits tax collected during the Second World War. This tax, imposed in 1939 at 60 per cent, was raised to 100 per cent in 1940. It was generally recognized that a tax at the latter rate must act as a deterrent to enterprise and economy in production and in 1941 it was provided that 20 per cent should be repaid on conditions, and at a date, to be determined by Parliament, which was done in later statutes. The refunds represented profits which, but for the excess profits tax, would have been liable to income tax at the time in the ordinary way and the refunds, when made, are therefore subject to a deduction for income tax. Because the tax so collected is balanced in each case by an equal part of the refund to cover it, both are treated as self-balancing items, the tax as revenue and the retained part of the refund as expenditure. Although the balances which are actually paid to the taxpayers are charged below-the-line, being met out of borrowed moneys if necessary, it would be inappropriate to enter an income tax transaction below-the-line, so that two self-balancing items have to be shown above-the-line.

[1] See page 97.

CHAPTER V

The Budget in Detail—(2) Expenditure (Above-the-Line)

(1) CONSOLIDATED FUND SERVICES

THE Consolidated Fund Services are, as we have already seen, those services which Parliament has decided, by statute once and for all, shall be met direct from the Consolidated Fund, as distinct from Supply Services which are met from annual Supply votes. It may be noted that they are the only item on the expenditure side of the Budget above-the-line for which estimates will not have been published before Budget Day. The main reason for this is that the debt services, unlike the Supply services, are already covered by standing Parliamentary authorities. Also, the main item, debt interest, may depend on factors affecting the volume of the debt or rates of interest which the Chancellor can properly reserve for explanation in his Budget statement.

After the end of every financial year the Treasury has to present to Parliament, under Section 21 of the Exchequer and Audit Departments Act, 1866, an account of all payments made for services which, in accordance with various Acts of Parliament, are charged directly on the Consolidated Fund. This account is published as the 'Consolidated Fund Abstract Account' and to it are appended the certificate and report of the Comptroller and Auditor-General on its contents.[1]

(a) NATIONAL DEBT SERVICES

(i) *Interest.* This represents the best estimate that can be made at Budget time of the interest payments that will have to be made above-the-line during the coming financial year. We have already seen[2] that some of the interest on the National Debt is charged

---

[1] By its definition the Account excludes supply expenditure. Moreover it is confined to payments and therefore excludes not only revenue but receipts below-the-line, some of which may be relevant to items on the payments side. An important case from the latter point of view is that of payments for redemption of debt (see Chapter VI, page 135). This particular Account must therefore be used with special care.

[2] See page 46.

below-the-line. The Government regularly borrows money in order to lend it to others: e.g. to Local Authorities and the National Coal Board. In such cases the interest paid to the Treasury by the bodies concerned is used to meet an equivalent amount of any interest the Treasury itself has to pay on the National Debt, and these two self-balancing items are shown as a receipt and a payment in the Exchequer account below-the-line. This procedure avoids the inflation of both sides of the Budget proper above-the-line. In 1957–8, out of a total interest charge of £826 million on the National Debt, £657 million fell within the Budget above-the-line and £169 million outside the Budget below-the-line. All interest payments on the Debt, whether shown above- or below-the-line are, of course, covered by once-and-for-all statutory authorities of the kind mentioned above.

For about two-thirds of the National Debt the total interest liabilities can be accurately calculated in advance from the known rates and dates of the contractual interest payments on the various categories of debt. But the balance of the estimate is more precarious: about a third of it may represent the interest payable on National Savings Certificates when they are encashed, and the remainder is the interest on Treasury Bills. As to National Savings Certificates it is difficult to form any close estimate of the extent to which they will be presented for payment in any year. For Treasury Bills, two variables have to be considered—the volume of Bills likely to be outstanding during the year; and the rate of interest they are likely to carry. The volume will again vary in three ways: first, according to the amount (if any) which it will be necessary to borrow to meet a deficiency on the overall Budget; secondly, according to how far that amount is likely to be provided by other forms of borrowing; and thirdly, according to movements in the gold and dollar reserves (see Chapter VII). Given the general outline of the Budget, the first factor can be allowed for with some confidence; the second becomes a matter of making assumptions as to the proportion of any new borrowing which will carry Bill rate, or other short or medium or long-term rates of interest; while the third must be based on estimates of the course of the balance of payments. The interest variable could be a much more difficult matter if any attempt were made to estimate in advance the course of interest rates during the year. Such an attempt, however, would be both fruitless and misleading. Not even the Chancellor of the Exchequer can foresee the course of Bank Rate and other interest rates for twelve months ahead; and any assumptions he made about them would be taken as an indication of his intentions and be invested with an importance and authority which they could not possibly possess. The Treasury avoids all such pitfalls by following the unheroic and necessarily rather unreal course of estimating on the basis of the Treasury Bill rate at the latest possible date just before the Budget. After the end of the financial year the amount of interest actually paid on each stock or other item of the Debt is shown in the Finance Accounts.

(ii) *Management and Expenses of the Debt.*[1] Apart from the 'Small Savings' securities (National Savings Certificates, Defence Bonds and Premium Savings Bonds) and the small amounts of securities registered in the books of the Bank of Ireland at Dublin and Belfast, the whole of the National Debt is managed for the Treasury by the Bank of England. The Bank issues prospectuses, receives subscriptions, makes allotments, keeps the registers of holding, executes transfers, pays interest and redemption moneys and carries out conversions. The Treasury repays the Bank's out-of-pocket expenses (e.g. for printing) in connection with issues, conversions and redemptions; and in addition pays it a fee for its other management services, which are of a continuing character, in accordance with an agreed scale. Thus on the unredeemed debt other than Treasury Bills and Victory Bonds the Bank receives £325 per million on the first £750 million of the Debt, £150 per million on the next £5,250 million and £50 per million on the rest—all of which amounts to just under £1½ million a year. (The Bank of Ireland receives £300 per million on the totals of its two registers.) For Managing Treasury Bills the Bank of England receives a fixed sum of £17,500; and for Victory Bonds £50 or £100 per million according to whether the Bonds are registered or unregistered.

The Post Office's costs for managing National Savings Certificates, Defence Bonds, Premium Savings Bonds, the Post Office register of marketable securities and the Government Annuity and Life Insurance Services are provided—along with the other costs of its Savings Department—in its annual Supply vote; but it receives repayment from the Treasury of its out-of-pocket expenses on the issue, conversion and redemption of Government stocks on the Post Office register.[2] The Trustee Savings Banks receive Commissions in respect of the Trustee Savings Banks part of the Post Office register, and

[1] In the Budget 'Financial Statement' and in the weekly Exchequer Returns the cost of management is included with interest in one figure. Details of management expenses are, however, shown separately in the Finance Accounts.

[2] The Savings Department of the Post Office also incurs expenses in connection with the business of the Post Office Savings Bank which are borne on the Post Office Vote and repaid to that Vote out of the Post Office Savings Bank Fund. But this is not relevant here because deposits in the Savings Bank are not included in the National Debt.

manage their part of the register.

'Expenses' of the Debt include the prize money on Premium Savings Bonds and any cash payments which may be made in connection with conversions of Government securities.

(iii) *Sinking Funds.* A small part of this represents the element of principal in terminable Life Annuities sold under the Government scheme[1]: every year's payment of such an annuity reduces, by the amount of the principal in it, the State's capital liability in respect of the annuities as a whole and therefore reduces equally the total of the National Debt. The rest of the item 'Sinking Funds' represents the cost of the 'specific' Sinking Funds attached, under the terms of the relevant prospectuses, to four particular Government stocks. They were originally referred to as 'specific' Sinking Funds in order to distinguish them from the more general 'Old Sinking Fund' and 'New Sinking Fund' which will be described in Chapter IX (The National Debt). The four stocks concerned and the Sinking Fund provisions attached to them are:

$3\frac{1}{2}$ *per cent Conversion Loan, 1961 or after*, issued originally in 1921 but added to since. For any half-year in which the average market price of the loan is below ninety, a sum not less than 1 per cent of the amount of the loan outstanding at the end of the half-year will be employed during the succeeding half-year to purchase the loan in the market for cancellation. The Sinking Fund operated continuously from 1922 to 1932 and from 1952 to date.

3 per cent Funding Loan, 1959–69, issued originally in 1934 but added to since. A sum equal to 2 per cent of the issue is set aside each half-year. After meeting the interest on the loan the balance is applied in the succeeding half-year to the purchase of the loan for cancellation if its price is at or under par. If the price is above par the said balance can be either so applied or invested under the control of the Treasury. In fact, whenever the price has been above par it has been applied in purchases.

4 per cent Funding Loan, 1960–90, issued in June 1919 and not added to since. A sum equal to $2\frac{1}{4}$ per cent of the original issue is set aside each half-year. After meeting the interest on the loan, the balance is applied in the same way as for the 3 per cent Funding Loan.

4 per cent Victory Bonds, also issued in June 1919 and not added to since. A sum equal to $2\frac{1}{4}$ per cent of the original issue

[1] See page 187.

is set aside each half-year. After meeting the interest on the bonds, the balance is applied to the redemption of the bonds at par by means of annual drawings.

It is not now the practice to attach Sinking Fund provisions like these to individual stocks. There does not seem to be good reason for promising to support the market for one or two out of all the Government stocks outstanding or to appear to give some special reassurance about their ultimate redemption. To do so is, indeed, something of a confession by the Government that it is over-anxious about the reception of an issue by the public.

(b) PAYMENTS TO NORTHERN IRELAND EXCHEQUER

The principal payment under this head arises out of the general financial settlement which led to the passing of the Government of Ireland Act, 1920, and to the setting up of the separate Government of Northern Ireland in 1921. Under the Act the levying and collection in Northern Ireland of certain taxes, known as the 'reserved taxes', were reserved to the United Kingdom Government: over the rest of the tax field the Northern Ireland Government took over the proceeds of existing taxes and are free to legislate about them or about new taxes as they think fit. In the Inland Revenue field, income tax, surtax, profits tax and the remanets of the various excess profits taxes are reserved; death duties and stamp duties were transferred. The Customs and Excise duties proper, the purchase tax and the licence duties relating to liquor and tobacco are reserved; but entertainments duty was transferred and Northern Ireland imposed and collects its own pool betting duty. Motor vehicle duties were transferred. The Post Office operates in Northern Ireland and its revenue is reserved. But although the reserved taxes continue to be collected by the United Kingdom Government, the Northern Ireland Government is credited in each case with that part of the revenue which is attributable to Northern Ireland.

On the expenditure side the procedure is rather different and the services involving expenditure are divided into three parts. First, there are certain 'Imperial' services which are wholly within the United Kingdom Government's control and of the cost of which Northern Ireland pays a share, not based on the cost of the individual services, but through one general 'Contribution to Imperial services' the amount of which is agreed annually. The Imperial services are the (UK) National Debt, defence, certain civil items (e.g. the Civil List, Foreign Office and Colonial Office), overseas trade and the

Royal Mint. Next there is a group of services which are 'reserved' to the control of the United Kingdom Government but the precise cost of each of which in Northern Ireland is recovered from the Northern Ireland Government. These services include broadcasting, the Supreme Court of Judicature in Northern Ireland, certain items connected with land purchase, the pensions of Civil Servants and police formerly serving in Northern Ireland and a number of others. With the cost of these reserved services there are also recovered appropriate shares of the expenses of the three Revenue Departments. Finally, all other services were 'transferred': they, and any new services since introduced by the Northern Ireland Government, are controlled and financed by that Government.

Northern Ireland has a Minister of Finance (corresponding to the Chancellor of the Exchequer), an Exchequer and a financial system which, in its parliamentary procedures and administrative practices, is modelled closely on ours. Financial adjustments between the two Governments take the form of payments between the two Exchequers, and the transactions just described above are brought together in the United Kingdom Budget in the item we are now considering. First, there is calculated the gross amount attributable to Northern Ireland of the reserved taxes. From this are deducted the cost of the reserved services and the Contribution to Imperial Services. The resulting net sum, being the Northern Ireland residuary share of the reserved taxes, is then paid by the United Kingdom Exchequer to the Northern Ireland Exchequer. The relevant figures (subject to later adjustment) are given after the end of each year in the Financial Statement issued on the United Kingdom Budget Day for the following year and later in the annual United Kingdom Finance Accounts. The figures for 1957–8 were:

		£ million
Gross proceeds of reserved taxes		84·0
Less—Cost of reserved services	7·6	
Contribution to Imperial Services ..	9·5	
	——	−17·1
Northern Ireland residuary share of reserved taxes		66·9

Two other payments may be made to Northern Ireland under this head of the Budget. First, under the Disabled Persons (Employment) Act, 1944, and the Employment and Training Act, 1948, the United Kingdom contributes the cost in Northern Ireland of certain services, similar to those provided by those Acts, for helping people to find, obtain and retain employment. In 1957–8, £47,100 was paid.

Secondly, the Social Services (Northern Ireland Agreement) Act, 1949, was passed with the object of maintaining parity, as between Northern Ireland and the rest of the United Kingdom, in the financial cost of certain social services, namely, family allowances, national assistance, non-contributory pensions and health services. The actual total cost to the United Kingdom and Northern Ireland Exchequers together is ascertained and is then reallocated on a national 'parity' basis, Northern Ireland's 'parity' being 2·5 per cent of the total[1] and that of the rest of the United Kingdom 97·5 per cent. Then, if either Northern Ireland's actual costs or those for the rest of the United Kingdom exceed the respective 'party' costs, the United Kingdom Exchequer or the Northern Ireland Exchequer, as the case may be, contributes 80 per cent of the excess to the other. The arrangement is a reciprocal one, but it has so far always fallen to the United Kingdom Exchequer to make the contribution. In 1957–8 Northern Ireland's estimatd costs for these social services were £26·1 million, and her 'parity' figure £20·1 million; so the United Kingdom Exchequer paid a contribution in respect of that year of £4·8 million.

How does the resulting financial position look from the Northern Ireland point of view? On the revenue side they have their residuary share of reserved taxes, the proceeds of the transferred taxes and of any new taxes they have themselves imposed, certain other items and the two special payments from the United Kingdom Exchequer just mentioned. On the expenditure side they have to meet the cost of all the transferred and new services for which they are responsible, including the service of Northern Ireland's own Public Debt (the total of which is about £52 million). The Northern Ireland Government publishes its own Finance Accounts which are broadly on the same lines as ours and which set out annually all the relevant figures. in summary form those above-the-line for 1957-8 were: Revenue— Residuary Share of Reserved Taxes, £66·9 million; Transferred and new taxes, £5·3 million; other revenue, £4·6 million; the two special United Kingdom contributions referred to above (including adjustments for other years), £4·7 million; Total, £81·5 million; against which expenditure above-the-line came to approximately the same total, there being a small surplus of revenue of £36,000.

It is not for us to discuss all the problems which face a Northern Ireland Minister of Finance at his Budget time; but one of them is relevant here, namely the amount he should agree to provide as the contribution to the cost of the Imperial services. The bulk of the

---

[1] This figure is slightly less than Northern Ireland's proportion of the total population of the United Kingdom.

revenue on which he can rely is settled for him at Westminster. On his outgoings, he may have to balance a desire to spend more on local services against his liability to provide a reasonable contribution to Imperial services. He need not give quite the same weight to broad economic considerations as a Chancellor of the Exchequer must do. On the other hand, he has different social considerations to take into account arising out of the lower standard of wealth and living and the chronically higher level of unemployment in Northern Ireland. There is, in fact, only one practicable working rule which can govern the relation between the United Kingdom and Northern Ireland Budgets. Northern Ireland must be allowed to provide in its Budget for standards of taxation and of state services—and particularly of the social services—which are broadly the same as those provided in Great Britain. If that broad relation is maintained, then a reasonable Imperial contribution will approximate to the resulting surplus above-the-line on the Northern Ireland Budget. The figures given above show that this is precisely what happened in 1957–8.

(c) OTHER CONSOLIDATED FUND SERVICES

The services here provided exhibit in detail the essential character of Consolidated Fund Services already noticed, namely that Parliament has by the relevant Statutes decided once and for all that they shall be met from the Exchequer without any need for further annual votes and for the discussions and sometimes disputes which such votes entail. The services are of a very varied nature and are listed in full—in some cases with the names of the beneficiaries concerned—in the annual Finance Accounts. At the head of them stands the annual payment for the Civil List, that is, the provision which Parliament makes by statute at the beginning of each reign for the Sovereign and the Royal Household. After this come the annuities payable under successive Civil List Acts to other members of the Royal Family. There follow pensions to former Prime Ministers, a former Speaker of the House of Commons, and former Lord Chancellors, Lords of Appeal and Judges; the salaries of the Speaker of the House of Commons, the Leader of the Opposition and the Comptroller and Auditor-General; the salary and expenses of the Governor of Northern Ireland; and the salaries of existing Judges and high officials of the Courts of Justice. Then, in a final miscellaneous group, come (with other items) the expenses of Parliamentary Elections; an instalment of a grant to Malta for the repair of war damage; and, largest of all, a sum of £4 million for the liability assumed by the United Kingdom Government in 1938 after the Government of Eire had refused to continue to meet certain Government obligations arising out of the long history of land purchase by Irish tenants.

(2) SUPPLY SERVICES

These are all services which, unlike the Consolidated Fund Services just described, are financed by annual votes of Parliament. Another name for these votes is 'moneys provided by Parliament': when a Supply service is the subject of legislation the latter will usually say that any expenses incurred under the legislation shall be met 'out of moneys provided by Parliament', thus leaving the actual provision for the service to future annual votes. The ways in which the Government settles the amounts of the Estimates for Supply services are described in Chapter X, and the procedure by which Parliament votes the money for them in Chapter XI. We are here concerned rather with the services which are the subjects of the votes.

In the Financial Statement issued on Budget Day the provision in the Budget for Supply services in the new financial year is shown under the heads—Defence, with separate figures for each of the Departments; Civil, with the total of each Class of the Estimates, including Tax Collection. All these figures, of course, have previously been published in the Estimates themselves.[1] As the financial year proceeds, however, the weekly Exchequer Returns do not divide the actual Supply issues from the Exchequer in that way but give only one figure for the whole of the Supply services to date. There is nothing obscurantist about this. The explanation is as follows. Except in the case of the Revenue Departments, Supply issues are not made direct from the Exchequer to the spending departments but in large lump sums to the Paymaster-General's Office, which is the departments' banker and which itself meets the cheques drawn on it by the departments to meet their commitments. For administrative convenience, the Treasury makes its issues during the first three weeks of each month in round sums against some of the larger votes, although the Paymaster-General uses the issues to meet orders on all votes, large and small. The matter is adjusted during the last ten days of the month to reflect the true position on all votes. Since for a large part of each month the votes against which issues are being made do not correspond with those against which funds are actually being spent, it is necessary, in the Exchequer Return, to show one

[1] It sometimes happens that important decisions of policy affecting expenditure are taken after the presentation of the Estimates but before Budget Day. In such cases, the Financial Statement will show the necessary addition to, or reduction of, the total for the Supply services.

lump sum for all issues to date throughout the year. But the supplement to the end-of-the-year Return divides the Supply issues made during the past year among the several Defence Departments and Civil Supply (including Tax Collection). The Financial Statement issued on Budget Day repeats this division. Three or four months later the Finance Accounts add a little more information by giving the issues to each Class of the Civil votes; but it is not until the departments' Appropriation Accounts are published some nine or ten months after the end of the year that it is possible to see exactly what each department has spent out of the vote or votes franted for it.[1]

But one further classified statement of the whole of the estimated Budget expenditure is published. In the Financial Statement, Table VI classifies it under six broad heads and not, in the case of the Civil services, according to the Classes of the Estimates. The six heads are: Debt Services; Defence Preparations; Assistance to Local Services; National Health Service, Insurance, Pensions, etc.; Agricultural and Food Subsidies; and Other Services. Subsidiary tables show how the figures under the third, fourth and sixth heads are built up.

(a) DEFENCE

This covers the requirements of the Army, the Navy and the Air Force, the Defence expenditure of the Ministry of Supply[2] and the expenses of the Ministry of Defence. Each of the three Defence Departments presents its Estimates, and accounts for its expenditure, on broadly the same pattern with about a dozen separate Estimates for, respectively, Pay, Reserve Forces, Headquarters, Supplies, Stores, Works, Pensions and so on. Taken as a whole the Defence Estimates reflect the current general defence policy of the Government and the various Estimates of the individual departments reflect the part of them has to play, in collaboration with the others, in carrying out that policy. The broad policy itself and the more detailed policies of the individual departments are set out each year in the White Paper on Defence Policy. This paper, normally published in February, is accompanied by a second White Paper on Defence Statistis, which contains the first announcement of the amounts of the Defence Estimates for the coming year and precedes by a week or two the publication of them in full detail. Subsequently,

---

[1] See Chapter XII. In particular for the difference between the amounts issued from the Exchequer and the actual expenditures of the departments see page 254.

[2] Although the bulk of the Ministry of Supply's expenditure is for defence purposes, it is a Civil department and its Estimate, like all other Civil Estimates, is presented by the Financial Secretary to the Treasury. See also page 121.

separate White Papers are published explaining the provisions made in the Navy, Army and Air Estimates respectively and the policies behind them.

It may be noted that the Estimate for the Ministry of Defence has to be published by itself since it could not appropriately go in the volume for any of the Defence Services or in that of the Civil Estimates. Only a relatively small part of the Estimate represents the expenses of the Ministry itself. The bulk is accounted for by the cost of British military staffs at the Headquarters of NATO and other international defence organizations: the British share of the expenses of those organizations: and—much the biggest of all—the British share of the cost of the military installations ('infrastructure') for the defence of the NATO area.

One important aspect of the Defence Estimates is the way in which the Defence Departments—subject to Treasury approval throughout —acquire and pay for the warlike and other stores they need. This subject has a long history[1] but the present position is very briefly as follows. The arrangements differ between the Navy on the one hand and the Army and Air Force on the other. We will take the latter first. It is for the Army and Air Force in the first place to state their requirements for a new weapon or piece of equipment—such as a gun, piece of ammunition, vehicle, aircraft or aero-engine—to the Ministry of Supply, setting out the type of thing required, its desired performance, quantity required and so on. Research and development may be needed before the required item can be put into production and these are carried out under the Ministry's control, either at its own research establishments or—as happens to something like three-quarters of the work—by industry under the Ministry's instructions. When a project is ripe for production the necessary contracts are placed by the Ministry who are responsible for paying the contractors, inspecting the finished articles and taking delivery of them. The Ministry then pass the articles on to the Army or Air Force, as the case may be, and receive payment from the relevant Army or Air Vote. The expenses of the Ministry on research, development and inspection remain charged to its own Vote, the Vote for the Ministry of Supply (Class VI, Vote 10). But the payments it has to make to contractors for actual production orders are charged to a separate Vote, to which are credited the payments received from the Army and Air Force: this is the Vote for Ministry of Supply (Purchasing (Repayment) Services). This latter Vote—which incidentally also bears the cost of transactions carried out by the Ministry for 'Non-

---

[1] See *The Organization of British Central Government*, 1914–56, by a Study Group of the Royal Institute of Public Administration (1957), pages 215–39.

Exchequer' customers, like Commonwealth or other Governments—
may be a 'token' Vote in that receipts balance or exceed payments.
This procedure governs the great bulk of the expenditure of the Army
and Air Force on warlike and other stores: it applies to a lesser
extent to the Navy. The Admiralty have always been allowed to
control the design and production of their ships and their armament,
and the corresponding research and development: the actual construction is carried out either in the Naval dockyards or by contractors. But the large Naval requirements of aircraft and air equipment generally, as well as a certain quantity of the stores required
for the shipbuilding and ship-repair programmes and otherwise, are
procured by the Ministry of Supply which receives payment for them
from Navy Votes.

Two points must be noticed about these arrangements. First, there
is necessarily a measure of central control over the combined requirements of the Defence Departments. This follows automatically from
the fact that the total expenditure on Defence each year is fixed at a
certain figure by the Government, But it applies with special force to
the Services' demands for research and development, partly because
the number of trained staff is limited and partly because these
activities can be notoriously expensive. Thus, if a demand comes
along for a new type of aircraft or nuclear weappn, either of which
may require the expenditure of many millions on research and development, it is necessary to make sure that it can be fitted into the
agreed financial programme and that there are staff and other
facilities available to cope with it. It may be, if the new demand is
clearly urgent and essential, that other items of lower priority have
to be dropped. The responsibility for the central control and co-
ordination of such matters lies with the Minister of Defence; but, of
course, the Treasury too will take a hand. In important cases, the
matter may go to the Cabinet.

The second point, which almost goes without saying, is that the
system by which the production of weapons and equipment is in the
hands of a department other than the 'user' departments can only
work if there is the fullest collaboration between the former and the
latter. This is achieved partly by appointing Army and Air Force
personnel to the staff of the Ministry of Supply and partly by close,
direct contact between the Ministry and the Defence Departments
themselves.

(b) CIVIL

After all the Civil and Revenue Departments' Estimates have been
published a separate booklet is published entitled *Memorandum by*

the Financial Secretary to the Treasury and Tables. Its contents are of threefold interest. First there is a long table showing the individual Estimates in which there are major variations compared with the previous year, and giving short explanations of those variations. Next come a series of tables, which Members of Parliament or parliamentary committees have asked for at different times, gathering together from different Estimates the total provision made for certain services —for example, research and development; subscriptions to international organizations; museums, libararies and galleries; Government information services; Civil Service superannuation. Finally, there is a series of tables giving the expenditure out of each separate vote over a ten-year period: incidentally, these show which old votes have been discontinued during the period and those which have recently been introduced. The form of this memorandum and of its tables has been much discussed, and many changes have been made, over the hundred years or so for which it has existed. There will probably always be nearly as many views about its worthwhileness as there are readers; but it is a useful document to have by one if one is particularly interested in the expenditure side of the Budget.

The Estimates for the Civil Supply Services are divided into ten Classes, for each of which a separate booklet is published. A 'Class' has no statutory or formal significance but is simply a convenient means of publishing together Estimates which all fall within a particular field of Government indicated by its title. The notes below give the main Estimates included in each Class and (in square brackets) pointers to elements which may be of interest in some of the Estimates. The titles in italics and inverted commas sometimes refer to an Estimate for England and Wales which may have a Scottish counterpart and occasional, an Irish one as well.

Class I (Central Government and Finance)
This includes Parliament, Treasury, Exchequer and Audit Department, Royal Mint, Royal Commissions, Secret Service, Scottish Home Department and a number of other departments or services, mostly small, which are concerned with the central machinery of government. ['*Treasury and Subordinate Departments*' includes besides the salaries and expenses of the Treasury and those other departments, a fee to the Bank of England in respect of the cost of exchange control, and also the expenses of the Capital Issues Committee. '*Crown Estate Office*'—that is, the Office of the Crown Estate Commissioners, formerly known as the Commissioners of Crown Lands—is for headquarters administrative expenses; the surplus revenue from the Crown Estates which they look after is paid into

the Exchequer under the item Miscellaneous Revenue. '*Royal Mint*' includes the withdrawal of silver coin and its replacement by cupro-nickel coin, the latter being largely financed by the sale of silver from the coin withdrawn. '*Secret Service*' is unique in that, when the expenditure is submitted for audit, it is supported not by vouchers but by certificates from the responsible Ministers. '*Scottish Home Department*' is included here rather than in Class III because its activities are wider than those of the Home Office in England.]

Class II (Commonwealth and Foreign)
These Estimates, with one exception, relate entirely to matters which are the responsibility of the Foreign Office or Commonwealth Relations Office or Colonial Office. The general form is to have one Estimate for each of those three Departments, followed by Estimates for the services for which it is responsible. ['*Foreign Office Grants and Services*' covers subscriptions to international organizations,[1] contributions to various internal funds of a charitable character, and a variety of grants by way of direct assistance to foreign countries. There is a separate Estimate for '*British Council*'. '*Commonwealth Services*' includes assistance to the defence of Malaya after she has attained independence. '*Colonial Services*' includes a long list of grants or loans to Colonies. Two Estimates cover assistance to '*Development and Welfare*' in the Colonies and in Rhodesia and other African territories respectively.]

Class III (Home Department, Law and Justice)
This includes the Home Office, Police, Prisons, the Courts, Public Trustee, and various legal expenses of Government. [After '*Home Office*' there is a separate Estimate for '*Home Office (Civil Defence Services*)': this relates to the Civil Defence organization and its equipment and stores, other expenditure on works and specialist services—like ports, railways, oil and food reserves—being included in Estimates for which the departments concerned with such services are responsible. '*Police*' is mainly for grants to Local Authorities and the Metropolitan Police Fund. '*Fire Services*' is mainly grants to Local Authorities for one-quarter of the cost of their fire services.[2] '*Public Trustee*' is a token vote, the expenses borne on the Estimate—but not, at any rate in 1958–9, the total cost of the Office, including Allied Services—being more than covered by receipts from fees.]

[1] A complete list of these subscriptions is given in a Table attached to the Financial Secretary's Memorandum on the Estimates.

[2] As from April 1, 1959, the grants to Local Education Authorities and a number of other grants to Local Authorities (including those for Fire Services) will be replaced by 'general grants' under the Local Government Act, 1958.

Class IV (*Education and Broadcasting*)

This includes the Education Departments, Museums and Galleries, grants for Science and the Arts, grants to Universities, and Broadcasting. ['*Ministry of Education*' consists, as to nearly 90 per cent of the gross Estimate, of the percentage grants to Local Education Authorities. [1],[2] The Estimates for all the Museums, Libraries and Galleries, with their respective grants in aid of purchases, are conveniently summarized in the table in the Financial Secretary's Memorandum referred to above.[3] '*Grants for Science and the Arts*' includes, besides grants to the Royal Society and other learned bodies, the funds distributed by the Arts Council.[3] '*Universities and Colleges, etc., Great Britain*' covers both the recurrent grants towards the current expenses of the universities, etc., and the non-recurrent grants for new buildings and other capital expenditure: schedules to the Estimate show the distribution of the grants. '*Broadcasting*' includes the payment to the British Broadcasting Corporation of the agreed share of the revenue from broadcast receiving licences: see page 101.]

Class V (*Health, Housing and Local Government*)

This includes the Ministry of Housing and Local Government, Housing, Exchequer grants to Local Revenues, the Health Departments, and National Health Service. ['*Ministry of Housing and Local Government*' includes, among the non-administrative items, compensation payments arising from 1955 onwards under the Town and Country Planning Act, 1954: payments arising from earlier decisions are charged to the Exchequer below-the-line as described on page 134. '*Housing*' covers the various subsidies on houses already built; annuities repaying the Exchequer loans for temporary houses (partly offset by receipts from Local Authorities); and grants to Local Authorities for requisitioned houses. '*Exchequer Grants to Local Revenues*' are the Exchequer Equalizatilon Grants made to Local Authorities whose rateable resources are below the average.[4]

[1] As from April 1, 1959, the grants to Local Education Authorities and a number of other grants to Local Authorities (including those for Fire Services) will be replaced by 'general grants' under the Local Government Act, 1958.

[2] A separate Memorandum is published annually on the Ministry of Education Estimate. (Cf. Cmnd 377 of March 1958.)

[3] Much useful information on these and kindred subjects is given in *Government and the Arts in Britain*, published for HM Treasury by HM Stationery Office, 1958.

[4] As from April 1, 1959, the Exchequer Equalization Grants will (under the Local Government Act, 1958) be renamed 'Rate Deficiency Grants', and the basis on which the Grants are calculated will be amended.

'*Ministry of Health*',[1] and to a less degree its Scottish counterpart, is mainly for the cost of the national milk scheme for children and expectant mothers and of other welfare foods. '*National Health Service*'[1]—with separate Estimates for 'England and Wales' and 'Scotland'—covers the expenses of the hospitals,[2] the general medical, pharmaceutical, dental and ophthalmic services,[3] and grants towards the various services of local health authorities. '*War Damage Commission*' is for the administrative expenses of the Commission; the actual War Damage compensation payments are charged to the Exchequer below-the-line, as described on page 133.]

Class VI (*Trade, Labour and Supply*)

This includes the Board of Trade and separate Estimates for three of its main activities, Export Credits, Ministry of Labour and National Service, Ministry of Supply and its Purchasing and Repayments vote and the Royal Ordnance Factories. ['*Board of Trade*' is entirely for administrative costs, covering its general, bankruptcy, companies (winding up) and patents services. Grants to various industrial organizations are in '*Board of Trade (Assistance to Industry and Trading Services)*'. '*Board of Trade (Strategic Reserves)*' is for the expenses of turning over stocks held as strategic reserves; when stocks are sold and not replaced—that is, in order to reduce the reserves—the proceeds are credited to the Exchequer as Miscellaneous Revenue (see page 103). '*Export Credits*' covers both administrative expenses and payments under gurantees of a normal commercial character; payments under Special Guarantees given in the national interest are provided for in an immediately following, separate Estimate. '*Ministry of Labour and National Service*' is mainly for administration but includes various grants for training and rehabilitation. '*Ministry of Supply*' covers both the Defence and Civil functions of the Ministry and some three-quarters of its represents expenditure on research and development, mainly carried out by industry on the Ministry's behalf. '*Ministry of Supply (Purchasing*

---

[1] The Ministry presents (as a Command Paper) an Annual Report covering the National Health Service and other health services.

[2] The accounts are published annually and separately, as a House of Commons Paper, of the Regional Hospital Boards, and Executive Councils and the Boards of Governors of the Teaching Hospitals. There is one paper for England and Wales and another for Scotland.

[3] The subheads relating to the pharmaceutical, dental and ophthalmic services show the extent to which their cost is covered by patients' payments. The National Health Service contributions payable by insured persons towards the cost of the National Health Service generally are shown in the Appropriations-in-Aid Subhead. See also note at end of Appendix D.

(*Repayment*) *Services*)' has already been explained in connection
with the Defence Estimates on page 115. '*Royal Ordnance Factories*'
is accounted for by the Ministry and represents the difference
between the Factories' expenditure and the value of the supplies they
produce, which are sold through or to the Ministry. Taking the
Ministry's three Estimates together, their total of £237 million for
1958–9 was divided as to £193 million Defence and £43 million Civil,
the balance of £1 million being attributable to the provision of
Industrial Capacity for Defence purposes, but reckoned as outside
the Defence programme. It is the second figure—the Defence
element—which is included in the published totals of Defence
expenditure.]

Class VII (*Common Services—Works, Stationery, etc.*)
This includes the Ministry of Works and a number of separate
Estimates of expenditure on the various types of buildings for which
it is responsible, Historic Buildings and Ancient Monuments, Rates
on Government Property, Stationery and Printing and the Central
Office of Information. The expenditure on buildings, rates, stationery
and printing and information is incurred on behalf of departments,
normally without repayment, and is concentrated in these Estimates
for the general reasons discussed on page 226. Appendices to the
Rates and Stationery and Printing Estimates show the costs expected
to be incurred for each department. ['*Ministry of Works*' is for
administrative expenses only, the cost of particular buildings and of
maintenance being provided in the succeeding Estimates. '*Public
Buildings, etc., United Kingdom*' is the most important of the latter,
giving details of new works in progress and proposed, and providing
for the maintenance, rent, furnishing, heating and lighting of existing
Government accommodation in the United Kingdom. Within this
Estimate, however, there is one subhead which involves a major
exception to the rule that the Ministry renders accommodation
services to departments without payment. Under this subhead there
is first a gross charge of expenditure incurred by the Ministry in
carrying out new works and other services for the Post Office and,
as a matter of convenience, some similar services in connection with
defence. This expenditure in fact exceeds that in the whole of the
rest of the Estimate. When the services are paid for by the departments concerned, their payments are credited to the subhead in
question, which is thus a net subhead. The reasons for this are that
expenditure for defence purposes ought not to remain as a final
charge to a Civil Vote; while, in the case of the Post Office, all other
capital expenditure has to be met from the Post Office Vote, even

though its cost is met from borrowed moneys,[1] and expenditure on new buildings should be dealt with in the same way. '*Rates on Government Property*' provides the contributions which are paid to local authorities in respect of Government buildings in lieu of rates, to which the Crown is not subject. '*Stationery and Printing*' covers expenditure on paper, printing, office supplies, etc., for Government departments generally and includes details showing the extent to which printing and binding are carried out at the Stationery Office's own Printing Works. In '*Central Office of Information*' the main items, after administration, are for press advertising, films and exhibitions. A large number of departments also provide for information services in their own Estimates: a full list of these departments' expenses, together with the expenses incurred for them by the Central Office of Information, is given in a table attached to the Financial Secretary's Memorandum on the Estimates.]

Class VIII (*Agriculture and Food*)
Includes the Agriculture Departments, separate Estimates for different aspects of the Government's agricultural, food and fishery services, Ordinance Survey, Development Fund and Forestry Commission. ['*Ministry of Agriculture, Fisheries and Food*' is for administrative expenses only and covers Kew Gardens and the Agricultural Land Commission. '*Agricultural and Food Grants and Subsidies*' covers farming grants and subsidies (e.g. fertilizers, ploughing up grassland, attested herds and calves) and the agricultural price guarantees (e.g. cereals, eggs, fatstock and milk). [2],[3] '*Agricultural and Food Services*' covers expenses incurred in such services as land drainage land settlement and agricultural education research and advisory services. '*Food* (*Strategic Reserves*)' is a Civil Defence service and covers the procurement and turnover of stocks of certain foods. '*Fishery Grants and Services*' is mainly for financial assistance to fishermen for boats engines, etc., a subsidy to the white-fish industry[4] and research and development. '*Development Fund*' is mainly for grants and loans recommended by the Development Commission

[1] See page 129.
[2] A Table attached to the Financial Secretary's Memorandum on the Estimates adds a little more detail and brings together the payments for England, Wales and Scotland.
[3] A White Paper on agriculture is published annually (usually in March) under the title 'Annual Review and Determination of Guarantees' which sets out in detail the price guarantees determined for the coming year and the reasons for them. (Cf. the 1958 paper, Cmnd 390.)
[4] The accounts of the White-Fish Authority are published annually as a House of Commons Paper.

for the improvement of the rural economy and for fisheries research by independent institutions.[1] '*Forestry Commission*' is for state forestry operations and grants; this, being a long-term undertaking, is as yet covered by sales of produce as to about only a fifth of the cost.]

Class IX (*Transport, Power and Industrial Research*)
Includes expenditure on roads, shipping and civil aviation, the Ministry of Power, Atomic Energy and the Departments of Scientific and Industrial Research. ['*Ministry of Transport and Civil Aviation*' is for administrative expenses only. '*Roads, etc., England and Wales*' includes the Ministry's expenditure on new construction, improvement and maintenance of trunk roads and grants to local highway authorities for similar operations on classified roads. An Appendix to the Estimate lists the new works and major improvements in progress or authorized under both heads. '*Ministry of Power*' is mainly for administration but also includes loans for installing fuel-saving equipment. '*Ministry of Power (Special Services)*' is mainly for works of a Civil Defence character in connection with oil storage and distribution. '*Atomic Energy*' provides, through the Atomic Energy Office (which is under the Prime Minister), grants to the Atomic Energy Authority for their operations, including new works and plant and machinery, and loans to enable it to advance money for the production of uranium; the Estimate takes account of receipts for certain products the figures for which are, for security reasons, not disclosed. '*Department of Scientific and Industrial Research*' includes grants to outside Research Associations, universities and others as well as a much larger expenditure in the Department's own research establishments (including the National Physical Laboratory); it also includes the United Kingdom's share of the expenses of the European Organization for Nuclear Research.]

Class X (*Pensions, National Insurance and National Assistance*)
The title is self-explanatory, except that this Class also includes Family Allowances. ['*Superannuation and Retired Allowances*' covers the pensions, etc., of Civil Servants, other than those lately serving in the Revenue Departments and civilians employed by the Defence Services.[2] '*Ministry of Pensions and National Insurance*' is for administrative expenses of the Ministry. '*War Pensions, etc.*' covers pensions to the armed forces arising out of the two world wars and

[1] The accounts of the Development Fund, with some details of the cases assisted, are published annually as a House of Commons Paper.

[2] A Table bringing together the cost of Civil Service superannuation from this Estimate and those for the Revenue Departments and the Defence Services is attached to the Financial Secretary's Memorandum on the Estimates.

of later service, pensions to the Mercantile Marine arising out of both wars, pensions to civilians arising out of the Second World War and grants to National Service officers and men and others to assist them to meet their financial commitments. '*National Insurance and Family Allowances*' covers the Exchequer payments to the National Insurance Fund[1] (both the 'supplement' based on the contributions paid by employers and employees and the additional grant in respect of the deficit on the Fund); the Exchequer contribution to the Industrial Injuries Fund; and Family Allowances. '*National Assistance Board*' includes the Board's administrative expenses but is mainly for National Assistance grants: it also includes non-contributory old-age pensions.]

(c) TAX COLLECTION

This covers the expenses of the '*Customs and Excise*' and '*Inland Revenue*' Departments, and Estimates for which are published together in a separate booklet. (The booklet also includes an Estimate for the expenses of the Post Office, but these are shown separately in the Budget accounts under 'Self-balancing Expenditure'—see below.) The organizations of the two Departments have already been described in Chapter IV.

(3) SELF-BALANCING EXPENDITURE

This consists mainly of Post Office expenditure, with a relatively small second item for that part of the Excess Profits Tax Post-war Refunds which is withheld to cover the recipients' tax liabilities on the Refunds. The reasons why these two items appear here and in this form have been explained in Chapter IV, pages 98 and 104.

The Post Office expenditure, as set out in the Post Office Estimate, includes provision for capital expenditure, which has already been described in Chapter IV in connection with the net Post Office revenue taken into the Budget.

[1] For a short description of the financial basis of the Fund see Appendix D.

CHAPTER VI

The Budget in Detail—(3) Below-the-Line

IN Chapter III we saw that, apart from the special case of the self-balancing interest which appears first on both sides below-the-line, the payments ('Issues') items relate either to the redemption of debt or to a variety of outgoings, mainly of a capital character, which Parliament has expressly authorized to be met from some source other than revenue; while the receipt items consist either of funds raised by borrowing or of repayments of loans previously made out of the Exchequer. In the present chapter it is proposed to give some short notes on the various items entered below-the-line in the order in which they appear in the weekly Exchequer Returns. The items described below may not all appear in any particular year's accounts, but any one of them is liable to appear on either the receipts side or the payments side or both. Some of those described will drop out in due course, and new ones will appear. The present list will at any rate illustrate the types of transactions which may at any time appear below-the-line. Since the amount of borrowed moneys appearing on the receipts side is largely in the nature of a balancing item, we will start with payments side.

(1) PAYMENTS

(a) INTEREST ON THE NATIONAL DEBT MET FROM RECEIPTS UNDER VARIOUS ACTS

This item has already been explained in Chapter V (page 106). On the payments side of the Exchequer Return only one figure is given for the total amount of National Debt interest met in this way; but details showing the amount of interest received into the Exchequer under each of the Acts concerned and building up to this payments figure are given in the Finance Accounts, on the receipts side of the main table (' Exchequer Receipts and Issues') and under the heading 'Interest received under the following Acts'.

(b) EXCESS PROFITS TAX, POST-WAR REFUNDS

These refunds have been explained in Chapter IV (page 104) in connection with Self-balancing Revenue. The amounts here charged below-the-line represent the balance of the refunds after deduction of income tax. They were authorized to be met out of borrowed moneys by the Finance (No. 2) Act, 1945.

(c) ISSUES UNDER THE FOLLOWING ACTS

General Note

Since 1937 all Acts authorizing the Treasury to provide repayable advances out of the Consolidated Fund have normally contained two general provisions. First, to provide the necessary funds, the Treasury may borrow in any way in which they are authorized to borrow under the National Loans Act, 1939 (see page 178). Secondly, repayments of the principal of the advances must be used to redeem debt; and interest received on the advances must be used to meet an equal amount of the annual charges for interest on the National Debt (see page 106). For most of the Issues about to be described receipts of interest and principal appear on the receipts side below-the-line under the respective headings 'Interest received under the following Acts' and 'Repayments under the following Acts.' Where this is not so that fact will be pointed out below.

The terms of repayment vary from case to case. In most long-term cases repayment is made by equated annuities or equal instalments of principal spread over a period of years. The period will depend broadly on the life of the asset created out of the advance. Thus, among the nationalized industries, the advances to the National Coal Board for investment purposes (mainly machinery) are repayable over fifteen years, those to the Electricity, Gas and Transport authorities over twenty-five years, and those to the Airways Corporations over seven years.

Where these issues are for the purpose of making repayable advances to bodies or persons other than Government departments, the amount of the advances outstanding at the end of the financial year in each case is shown in the statement of Estimated Assets contained in the annual Finance Accounts.

In most of these cases the relevant statutes provide that the Minister concerned shall present annual accounts of the transactions, with, generally, an explanatory foreword. Also, where the borrowers are public corporations, the latter present annual reports and statements of their own accounts, which are published as House of Commons papers.

Tithe Act, 1936
This Act extinquished tithe rent-charge and gave the tithe-owners stock in compensation. The former tithe-payers now pay 'redemption annuities' in lieu of rent-charge, and the annuities are paid into the Redemption Annuities Account and are there charged with the service of the stock. In so far as the Account is insufficient from time to time to meet the service of the stock, advances are made from the Colsolidated Fund. These advances are mostly of a temporary character and are quickly repaid; interest is compounded and paid with the principal.

Export Guarantees Acts, 1949 to 1957
These Acts, which superseded previous legislation on the subject, enabled the Board of Trade to give guarantees of two kinds—first, after consultation with an Advisory Committee, guarantees in connection with exports and in other ways for the purpose of encouraging overseas trade (up to £750 million), and, secondly, without such consultation but with Treasury approval, and if expedient in the national interest, to give guarantees for the same purpose or for the purpose of rendering economic assistance to overseas countries (up to £250 million). The cost of implementing any of these guarantees is borne on annual Supply votes: but the Act provides that if it is not to met in any case it shall be charged on and issued out of the Consolidated Fund. (No guarantee has in fact yet had to be met out of the Consolidated Fund.) In addition, the Board of Trade has power to acquire any securities it has guaranteed—that is, it can provide finance as well as guarantees. To enable it to do this, advances are made from the Consolidated Fund to the 'Acquisition of Guaranteed Securities Fund', from which the cost of acquiring securities is paid, into which all receipts of interest and principal are paid and from which payments of interest and principal to the Exchequer are made. If the interest due to the Exchequer on its advances exceeds that received on the guaranteed securities, the difference is charged to annual Supply votes. An annual account of the Fund, after examination by the Comptroller and Auditor-General, is submitted to Parliament and published in the annual volume of Civil Appropriation Accounts. The 'below-the-line' item now being noticed consists of such advances for the acquisition of guaranteed securities.

Housing (Scotland) Acts, 1950 to 1957
Advances may be made by the Secretary of State for Scotland, not exceeding £100 million in all, to the Scottish Special Housing Association to enable or assist it to provide houses. The Treasury may issue

the necessary funds from the Consolidated Fund and out of borrowed moneys. (Certain annual and other grants to the Association in connection with the provision of housing are borne on the vote for Housing, Scotland.) The Minister's accounts are published with the Civil Appropriation Accounts.

Armed Forces (Housing Loans) Acts, 1949 and 1953
In order to supplement what could be provided out of revenue for housing married persons in the Armed Forces, the Treasury was authorized to advance out of borrowed moneys up to £75 million over the ten years to 1960. Expenditure out of these advances is included in Defence votes and the advances are applied as appropriations-in-aid of the votes containing provision for the houses in question. (In addition, savings on Defence Works votes can be applied to this service by virement[1]; but such transfers count against the £75 million.) The votes provide for the repayment of the advances by means of sixty-year annuities.

Local Authorities Loans Act, 1945
This is the Act under which advances are made to the Local Loans Fund, from which, in turn, the Public Works Loan Board make loans to local authorities for capital purposes. It seemed as well to give a fairly full explanation of this item and this is to be found in Appendix E.

Miscellaneous Financial Provisions Acts, 1950 and 1955: Northern Ireland Exchequer
The Treasury have power to make advances to the Government of Northern Ireland to enable that Government to make loans to local authorities and others from the (Northern Ireland) Government Loans Fund. (That fund is the Northern Ireland equivalent of the United Kingdom Local Loans Fund.) The advances outstanding at any time must not exceed £30 million. They are normally repaid by sixty-year annuities.

New Towns Acts, 1946 and 1955
Advances, not to exceed £250 million in all, are made through the Minister of Housing and Local Government to the dozen or so Development Corporations which are constructing the New Towns, to finance their capital expenditure. The advances are repayable by sixty-year annuities. (The Corporations also receive grants from the

[1] See page 236.

Ministry's Supply vote for non-capital expenditure on water supply, sewerage and other services and from the votes for Housing towards housing expenses.)

Post Office and Telegraph (Money) Act, 1958
This Act is the latest of the series of periodical Money Acts under which the Treasury is authorized to provide finance for the capital development of the various Post Office services.[1] Each Act provides for advances up to a certain amount—£75 million in the Act of 1958—and authorizes the Treasury to raise the necessary money either by terminable annuities for periods not exceeding twenty years or in any manner authorized by the National Loans Act, 1939. As the amount authorized by one Act approaches exhaustion a fresh, similar authority is sought from Parliament. Until 1953 it was customary for the Treasury to borrow funds in the custody of the National Debt Commissioners (mainly from the Post Office Savings Bank) and to repay them by terminable annuities. But at that date that source of funds seemed likely to become inadequate and the general power was taken to borrow in any other way. This new provision enables the Treasury to consider how best to finance this service in the light of its total capital commitments and the resources (e.g. the above-the-line surplus) available to meet them. All the capital expenditure of the Post Office is included in its Supply vote, and the Treasury advances are appropriated in aid of the vote. An appendix to the Estimate, and later to the Appropriation Accounts, shows the amount of capital expenditure met from these advances. The Post Office's accumulated net liability to the Exchequer for capital advances is shown in the Balance Sheet included in the Department's Commercial Accounts.[2] All Post Office borrowings from the Treasury—however the Treasury may have raised the money—are repaid by twenty-year annuities, which are borne on the Post Office vote.

Cinematograph Film Production (Special Loans) Acts, 1949 to 1954
The first Act (1949) established the National Film Finance Corporation to finance the production and distribution of films by persons able to produce and distribute on a commercially successful basis who cannot obtain adequate finance elsewhere. Under the Act, as subsequently amended, the Board of Trade could within eight years from 1949 make advances to the Corporation up to a total of £6

[1] The Post Office finances a considerable part of its development expenditure by using depreciation moneys: see page 97.
[2] See page 98.

E

million and for this purpose the Treasury could advance money from the Consolidated Fund.

Development of Inventions Acts, 1948 and 1954

The National Research Development Corporation was set up under these Acts to secure the development and exploitation of, and hold rights in, inventions resulting from public research and other inventions when the public interest requires it. The issues from the Consolidated Fund are to enable the Board of Trade to make advances to the Corporation for capital expenditure within a period of ten years from 1949. The amount outstanding at any time is not to exceed £5 million, and advances are free of interest for ten years.

Coal Industry Acts, 1946 to 1956

These Acts authorise the Treasury to make advances to the National Coal Board to enable the Board to defray expenditure chargeable to capital account. The first Act of 1946 authorized advances up to £150 million in the first five years. Subsequent statutes extended this limit and the Act of 1956 altered its form. It provided that the aggregate amount of the advances outstanding may not at any time exceed by more than £75 million (or such greater sum as the Ministry specify) the highest amount outstanding at any time during the previous financial year nor £650 million in all. Under this new provision the Board can use temporary cash surpluses to repay Exchequer advances and then draw further advances as and when required. The Exchequer Account and the Finance Accounts therefore show a gross total of advances on the payments side offset by repayments on the receipts side, and only the net additional outstanding with the Board counts against the statutory limits. Since the advances are for capital purposes, repayment terms are linked to the Board's depreciation provisions; that is, with minor exceptions, the advances are repaid by fifteen-year annuities or (in the case of working capital) from day to day.

Finance Act, 1956, and Nationalized Industries Loans Act, 1958: Advances to Nationalized Industries

When each of these industries was nationalized the relevant statute gave the newly-created authority power to borrow for capital purposes. (This also applied to the bodies created before the era of nationalization, namely, the two Air Corporations and the North of Scotland Hydro-Electricity Board.) In the case of the National Coal Board it was provided at the outset that the Board should borrow from the Government; but in all the other cases the authorities were left to raise long-term capital by the issue of stocks in the market, the stocks being guaranteed by the Government. (A list of the stocks so issued and guaranteed is given in the annual Finance Accounts in the 'Statement of Loans Guaranteed by the British Government'.) In course of time occasions arose when, owing to market conditions, authorities found difficulty in issuing stocks to raise money when they needed it and had to borrow temporarily from the banks. Not only was this inconvenient to the industries concerned; it was also un-satisfactory to the banks that they should have to advance large sums for capital purposes, particularly as such advances came at a time when they were being asked, as a matter of policy, to restrict their advances generally. Accordingly, as a temporary alternative to—not in substitution for—the existing power to make stock issues, the Finance Act, 1956, provided that any sum which a nationalized undertaking had power to borrow could be raised by taking an advance from its appropriate Minister: e.g. the Central Electricity Authority and the Gas Council from the Minister of Power; the British Transport Commission and the two Air Corporations from the Minister of Transport and Civil Aviation. The Treasury was then authorized to issue the necessary moneys out of the Consolidated Fund to enable the respective Ministers to make such advances. The total of all advances was not to exceed £700 million and these new arrangements were to operate until March 31, 1958, only. Sub-sequently, by the Nationalized Industries Loans Act, 1958, and the Finance Act, 1958, the period of operation was extended to August 31, 1959, and the maximum total of advances was increased to £1,070 million. These arrangements mean, on the one hand, that the nationalized undertakings are able to draw capital finance for their approved programmes from the Government as and when they need it, irrespective of the state of the market; and on the other hand, that the Treasury can, in so far as it needs to borrow for this and other purposes,[1] raise money when market conditions are favourable and at times which are convenient having regard to its other debt trans-actions. A statement of the amount issued to the nationalized in-dustries is included in the weekly Exchequer Returns and in the annual Finance Accounts.

Transport (Railway Finances) Act, 1957
This Act was passed at a time when the British Transport Com-mission was faced with the prospect of a current deficit on British Railways for a number of years and had also undertaken a large

[1] E.g. after taking account of all its liabilities below-the-line and of the Budget surplus above-the-line.

programme for the modernization of the railways at a total cost estimated at some £1,200 million. The Commission have power to borrow for capital purposes under their original statute. The Act of 1957 further empowered them, firstly, for ten years to borrow to meet not more than three years' interest on their capital borrowings; and, secondly, for seven years, and up to not more than £250 million in all, to borrow to meet the railways' annual deficits with interest thereon. The borrowing power to meet interest on capital borrowings can be exercised by taking advances under the Finance Act, 1956, referred to in the previous paragraph. The Act of 1957 authorized issues from the Consolidated Fund to enable funds to be advanced to the Commission to meet the railway deficits. Repayments of these latter advances will begin not later than 1963.

Cotton (*Centralized Buying*) Act, 1947, and Cotton Act, 1954

The Act of 1947 set up the Raw Cotton Commission to buy, import, hold and distribute all raw cotton required by the cotton industry and the re-export trade. The Board of Trade were empowered to advance initially to the Commission the funds required to pay for the stocks of cotton taken over from the Board, up to a further £75 million to finance current outgoings, and up to a further £10 million for capital expenditure; and the Treasury were authorized to issue these sums from the Consolidated Fund. The Act of 1954 made provision for the winding-up of the Commission. For this purpose the Board of Trade were empowered to cancel, if necessary, advances already made and make further advances in connection with the winding-up. The position at March 31, 1958, was that the liquidation which commenced on September 1, 1954, was not yet complete and advances by the Board of Trade of rather more than £8¼ million remained outstanding.

Overseas Resources Development Act, 1948

This Act established two Corporations—the Colonial Development Corporation to investigate and carry out projects for developing the resources of the Colonies; and the Overseas Food Corporation to investigate and carry out projects for the production and processing outside the United Kingdom of foodstuffs and other agricultural produce. Issues from the Consolidated Fund were authorized to enable the Secretary of State for the Colonies to advance up to £100 million for the capital expenditure of the Colonial Development Corporation, and the Minister of Food (as he then was) to advance similarly up to £50 million to the Overseas Food Corporation. Advances are still being made to the Colonial Development Corporation. The Overseas Food Corporation was wound up in 1954 and outstanding advances amounting to £39 million were written off under Acts passed in 1951 and 1954.

Miscellaneous Financial Provisions Act, 1946: War Damage

The War Damage Act, 1941 (as amended by later Acts) made provision for two schemes of compensation for war damage. The first related to damage to land and buildings and is being administered by the War Damage Commission: it was accompanied by the levying of annual contributions on property owners for five years. The second scheme related to damage to goods (business and private chattels) and is administered by the Board of Trade: in this case the compensation was partly free and partly dependent on the payment of contributions.[1] In view of the abnormal character and capital nature of these compensation payments, the Act of 1946 authorized them to be met out of borrowed moneys. (No question arises here, of course, of receipts from interest or repayments.)

Miscellaneous Financial Provisions Act, 1955: Potato Marketing

A scheme for guaranteeing prices or assuring markets to potato growers having been drawn up under other ligislation, this Act empowered the Ministry of Agriculture, Fisheries and Food to make advances not exceeding £30 million to enable the Potato Marketing Board to implement the scheme. Issues from the Consolidated Fund were authorized for this purpose. The advances provide the Marketing Board with working capital: they are temporary only and are repaid as cash becomes available. If the Board incur a deficiency in implementing guaranteed price schemes, they are reimbursed 95 per cent of the deficiency from the Supply vote for Agricultural and Food Grants and Subsidies.

Sugar Act, 1956

This Act established the Sugar Board with the duty of purchasing supplies of Commonwealth sugar in fulfilment of the Government's obligations under the Commonwealth Sugar Agreement, and, when directed to do so, of purchasing Commonwealth sugar outside those obligations. Normally the Board buy and sell sugar as principals and, taking one year with another, have to balance their revenue account. The Act contains provisions, including those for a 'sugar surcharge', to help them to do this. But the Minister of Agriculture, Fisheries and Food is empowered to advance to the Board, out of issues from

---

[1] The contributions under both schemes were credited to Revenue. Wartime expenditure under the schemes was met from Votes of Credit.

the Consolidated Fund, moneys required for revenue or capital purposes not exceeding £25 million. He may also advance up to £30 million, similarly provided, through the Board to the British Sugar Corporation to enable the latter to carry out duties regarding the purchase of home-grown beet.

Town and Country Planning Act, 1954, and Town and Country Planning (Scotland) Act, 1954

The subject matter of these Acts and the earlier Acts of 1947 is very complicated; but, broadly, the Acts of 1954 provided that payments of compensation arising out of planning decisions or action taken before January 1, 1955, could be made out of borrowed money advanced from the Consolidated Fund. The object of this was to spread over future years' revenues the burden of certain large payments accumulated from previous years; and the spreading is achieved by the fact that repayment of the Consolidated Fund advances is made through twenty-year annuities borne on the votes for the Ministry of Housing and Local Government and for the Department of Health for Scotland. (Similar payments arising out of decisions or action taken on or after January 1, 1955, are borne direct on the votes for the two departments just mentioned.)

Finance Acts, 1946, 1947 and 1954 : Post-war Credits

These credits date from the wartime Budget of 1941, when the personal allowances and the earned income allowance for income tax purposes were reduced. The then Chancellor was unwilling to make the reductions permanent; at the same time the need to combat wartime inflation made it necessary to withdraw purchasing power immediately. The extra tax payable as a result of the reductions in allowances was therefore credited to the taxpayers, to be repaid after the war at such date as Parliament might determine. This applied to the extra tax paid in the five years 1941–2 to 1945–6, and the total amount of credits originally created was £765 million. It was generally expected at the time that the repayments of these credits would form a useful addition to personal expenditure if post-war adjustments of the national economy resulted in any falling off in consumers' demands. In fact, there having been no such falling-off but rather an inflationary excess of demand, successive Governments have judged it unwise to add to the inflationary forces by repaying any appreciable proportion of the credits in any one year. In the three Finance Acts mentioned above, however, Parliament authorized the repayment of the credits to limited classes of taxpayers and by March 31, 1958, about £300 million had been repaid. Further, the

Finance Act, 1946, empowered the Treasury to meet these abnormal outgoings out of borrowed moneys.[1] (No question of interest or repayments arises in this case.)

International Finance Corporation Act, 1955

This Corporation is an offshoot of the International Bank for Reconstruction and Development and was established by an international agreement of 1955 in order to provide funds for development by methods which the Bank itself (under the terms of the Bretton Woods Agreement by which it was established) was precluded from using. The purpose of the Corporation is to supplement the work of the Bank by encouraging the growth of productive enterprise in member countries, particularly in the less developed areas. With other member countries, the United Kingdom was committed to subscribe part of the stock of the new Corporation—$14,400,000 out of a total capital of $100 million—and this Act of 1955 provided that the subscription should be charged on the Consolidated Fund and could be met out of borrowed moneys. It is too early to say what receipts will arise from this subscription.

Television Act, 1954

Under the Act the Postmaster-General was empowered to make advances to the newly-established Independent Television Authority to defray initial expenses, to meet capital expenditure and to provide working capital. The advances were not to exceed £1 million in the year beginning July 30, 1954, or £2 million in all. The advances were to be made out of the Consolidated Fund and are repayable by annuities within ten years from 1954.

(d) REDEMPTION OF DEBT

This list of debt redeemed should be read in conjunction with two other statements. First, on the receipts side, under the heading 'Money raised by the creation of debt', will be found a list of securities containing many of the same names which appear in the redemption list. At the top of both lists is a huge figure for Treasury Bills: this is due to the fact that these Bills have a currency of only three months or less, so that the whole issue (amounting to over £4,000 million) is turned over many times each year, involving redemptions of existing Bills and issues of new Bills on each occasion. Similarly,

[1] For an account of the 1941 discussions see R. S. Sayers, *op. cit.*, pages 80–5. For details of the post-war credits and repayments see the Annual Reports of the Commission of Inland Revenue.

at the bottom of each list is a large figure for Ways and Means Advances: these Advances also are turned over many times each year. The other securities appearing in both lists are the 'Small Savings' securities (National Savings Certificates,[1] Defence Bonds and Premium Savings Bonds) and Tax Reserve Certificates.[1] All of these are continuously 'on tap' for new subscriptions; but at the same time some existing holdings are repaid every day under the terms of the prospectuses governing the different issues.

The other statement to be read with this redemption list appears after the end of the year in the Finance Accounts under the title 'Transactions in connection with the National Debt'.[2] This shows for each security how far, and for what reason, the nominal amount outstanding has been increased or reduced during the year. The 'Transactions' statement will often show that part of the total of a maturing security has been converted into some other security, so that the amount to be paid off in cash and charged in the Exchequer Account for redemption of debt is only a portion of the total issue. A smaller point to notice is that secutities are sometimes repayable at a premium over their nominal amount. In such cases the premiums will be charged in the Exchequer Account under redemption of debt; but they are not included in the figures in the 'Transactions' statement, which relates only to the nominal amounts of the securities concerned. (Such premiums arise in the case of Defence Bonds, which are repayable at certain premiums after being held for given periods of years.)

Two other items in the redemption list remain for mention. The three figures against Terminable Annuities represent the element of principal in the annuities by which the Treasury is repaying certain moneys borrowed from funds held by the National Debt Commissioners[3]; the interest element is charged to National Debt interest.

The figures under 'Other Debt', both 'Internal' and that payable in external currencies, represent the principal repaid during the year under the respective agreements governing a number of loans from overseas sources.[4] Either of these two subheads of 'Other Debt' may appear also on the receipts side of the account under 'Money raised by the creation of debt' because some debts may be increased during the year while others are being reduced. A convenient summary of

[1] In both lists the figures for National Savings Certificates and Tax Reserve Certificates include only principal (that is, the purchase price). When Certificates are repaid the accumulated interest is charged as National Debt interest.

[2] It also appears, in rather different form, in the National Debt Returns. See page 185.

[3] See page 190.

[4] See pages 197 and 199.

the changes in the different loans during the previous year is given with Table III of the Financial Statement.

(e) MISCELLANEOUS FINANCIAL PROVISIONS ACTS 1946 AND 1955: CIVIL CONTINGENCIES FUND

The purposes of this Fund are explained in Chapter XI below. The Act of 1946 permitted a temporary increase in the capital of the Fund after the Second World War by up to £250 million. This was later reduced and the maximum capital is now fixed by the Act of 1955 at £75 million. Within this limit additional capital is issued as and when required and is repaid when no longer required. (Cf. the item on the receipts side.) Since the Fund earns no interest from any source, it pays no interest on the capital provided by the Consolidated Fund.

(f) BRETTON WOODS AGREEMENTS ACT, 1945

Under the Bretton Woods Agreements the International Monetary Fund and the International Bank for Reconstruction and Development were established. The United Kingdom, like other member countries, was committed among other things to subscribing, partly in gold and partly in sterling, a share of the capital of each institution and to maintaining the gold value of the sterling element in those subscriptions. The Act of 1945 provided that the payments to meet these commitments should be charged on the Consolidated Fund and could be met out of borrowed moneys. Small amounts may appear in the accounts year by year by way of adjustments to maintain the gold value of the subscriptions.

(g) SUEZ CANAL DRAWN SHARES

See the item on the receipts side, 'Suez Canal Shares', on page 141.

(h) ISSUES TO THE EXCHANGE EQUALIZATION ACCOUNT

Such issues may be needed at any time. See the description of the Account in Chapter VII.

(2) RECEIPTS

(i) INTEREST RECEIVED UNDER THE FOLLOWING ACTS

In all but four cases, these interest receipts (as set out in detail in the Finance Accounts) arise under Acts which have already been described above under 'Issues made under the following Acts'. The four exceptions are the following:

Housing (*Temporary Accommodation*) *Act, 1944, and Requisitioned Houses and Housing* (*Amendment*) *Act, 1955*

Advances, amounting to £207 million in all, were made under these Acts to enable the Ministry of Works to provide temporary houses for local authorities. The advances were originally to be repaid by ten-year annuities borne on the votes for the Ministry of Health and the Department of Health for Scotland—now on the votes for Housing, England and Wales, and Housing, Scotland—where they are partially offset by receipts from the local authorities. As the houses lasted for longer than the ten years originally assumed, the Act of 1955 extended the period of repayment of the advances. The amount of the advances outstanding on April 1, 1955 (£51 million) is being repaid by seven-year annuities ending in 1961. The interest receipts under the present heading represent the interest element in the annuities.

Bank of England Act, 1946

This Act transferred the Capital Stock of the Bank to the Treasury from the existing holders, who received in return such amount of 3 per cent Treasury Stock, 1966, or after, as would give them an annual amount of interest equal to the average annual gross dividend on the Capital Stock during the twenty years ended March 31, 1945. The amount of the Capital Stock was £14,553,000 and over the twenty years in question had always received a gross dividend of 6 per cent per half-year. The total amount of Treasury Stock issued was £58,212,000[1] and represented £400 nominal for each £100 nominal of Capital Stock. The Act further provided that each half-year the bank should pay to the Treasury, in lieu of dividend on the Capital Stock, £873,180 or such other sum as might from time to time be agreed between the Treasury and the Bank.[2] Receipts from these payments at the above figure are exactly equal to the annual interest due on the original issue of Treasury Stock.

Cable and Wireless Act, 1946

This Act transferred to the Treasury the shares of Cables and Wireless Ltd (in so far as they were not already held by the Treasury) in return for which the shareholders received Government securities of equivalent value. The receipts under this head represent dividends

---

[1] It has since been reduced by £20,016 as a result of National Debt operations.
[2] At the time of writing, the figure has never been changed.

paid by the Company on shares acquired by the Treasury in 1946.

European Payments Union (Financial Provisions) Act, 1950
For a short account of the working of the Union see Chapter VII, page 156. Under a bilateral agreement with this country, Denmark is reducing by instalments her accumulated sterling debt in the same way as the United Kingdom is reducing its accumulated debt to certain other countries with whom it has made bilateral agreements. The interest here in question is that paid by Denmark; repayments of principal are credited under 'Repayments under the following Acts'.

(j) REPAYMENTS UNDER THE FOLLOWING ACTS

These Acts also form very much the same list as 'Issues under the following Acts' on the Issues side of the Account; but the following cases do not appear there:

Land Settlement (Facilities) Acts, 1919 and 1921
These Acts provided for loans by the Public Works Loan Board to local authorities in connection with schemes for land settlement. The loans were made, not from the Local Loans Fund, but out of moneys advanced to the Board from the Consolidated Fund, the last loan being made in 1926. They amounted to £17 million in all, repayable over periods up to eighty years and about £7½ million has been repaid. (The interest received by the Exchequer is taken in as revenue above-the-line under 'Receipts from Sundry Loans, etc.'; these Land Settlement Acts were passed before the practice arose of crediting such interests receipts below-the-line.)

Housing (Temporary Accommodation) 1944, and Requisitioned Houses and Housing (Amendment) Act, 1955
See above, under 'Interest Received'. The figures here represent the element of principal in the annuities.

Iron and Steel Act, 1953
The Iron and Steel Holding and Realization Agency was established under this Act to secure the return of the nationalized iron and steel undertakings to private ownership.[1] Moneys accruing to the Agency which are not needed for the exercise of its functions are paid into the Iron and Steel Realization Account and any moneys standing to the

[1] See page 162.

credit of the Account which are not needed to meet commitments of the Agency are to be paid into the Exchequer and applied to the redemption of debt. Annual statements of the Account are published as House of Commons papers, as is also the annual Report of the Agency.

Anglo-Turkish (Armaments Credit) Agreement Act, 1938
The Act confirmed an armaments Agreement between the British and Turkish Governments and authorized the Treasury to advance up to £6 million under the Agreement to the Turkish Government to enable it to meet payments due under contracts for purchasing defence material in the United Kingdom. The advances were to be repaid over the ten years 1952–62. Under an agreement of 1939, Turkey received further arms which were financed out of Votes of Credit. As a result of a later agreement, most of the cost for the Vote-of-Credit supplies was written off and the total debt reduced to £7½ million, repayable in Turkish currency over the years 1954 to 1960.

(*k*) MONEY RAISED BY THE CREATION OF DEBT

The list of securities under this heading relates entirely to those which were issued in return for *cash* subscriptions. Conversion operations do not bring in cash to the Exchequer and so do not find a place in the item 'Money raised'. Like the redemption list on the opposite side of the accounts, this list should be read in conjunction with the statement of 'Transactions in connection with the National Debt' in the annual Finance Accounts. When a new stock is issued, the figure in the Exchequer Account, under 'Money raised', for the cash received will often differ from that shown in the 'Transactions' statement for the nominal amount of stock created. The explanation of the difference will normally be that the stock was issued at a discount.

The item in this list, 'Other Debt'—like the corresponding item in the redemption list on the other side of the account—covers debts incurred to overseas governments and institutions. The particular debts concerned each year are given in summary form with Table III of the annual Financial Statement.

In form, this item on the receipts side of the account is of some interest as showing how, after taking account of the balance above-the-line, and all the Exchequer's liabilities and other receipts below-the-line, the cash position of the Exchequer was balanced over the year. But the figures are not in themselves of great significance. In the first place, for a number of items (e.g. the floating debt and the Small Savings securities) net balances must be struck with the corresponding items on the payments side for redemption of debt. More important, the figures give no indication of the extent to which, during the year, the money raised came from official institutions and funds as distinct from outside sources like the money market and the stock market. The point of this distinction will appear in Chapter VIII.

(*l*) MISCELLANEOUS FINANCIAL PROVISIONS ACTS, 1946 AND 1955: CIVIL CONTINGENCIES FUND

This represents repayment of capital no longer required by the Fund: see the note above on item (*e*) on the payments side.

(*m*) EUROPEAN PAYMENTS UNION (FINANCIAL PROVISIONS) ACT, 1950

This represents repayment of capital from the same source as the interest described under item (*i*) above.

(*n*) SUEZ CANAL SHARES

The British Government's interests in the Suez Canal Company—the acquisition of which was authorized *ex post facto* by the Suez Canal (Shares) Act, 1876—have been changed as a result of the nationalization of the Canal by the Egyptian Government in 1956.

Before the change the Company's capital consisted of 800,000 shares of 250 francs each, amounting in all to 200 million francs. Part of the Company's earnings each year had to be set aside in the form of a sinking fund sufficient to redeem the shares (by annual drawings) by 1969, the date on which the original concession was due to end. Shares so redeemed were known as *actions de jouissance* and, although they were paid off in cash, they continued to rank for dividend. Unredeemed shares (known as *actions de capital*) ranked not only for dividend but also for an annual interest payment at the rate of 5 per cent. On January 1, 1957, the total capital consisted of 357,384 *actions de capital* and 422,606 *actions de jouissance*; and of these the British Government owned 161,616 and 191,888 respectively. Dividends on both types of capital are credited to revenue under 'Receipts from Sundry Loans, etc.' Under the Finance Act, 1898, all moneys received by the Exchequer in respect of shares drawn for repayment have to be applied 'in like manner as the New Sinking Fund', that is, to repayment of debt, and each year this item on the receipts side below-the-line is balanced by an equal one on the payments side in the form of an 'issue to reduce debt'.

Following the Egyptian act of nationalization the statutes of the Company were amended in June 1957 and April 1958. On the former occasion the Company was enabled to continue as a French investment company in control of extensive assets outside Egypt. On the second occasion the capital structure was reorganized into ordinary shares (one each for each old share, redeemed or unredeemed, plus allotments for certain founders' and other interests) and debentures (one for each unredeemed share). After this reorganization the British Government owned 353,504 ordinary shares (out of a total of 1,075,000) and 161,616 debentures (out of a total of 357,384). The ordinary shares are entitled to whatever dividend is declared by the Company; the debentures carry 5 per cent interest and will be redeemed by annual drawings before January 1, 1969. Thus, in effect, the old *actions de jouissance* and the equity elements in the old *actions de capital* are represented by the new ordinary shares and the fixed-interest element in the *actions de capital* is represented by the new debentures.[1]

(*o*) EXCHANGE EQUALIZATION ACCOUNT—REPAYMENTS

These repayments occur when the Account holds more sterling capital than it requires for the time being and returns the excess to the Exchequer, which originally provided it. See the description of the Account in Chapter VII.

[1] The title and form of this item in the account, and of the corresponding item on the Payments side, may have to be amended as a result of the new capital structure of the Company.

CHAPTER VII

A Digression—The Issue Department of the Bank of England and The Exchange Equalization Account

HAVING looked at all the multifarious items which can affect either the receipts side or the payments side of the Exchequer during the financial year, we shall have to consider what problems they create, when they are brought together, in the day-to-day management of the cash position of the Exchequer. But before we do that we must digress for a while to describe two institutions which, though not strictly parts of the Budgetary system, have very close relations with the Exchequer and play prominent parts in the management of it. The first is the Issue Department of the Bank of England and the second is the Exchange Equalization Account. The extensive history, theory and practice of these two institutions would be far beyond the compass of a chapter of this book: we shall notice only such points as are necessary to understand their general nature and the parts they play in the transactions described later in this book.

(1) THE ISSUE DEPARTMENT

As is shown by the published weekly Bank Return, of which a specimen (the Return for July 16, 1958) is given in Appendix F, the Bank's functions are divided between the Issue Department and the Banking Department.

It is not necessary for our purposes to describe the Banking Department at any length, it acts as banker for the Government, for the commercial banks and for other non-Government customers. The total deposits held by the Bank from time to time for each of these three groups appear in the Return against the items 'Public Accounts', 'Bankers' and 'Others' respectively. On July 16, 1958, the totals of these three items were £10·7 million, £212·1 million and £72·9 million. 'Public Accounts' cover not only the balance on the Exchequer Account, which is normally kept to about £2 million, but other important accounts of Government departments such as those of the

Paymaster-General (holding supply issues to be drawn on by the spending departments), the Inland Revenue and the Customs and Excise (revenue on its way to the Exchequer), the National Debt Commissioners (sums awaiting investment), the Post Office and others. The commercial banks keep large balances at the Bank out of which—apart from other purposes—they make transfers to the Government revenue accounts in respect of their customers' tax payments and transfers to each other to settle their balances on the daily bank-clearing; these accounts are also used when the banks have to pay the Bank for bank notes or when they receive payment for notes paid into the Bank. The third group, 'others', represents a great variety of customers, including central banks of overseas countries. The assets which the Banking Department holds against all these deposit liabilities consist for the most part (80–90 per cent) of Government securities; but they also include the balance of the total issue of bank notes which is not for the time being in circulation.

MECHANISM OF THE NOTE ISSUE

The part of the Bank Return which relates to the Issue Department is the account of the country's note issue, for which the Bank of England, subject to certain statutory conditions, is responsible.[1] All notes are now 'Bank Notes'. When the public requires notes—as when individuals want them for personal expenditure or employers want them to pay wages—they take them from their own banks by drawing down their deposits correspondingly, and the banks provide the notes out of that part of their cash balances which they keep in that form. As and when the banks have to replenish their stocks of notes they in turn draw notes from the stock in the Banking Department of the Bank of England, paying for them out of their deposits at the Bank. If the public wish to pay notes into their banks and increase their deposits accordingly, and if the banks then find themselves with more notes than they need, the two converse transactions take place. The total of notes in circulation at any given time, and the fluctuations in that total from day to day, therefore reflect public demand. This is strikingly demonstrated by the sharp increase in the total just before times of high spending at Christmas, Easter, Whitsuntide and the August Bank Holiday, and the corresponding decreases in the total just after those seasons. Over longer periods there is a tendency for the total issue to rise in times of rising economic

---

[1] The issue of coinage is the responsibility of the Royal Mint. The Mint issues an annual report on its operations, which is published as a non-parliamentary paper.

activity or of rising prices and wages, and a tendency for it to fall in the converse conditions. In practice the Bank responds automatically to such changes, issuing more notes to the extent that there is a demand for them and redeeming them for cash when the public wishes to pay them in.

The transactions in notes with the commercial banks are actually handled by the Banking Department. The stock of notes which it holds among its assets forms a reserve from which new demands are met and to which notes handled in are added. When the reserve is running low—say, below £15 million—the total issue is increased. In that event all the additional notes are sold by the Issue Department to the Banking Department and added to the latter's reserve. The Banking Department pays for them by a transfer of securities (Treasury Bills) of equivalent value to the Issue Department which adds those securities to the assets already held against the whole issue. When the Banking Department's reserve of notes becomes unnecessarily large the whole issue is reduced by a series of transactions which are the converse of those just described.

CONTROL OF THE NOTE ISSUE UP TO 1939

But although such movements in the total issue are in practice automatic so far as the Bank is concerned, certain statutory formalities have nevertheless to be observed. Before the First World War, notes could be obtained from the Bank only against gold coin and bullion, and gold coin and bullion could be had from the Bank against notes. The smallest note was for £5. The total issue was, with small and limited exceptions, covered by gold, During that war and until 1928 the need for a greatly increased volume of notes was met by the Treasury, which supplemented the Bank's issue by its own issue of 'Currency Notes' (including notes for £1 and 10s), though this latter issue was, in fact, managed for the Treasury by the Bank. Currency notes were issued against cash, that is, against bankers' cheques, because, as a war measure, the circulation of gold coin was stopped and all gold and bullion was concentrated in the hands of the Bank so that it could be used to greater advantage for national purposes. The moneys received in payment for Currency Notes were invested in Government securities and held against the issue in that form. In 1928 the two issues were amalgamated, under the Currency and Bank Notes Act of that year, into one new Bank of England issue. But it was a very different issue from that which existed before 1914, since a large part of it was uncovered by gold. This uncovered part was known as the 'Fiduciary issue' and the position immediately after the amalgamation was that out of a total issue of £419 million, only £159 million was covered by gold coin and bullion, so that the fiduciary issue was £260 million. The Act of 1928 sought to control the total of the fiduciary issue by providing that any increase of it over £260 million should be subject to Treasury approval which was to be given for not more than six months at a time and was to be conveyed by a formal Treasury Minute presented to Parliament; but no increase so approved could remain in force for more than two years unless Parliament otherwise determined. Moreover, the profits derived by the Bank from the note issue *less* the expenses of the whole issue (which were taken to include any depreciation of the securities) were to be paid to the Exchequer. In 1932, by the Finance Act of that year, the Exchange Equalization Account was established for the reasons, and with the functions, described below. Since the Account was to be used primarily to prevent undue fluctuation in the exchange value of sterling, and since that was also the main purpose for which the Bank then held gold, there was much to be said for concentrating the country's gold reserves in the Account: but this result was not completely achieved until the outbreak of war in 1939. In the meantime it was largely a matter of convenience whether gold was held by the Department or in the Account. Between 1932 and 1936 transfers of gold were made, in exchange for sterling, from the Department to the Account; but from 1936 onwards, when the Account found itself over-full of gold and short of sterling transfers took place in the opposite direction. The Finance Act of 1932 also provided that when the Department sold or bought gold it should respectively pay to, or receive from, the Account the excess of the market price of the transaction over the old statutory prices of 85s a fine ounce, at which gold continued to be valued in the Bank's weekly Return. (There was no need to provide for any deficiency below 85s since the market price had clearly exceeded that figure for good.) This was a logical consequence of establishing an official Account for exchange operations and of the interchangeability of gold between the Department and the Account.

In 1938 a review of the whole position led to the passing of the Currency and Bank Notes Act, 1939, which came into force on March 1, 1939. The main result of the review was a revision of the existing arrangements for valuing the Issue Department's assets. In particular it was an anachronism to go on valuing gold at the old price of 85s; and the opportunity was taken to change the system whereby any depreciation in the other assets of the Departments was a charge against the profits to be transferred to the Exchequer. Some means should be found of ensuring that the assets should be regularly valued at current prices and that they should at all times be sufficient, but no more than sufficient, to cover the note issue. It was natural and appropriate that the Exchange Equalization Account should be brought in for this purpose as it was already taking the Department's book profits, and covering its book losses, on current transactions in gold. The new Act, while making no change of principle in the 1928 law about Treasury approval of increases in the fiduciary issue, increased the statutory limit to that issue, above which Treasury approval was necessary, to £300 million. But it also made fundamental changes in the arrangements between the Department and the Account. In the first place it provided that the gold remaining in the Issue Department should be revalued at its current market price (then about 148s an ounce—and now about 250s) instead of at the old statutory but ineffective price of 85s an ounce. (One result of this revaluation upwards of the Department's gold holding was a reduction in the fiduciary issue—but not, of course, the total note issue—by some £100 million.) Secondly, the Act provided that, beginning on March 1, 1939, the gold and securities in the Department should be valued each week at current market prices, that week by week any excess shown by such valuation over the total amount of notes outstanding should be made over by the Department to the Account and any deficiency made good to the Department by the Account. Since the Account was thus in effect to guarantee the value of the Department's assets there was an equal propriety in the further provision of the Act that the profits of the Department should thenceforth be paid to the Account instead of to the Exchequer.

THE FIDUCIARY ISSUE TODAY

At the outbreak of war in September 1939 the whole of the gold remaining in the Issue Department, except a token amount of about £100,000, was transferred to the Account, and for practical purposes the whole of the note issue, amounting to £580 million, then became a fiduciary issue.[1] This complete transformation of the nature of the note issue, as compared with that laid down in 1844, took place ostensibly by virtue of the development and activities of the Exchange Equalization Account. But it would scarcely have been possible if public opinion and sentiment has not grown ready to accept the idea

[1] During and after the war, the period of two years for which, under the 1928 Act, the Treasury could authorize an increase in the fiduciary issue without recourse to Parliament was extended to four years, then to six years and finally indefinitely—first under emergency powers and later (in 1945) under the Supplies and Services (Transitional Powers) Act, 1945. These special arrangements were superseded by the provisions of the Act of 1954 about to be referred to.

that a note issue backed even in part by gold had become an out-moded concept. Either because of the change of sentiment or in spite of it, the question arose after the Second World War whether the arrangements for the control of the fiduciary issue laid down in 1928 were appropriate to the new conditions. There was clearly a case for waiting awhile and for watching how they worked as the national economy adapted itself to peacetime conditions and it was not until 1954 that Parliament legislated on the subject again. Under the Currency and Bank Notes Act of that year the structure of the 1928 control was modified. The new Act first fixed the fiduciary note issue at £1,575 million and then made the procedure for varying that figure rather more flexible. If the Bank so represent, the amount of the fiduciary note issue may be varied (up or down) by Treasury Minute to such specified figure as may be agreed between the Treasury and the Bank and for not more than six months at a time. If it is desired that a Treasury direction authorizing an increase above £1,575 million shall remain in force for more than two years the Treasury may by Order extend the period by two years at a time,[1] but such Order is subject to annulment by resolution of either House of Parliament. Thus a continued increase in the fiduciary issue no longer requires the positive approval of Parliament; but either House can annul it if it wishes and can, therefore, make any Treasury Order the occasion for a debate.

It may be thought that there is some illogicality in the arrange-ments for Treasury and parliamentary control over the amount of the fiduciary issue. Undoubtedly the Bank must issue what notes the public needs: and any attempt to restrict the issue arbitrarily would cause serious inconvenience and confusion, Nor would such arbitrary action serve any useful purpose, since fluctuations in the total of the note issue reflect economic causes which should be attacked, if necessary, where they arise. On the other hand, it would certainly be odd if the ultimate control of so basic a national service as the note issue were altogether divorced from the Government and Parliament; and that is the justification for the present arrangements. The latter have never been used to interfere with the natural course of the note issue; but they do at least afford formal occasions on which either the Treasury or Parliament could, if it thought fit, require a review of the situation.

One last point may be made about the fiduciary issue. When the note issue is increased in response to public demand, the Issue Depart-ment receives securities in exchange for the additional notes from the

---

[1] This has been done on two occasions—by the Fiduciary Note Issue (Exten-sion of Period) Orders of 1956 and 1958 respectively.

Banking Department which in turn sells the notes to the commercial banks. This increases the Issue Department's total income from its investments; but—assuming the increase in its expenses is negligible —the profit which it is later due to pay over to the Exchange Equalization Account is increased by the same amount. The Exchequer has, of course, to pay the interest on the securities newly acquired by the Department; but, tsking the Exchequer and the Account together, the net effect of the increase in the note issue is that the Treasury borrows the amount of the increase from the public free of interest. Conversely, when the note issue is reduced, the Treasury has to repay a corresponding amount of similar debt.

THE ISSUE DEPARTMENT'S TRANSACTIONS IN GOVERNMENT SECURITIES

On July 16, 1958, the fiduciary issue, that is all but £361,000 of the total issue, stood at £2,100 million. Against this, no less than £2,085 million of Government securities were held, details of which are not published. For a national note issue of this size, there is no practicable alternative to investing in such securities; and the size of the total investment allows room for much discretion on the part of the Bank as to the types and periods of the securities to be bought. This situation has two particular implications. First, it requires the closest day-to-day collaboration between the Bank and the Treasury. Secondly, given that collaboration and mutual consideration, the Treasury has available, with the help of the Bank, a *masse de manoeuvre* which is of the greatest assistance in dealing with questions of Exchequer and debt management. To appreciate the second fact, one needs to realize that when the Treasury borrows or redeems debt it makes a vast difference whether the transaction is with the public—that is, the commercial banks, financial and other business undertakings and private individuals—or with some Government department or official institution. Its offers and obligations to the public are always absolute and are not in any way the subject of bargains or understandings. It does not actively concern itself, for instance, with what a member of the public does with the security he accepts or the redemption moneys he receives. But Government departments and official institutions are, so to speak, within the family and it is possible for the Treasury to come to mutual arrangements with them, due regard being paid, of course, to their respective needs and responsibilities. Thus, if they are going to receive redemption moneys, the Treasury may be able to arrange that they immediately lend the moneys, or part of them, back again; or, if a conversion offer is made, that they accept that offer and do not ask to be paid off in cash.

The Issue Department is one of the family and works closely with the Treasury in a number of ways. For example, the Department can buy in the market over a period an existing security which is due for repayment some time ahead and so reduce the amount which the Treasury has to pay out to the public on the maturity date. On maturity the Department will take the redemption moneys but will immediately re-lend them to the Treasury. Or, if a conversion is offered, it will accept the offer. In either case the dimensions of the Treasury's real problem—that of dealing with the debt in the hands of the public—are very much reduced. The larger the proportion of any maturing security which is in the hands of the Department, the easier it is for the Treasury to suit its own convenience and advantage in deciding whether simply to redeem in cash or whether to offer the alternative of conversion on the cheapest possible terms. Again if, as part of its longer-term operations the Treasury desired to issue a new market security for cash, the issue could be bigger if the public could take it up gradually over a fairly long period ahead—that is, if the issue were in effect 'on tap'—than if it has to be wholly subscribed in a much shorter time. With the help of the Issue Department both parties' interests are met: the Treasury gets its money quickly and the public can take up the new security at leisure. This is achieved by the Department subscribing to a large part of the new issue and subsequently selling its holding to the public by degrees, as and when market conditions allow. Finally, the Department can conduct 'market operations' of a more general character, not necessarily connected with specific maturities or new issues. It has a very varied portfolio of Government securities. If it can sell a medium-term or long-term existing security in the market and at the same time buy up shorter-dated securities, it is achieving the very salutary result of postponing to that extent the date when the Treasury will have to pay out cash *to the public*. If the shorter-dated securities are Treasury Bills it is performing the very useful function of 'funding' part of the Floating Debt in the hands of the public. Again, the purchase and sale of Treasury Bills can be used to even out day by day the supply of money to the market when the Government is on balance drawing funds from the market or paying out funds to it.

One further point, however, must be noticed. Market operations which involve simultaneous buying and selling can be more or less self-financing: the cash required for buying up the shorter securities is provided by the sales of the longer ones. But this may not hold good when the Department subscribes a large sum in a day or two to a new cash issue. When it has to find cash on such occasions it will do so by letting Treasury Bills, of which it holds a large quantity, run off—that is, it does not renew them when they mature. When it is a question of a new cash issue the Treasury is in no difficulty because its repayments of the Bills are balanced by the Department's subscription to the new issue. But where the Department is buying up a security against maturity the Treasury has to look elsewhere to borrow cash with which to repay the Department. The ease with which it can do this will depend on a variety of circumstances at the time; but any difficulty in that respect will normally be regarded as being outweighed by the advantages of the particular operation which the Department is conducting.

There are two other aspects of the Department's market operations. First, the sale of securities other than Treasury Bills tends to reduce the liquid assets of the banks: because it enables the Treasury to reduce the outstanding volume of market Treasury Bills, of which the banks are the biggest holders, and also because, if the banks themselves buy the securities, their cash holdings are reduced. Secondly, the purchase and sale of securities could be used to influence the market prices of the securities and so to influence yields and interest rates. There is no evidence that this is ever the objective of the Issue Department, though some people would say that there are occasions when it should be. Discussion of either of these points, however, would lead us well beyond the scope of this book.

(2) THE EXCHANGE EQUALIZATION ACCOUNT

ORIGINS AND FUNCTIONS

The abandonment of the gold standard by this country in the exchange crisis of September 1931 not only had the result that the exchange value of sterling was free to fluctuate without limit either way but also opened up the prospect of considerably greater speculation on the exchanges than when sterling was linked to gold. It was clearly desirable that the authorities should do what they could to minimize the resulting exchange fluctuations, if only because of the serious inconvenience which a constantly fluctuating rate would cause to trade and commerce. The problem was how to do this without causing undue disturbance to the internal credit system of the country. To steady the exchange rate the Bank of England would have to be prepared to buy foreign exchange when there was a heavy demand for sterling and to sell foreign exchange when sterling was being widely offered. But if the Bank bought foreign exchange it must pay out sterling to the banks and that would immediately increase their credit base. Conversely, if it sold foreign exchange it would immediately cause a contraction of the credit base. When the exchange fluctuations might be due largely to speculative movements of capital it would be wrong that remedial measures should involve interference with the domestic credit system which might have serious effects on the country's economy and in particular on its industries and trade. Some machinery was required which would enable the authorities to insulate the domestic credit system as far as possible from the results of official operations on the exchanges. Such machinery was provided by the Exchange Equalization Account.

The Account was set up by the Finance Act, 1932, which provided that it should be under the control of the Treasury and that its funds could be invested in securities or gold in such manner as the Treasury thought best adapted 'for checking undue fluctuations in the exchange value of sterling'. On the outbreak of war, the Currency (Defence) Act, 1939, extended the function of the Account so as to cover the more varied and extensive needs of wartime by providing that the funds in the Account could be invested in securities or gold, as the Treasury thought 'expedient for securing the defence of the realm and the efficient prosecution of any war in which this country may be engaged'. After the war, the Finance Act, 1946, repealed this last provision but extended the original function of the Account by providing that the purpose for which it might be used should 'include the conservation or disposition in the national interest of the means of making payments abroad'. This last extension of the ambit of the Account enabled it to be used, not merely to check day-to-day fluctuations in the exchanges, but to build up and husband the country's foreign exchange reserves in the best interests of its trade and external financial position, whether in the short term or the long. Any discussion of the actual operations by which the Account has fulfilled its purposes, even if those operations could be publicly disclosed, would take us far beyond the scope of the present book. We are, however, closely concerned in the overall total of the capital of the Account and in the way in which its operations change the distribution of that capital between sterling and sterling securities on the one hand and gold and foreign currencies (including securities in such currencies) on the other.

PROVISION OF CAPITAL

The Finance Act of 1932 provided that to give the Account working capital £150 million should be issued from the Consolidated Fund.[1] As the Account's operations extended, two further issues of £200 million each were authorized by the Exchange Equalization Account Acts of 1933 and 1937 respectively. On the outbreak of war, the Currency (Defence) Act, 1939, removed any limit to the issue of capital from the Consolidated Fund, but provided, on the other hand, that if at any time the Treasury thought the sterling assets of the Account were for the time being in excess of requirements they might direct that the excess should be applied to the reduction of debt. These two provisions of the Act of 1939 remain in force. Since the beginning of the Account the amount of the net outstanding issues to it from the Consolidated Fund has risen and fallen on numerous occasions and often by very large figures. At March 31, 1958, the net outstanding issues of sterling to the Account from the Consolidated Fund amounted to £700 million. This was not, however, the actual amount of capital at the disposal of the Account on that date. The latter would reflect, in addition, not only the two transactions mentioned in footnote 1 on this page, but also the cumulative effect to date of other transactions for which figures have not been published, such as interest and dividends on holdings of securities; profit or losses on transactions in gold, foreign exchange and securities; the profits of the Issue Department; and the weekly adjustments on the valuations of the Department's assets. In addition to all this the Account holds the dollar securities, of unpublished amount and value, which remain in the Treasury's hands after being requisitioned during the Second World War.[2]

MONETARY EFFECTS OF THE ACCOUNT'S OPERATIONS

It will be apparent from the nature of the Account's activities that its capital will at any given time be divided between sterling, sterling

---

[1] Two further provisions were made in 1932 which respectively added to and reduced this capital. First, the Account received the assets (valued at some £25 million) of the old Exchange Account set up during the First World War. Secondly, the new Account was required to pay some £8 million to the Bank of England to make good the loss sustained by the Bank in raising certain foreign credits during the exchange crisis in the autumn of 1931.

[2] On these securities see statements by the Chancellor of the Exchequer in the House of Commons on July 3, 1951 (*Hansard*, Cols, 200–1), and February 3, 1955 (*Hansard*, Col. 136) by the Economic Secretary to the Treasury on July 26, 1955 (*Hansard*, Cols. 1122–3) and by the Chancellor of the Exchequer on December 4, 1956 (*Hansard*, Col. 1052), and December 18, 1956 (*Hansard*, Col. 1078).

securities, gold, foreign exchange and securities expressed in foreign currencies. Whatever it holds in sterling, apart from its relatively small working cash balance, is invested temporarily with the Exchequer, in 'tap'[1] Treasury Bills. When, in the course of its operations, the Account buys gold or dollars or other foreign exchange, it has to pay sterling to the sellers; and in order to do this and maintain its working balance of sterling it requires repayment of some of the Treasury Bills, the maturity dates of which are, of course, appropriately spread. Conversely, when the Account has to sell gold or dollars or other foreign exchange, it receives sterling and can increase its investment in Treasury Bills. Thus, when the country's gold and dollar reserves are increasing, the Account's sterling assets are falling; when the reserves are falling, the Account's sterling assets are increasing.[2] Now let us look a little more closely at what takes place when the sterling assets are falling. On the one hand, the Account has called in some of its investments in Treasury Bills: and that means that, other things being equal, the Exchequer, in order to repay the Account, must borrow somewhere else. On the other hand, the Account pays out the sterling repaid by the Exchequer into the banking system, for the crdit of the banks' customers who are selling the gold or foreign exchange to the Account; and that means that, for the time being, the banks' deposits and their cash holdings are each increased by an equal amount, their cash ratio is increased and, under the traditional practice, they could increase the amount of credit they could give.[3] We are back to the problem noted at the beginning of this story of the Account—that of insulating the domestic credit from the effects of movements in the country's gold and dollar reserves. Now we have just seen that at the same time that these things are happening to the banks the Exchequer has been forced, in order to provide the Account with sterling, to borrow it. If the Exchequer can arrange to borrow it 'outside the family'—that is, from the public (including the Banks)—it will reduce the amount of money in the banking system and so achieve that insulation of the system of which we have spoken. It may not be easy for the Exchequer

[1] See pages 166 and 196.

[2] Such transactions in gold and foreign currencies and the resulting changes in the reserves will, of course, reflect not only the current balance of payments but capital movements as well.

[3] It should be noted that when the Government itself buys gold, dollars or other foreign exchange to meet its own expenditure abroad, none of these monetary effects follows. The Exchequer itself buys the dollars, etc., from the Account and after borrowing the sterling back again in the normal way has neither more nor less sterling cash than it had before. Bank deposits and the supply of money in the country at large are unaffected.

to do this directly, e.g. by increasing the amount of the weekly offer of Treasury Bills by tender, because that could only operate after a delay of a week or so. More likely, the desired objective can be secured through the Issue Department by the immediate sale of Treasury Bills to the market. By such sales the Department abstracts funds from the market—and that is, in effect from the banks—and can immediately lend such funds to the Exchequer on fresh tap Treasury Bills. Thus the additional gold and dollar reserves can be secured without any change in either the total debt of the Exchequer or in the total assets of the Issue Department or in the total money supply in the market, including the banks. Of course, events may not work out quite so smoothly or perfectly as that: there may be differences between the amount of the Exchange Equalization Account's operations and the extent of the countervailing action which the Issue Department can take, and it is possible that there may sometimes be delay between the action and the counteraction. But, broadly, that is the fashion in which the establishment of the Account has justified the hope and expectation of 1932.

ADJUSTMENTS OF CAPITAL

It will be understood that the movements in the Account's holding of sterling, gold and other currencies, etc., which have just been referred to do not in themselves directly affect the total capital of the Account. They all take place within whatever is the capital outstanding for the time being. But heavy or long continued trends in the reserves can, and do, require changes in the sterling capital. A continued rise in the reserves can require the issue of more capital to the Account from the Exchequer in order to enable it to go on acquiring gold and dollars for sterling. On the other hand, a drain on the reserves may result in the Account acquiring more sterling than it is likely to require in the foreseeable future, in which case the unwanted surplus can be returned to the Exchequer where, under the Act of 1939 referred to above, it can be used to repay debt. (The debt so repaid will be the Treasury Bills in which the unwanted capital has up to that point been invested.) Until recently it was the practice to make advances or capital from the Exchequer or repayments by the Account in large round sums at as long intervals as possible. Latterly, however, advantage has been taken of the fact that such operations can be carried out at any time and at short notice, to adjust the capital of the Account either way by smaller amounts and at more frequent intervals.

THE ACCOUNT AND THE EUROPEAN PAYMENTS UNION

One function of the Account is to give effect to the financial transactions between the United Kingdom and the European Payments
Union. This was authorized by the European Payments Union
(Financial Provisions) Act, 1950, which confirmed the country's
participation in the agreement setting up the Union (Cmd 8064). The
Union works on the general principle that at the end of each month
the credits and debits which have accumulated bilaterally during the
month on the trade and payments between members of the Union
are converted into a single credit or debit for each member in the
books of the Union.[1] These net credits and debits are expressed in
units of account, each unit at present having a gold value equivalent
to one United States dollar. They are settled partly by interest-bearing
credit and partly by gold or dollar payments between each member
and the Union, subject to an agreed ceiling for the cumulative net
credit extended to each member since July 1, 1950. At present 75 per
cent of each monthly credit or debit must be settled in gold or dollars
and credit is given for the remaining 25 per cent. (Apart from such
settlements, certain countries who have in the past accumulated substantial debits—of which the United Kingdom is one—have agreed
to reduce their debits by special payments in gold over periods of
five to seven years to the countries which extended the corresponding
credits. The debtor countries' debits in the books of the Union are
reduced as the amounts covered by these bilateral agreements are
repaid.) The gold and dollars due to or from the United Kingdom in
the monthly settlements with the Union are paid into or out of the
Exchange Equalization Account. But it is a basic principle that if the
British Government borrows for any purpose such borrowings must
be brought to account in the Exchequer, shown as part of the
National Debt and charged on the Consolidated Fund. The Exchange
Equalization Account cannot itself receive credit from the Union or
any individual country. When therefore the United Kingdom receives
credit in a monthly settlement the Account pays the sterling equivalent
to the Exchequer, which shows the receipt below-the-line as 'Money
raised by the creation of debt,' and a corresponding amount is included in the National Debt accounts under 'Internal Debt'. When
the country is in surplus with the Union in any month, but still

---

[1] The credit or debit for each member is really a credit or debit in respect of
that member's currency. Thus the United Kingdom is credited or debited with
the net result of all transactions in sterling by members of the Union, whether or
not the United Kingdom is a party to such transactions, and with the net result
of its transactions in the currencies of other members of the Union, whether they
be with the country of issue or not.

cumulatively in debt to the Union, the sterling equivalent of the amount of credit it has to allow at the settlement is paid by the Exchequer to the Account and is shown as 'Redemption of Debt' below-the-line, and the entry in the National Debt for debt outstanding to the Union is correspondingly reduced. If the country is in surplus after we have cleared off all the debit in the books of the Union, the credit we shall have to give will be provided by the Account under the special powers given in the Act of 1950. The Account will pay out sterling to the Union and count the resulting debt due to the United Kingdom as one of its assets. The accounting arrangements for the debts being repaid under the special bilateral agreements referred to above are slightly different. These outstanding debts, being payable otherwise than in sterling, are shown in the National Debt accounts as 'Debt payable in external currencies'.[1] The periodical payments of interest and principal are made from the Exchequer in sterling in the first place to the Account and there converted into gold or dollars for transmission to the creditors.

ADMINISTRATION OF THE ACCOUNT

The Account is managed by the Bank of England in accordance with lines of general policy agreed from time to time with the Treasury. That is, the Bank conducts the day-to-day operations in the gold and foreign exchange markets and carries out any necessary investment of the Account's funds. It informs the Treasury daily of the transactions on the Account. The Bank's costs and out-of-pocket expenses are charged to the Account.[2] The issues or repayments of sterling capital from and to the Exchequer are published when they occur in the current weekly Exchequer Return; and the amount of the country's gold and dollar reserves and the United Kingdom's account with the European Payments Union are published monthly. Apart from those items, no details are published of the Account's current transactions, and the nature of the operations would seem fully to justify such secrecy. That is not to say, however, that there is no check of any kind on these activities or on the accuracy and regularity of the accounting records. In the first place the Finance

---

[1] As a converse case, Denmark is repaying in sterling, by instalments, an accumulated debt to the United Kingdom. The interest and principal received from Denmark are included below-the-line under, respectively, 'Interest received under the following Acts' and 'Repayments under the following Acts', the Act in this case being that of 1950 mentioned above.

[2] These costs and expenses are quite separate from those which the Bank incurs in the administration of the Exchange Control and for which it receives a fee charged to the Vote for Treasury and Subordinate Departments.

Act of 1932, in setting up the Account, provided that it should each year be 'examined by the Comptroller and Auditor-General in such manner as he, in his discretion, thinks proper with a view to ascertaining whether the operations on and the transactions in connection with the Account have been in accordance with the provisions of this part of this Act and he shall certify to the Commons House of Parliament whether in his opinion, having regard to the result of the examination, the operations on and transactions in connection with the Account have or have not been in accordance with the provisions of this Part of this Act'. The Comptroller and Auditor-General's certificate is included in his annual report on the Consolidated Fund Abstract Account[1] and, since 1932, has been extended to cover the extensions of the Account's activities by later Acts. Secondly, in addition to the Comptroller and Auditor-General's examination, it was agreed in 1937 that a statement of the Account as at the end of each financial year should be communicated confidentially to the Public Accounts Committee who should be free to question Treasury witnesses on it and, if they found anything which they considered irregular or calling for special mention, to report on it to the House of Commons.[2] (So far the Committee have not found it necessary to make any such report.)

[1] See page 105.
[2] See the statement by the Chancellor of the Exchequer in the House of Commons on June 28, 1937 (*Hansard*, Cols. 1663/4).

ADDENDUM TO CHAPTER VII, PAGES 156-7

Following the announcements on December 27, 1958, of the convertibility of ('external account') sterling and of other European currencies, the European Payments Union ceased to operate. It is replaced by the European Monetary Agreement, which was drawn up in August 1955 against such an eventuality and which comprises (1) a new system of multilateral monthly settlements and (2) a more discretionary system of credit facilities through a new European Fund.

CHAPTER VIII

Financing the Exchequer

EVERY day revenue is received into the Exchequer from all or most of the taxes and from the other sources of revenue already described. The receipts are, as we have seen, spread by no means evenly over the year. The rate of expenditure above-the-line also varies, though not so much as the revenue. The net surplus or deficit above-the-line varies consequentially. Even when a large surplus is expected over the year as a whole there is a strong probability that there will be a deficit in each of the first three quarters and a very large surplus in the fourth quarter. And within any quarter the deficit or surplus will vary considerably from day to day. Even in the fourth quarter the heavy inflow of revenue is likely to cause big surpluses in the first few weeks, then to tail off and to be outweighed by heavy end-of-the-year expenditure in the later weeks. Below-the-line, receipts and payments will vary even more, the payments being for the most part of a capital nature. These capital payments may, by arrangement and for the general convenience, be made at agreed intervals throughout the year, but even so they cause big fluctuations from day to day. Taking above-the-line and below-the-line together, the normal pattern is still that of a deficit in each of the first three quarters and a surplus in the fourth, and of big variations from day to day. Thus on one day the Exchequer will find itself short of cash to finance all its outgoings: the problem is then how to raise the cash required *that day*. On another day the Exchequer has more cash than it needs: the problem is then how to dispose temporarily of the surplus cash to the best advantage *that day*. In each case the object will be to achieve, at the end of the day, an Exchequer balance at the Bank of England of about £2 million and at the Bank of Ireland of rather over £1 million. All this is not to say that the outcome of any day's Exchequer transactions always takes the Treasury by surprise. Of course, it is constantly looking ahead; and, applying its long experience to such indications of future incomings and outgoings as are available, it tries to estimate the course of the Exchequer balance for weeks in advance. Even so, although this may illuminate, it does not solve, the problems of the day-to-day management of the Exchequer.

Let us first consider the possible sources from which the Exchequer, if in need of cash, may be able to borrow. For this purpose we can divide the sources into two broad groups. The first group consists of what can all be described as 'extra-budgetary funds'. With one exception[1] they are all Government moneys and, although some of them may have been derived from or be destined for the Exchequer, they are, at the moment of any borrowing of them, outside the Budget accounts. And they are all under the control either of the Treasury or of other Government departments or of other public bodies with whom the Treasury is in close day-to-day contact. The second group of sources involves difference aspects of borrowing from the public through channels of saving or offers of securities which are open to the public generally. Under both heads we shall have to refer to different kinds of securities on which the Treasury is accustomed to borrow. In this chapter we shall not normally describe the securities in detail but shall leave that for the next chapter where they will fall into their places in the description of the National Debt.

THE 'EXTRA-BUDGETARY FUNDS'

It is one of the Treasury's cardinal principles that it should make the fullest use of idle balances within the system of Government finance— that is, by borrowing from the extra-budgetary funds—before it borrows from the public. That is not to say that it will in fact always be able to borrow from any particular extra-budgetary funds on any given day: that will depend on all the relevant circumstances at the time. Some of these sources are not always potential lenders; those in charge of them have their own duties, liabilities and contingencies, and if they have been able to lend temporarily to the Exchequer on one day they may have to withdraw some or all of their loans another day. When they are approached, each of them has to consider when funds which are then surplus will be required for use and this will determine how much of them can be lent, for how long and in what form. So, on any particular day, the Exchequer may be borrowing from one or more extra-budgetary funds and repaying debt to others. Subject to that, here is the list of the principal extra-budgetary funds:

(a) *The Paymaster-General* has in his hands moneys (apart from Supply grants) arising from a great variety of sources. Thus, he holds balances awaiting eventual transfer to the Exchequer as Exchequer Extra Receipts[2] as well as other departmental receipts. He also holds

[1] The Issue Department. See note 1 on page 162.

[2] See page 228.

various Deposit Accounts on behalf of departments, which represent the current credit balances on a number of statutory funds, including some of those referree to below. Again, he holds Supply grants which are issued to him from the Exchequer and from which the voted expenditure of departments will be met[1]: these issues are limited as far as possible to the departments' immediate needs but some portion of them will always be lying temporarily unused. Whatever balances may be available from time to time on all these various accounts are lent by the Paymaster-General to the Exchequer on a day-to-day basis in interest-free Ways and Means Advances.[2]

(b) *The Post Office* receives moneys on behalf of the Exchequer (e.g. subscriptions to Small Savings securities) and other departments- It settles weekly with the Exchequer and the other departments and in between settlements it lends such receipts to the Exchequer on a day-to-day basis in interest-free Ways and Means Advances.

(c) *The National Debt Commissioners* are the investment experts within the Government system and are in charge of the assets of a number of funds which they have a statutory duty to invest in the best interests of the respective funds. (The important funds are the National Insurance Funds, the Local Loans Fund and the Savings Banks Funds.) A proportion of some of these assets must be kept permanently liquid and the Commissioners may be ready to that extent to invest moneys in Treasury Bills and keep them in that form. In addition they will generally have in their hands money belonging to some of these funds which is due for investment in longer-dated securities but which, for one reason or another, will not be invested for a while. Such money will be lent to the Exchequer on a day-to-day basis in interest-bearing Ways and Means Advances.

(d) The *National Insurance Fund* had, for a long time, a continuous surplus of current income from employers' and employees' contributions and other sources over current expenditure on pensions, other benefits and administrative expenses. This surplus was lent temporarily to the Exchequer through the Paymaster-General (who holds the Fund's current cash balances) in interest-free Ways and Means Advances. (As and when it was decided that any part of these surpluses should be invested, the moneys concerned were put in the hands of the National Debt Commissioners and fell under the reference to such moneys in (c) above.) Now, however, the tide has turned: the Fund has begun to incur growing annual deficits and will require the assistance of the Exchequer. (See Appendix D.) There will be no surplus funds to invest; but the Fund will, of course,

[1] See page 245.
[2] For Ways and Means Advances see pages 178 and 240.

F

continue to carry cash balances and these will continue to be lent temporarily to the Exchequer through the Paymaster-General as above.

(e) The *Issue Department of the Bank of England* and its functions have been described in Chapter VII.[1] We there saw that whenever the fiduciary issue is increased the Department invests the proceeds with the Exchequer and that when the issue is reduced the Exchequer has to repay debt to the amount of the reduction. The Department may also be a potential lender to the Exchequer at other times. If, as part of its market operations, it has sold existing securities (including Treasury Bills) and does not at once reinvest all the proceeds by buying other existing securities (including Treasury Bills), it will have free cash which it can lend temporarily to the Exchequer on new Treasury Bills. Conversely, when the Department buys, on balance, more securities than it sells, it must find the necessary cash by calling in some of its loans to the Exchequer.

(f) The *Iron and Steel Holding and Realization Agency* is a relatively new source of borrowing for the Exchequer. The Agency was set up under the Iron and Steel Act, 1953, to 'denationalize' the iron and steel industry. For this purpose the Act vested the then nationalized undertakings in the Agency, which has proceeded to sell most of them by public offer or private treaty. So long as an undertaking remains in its hands the Agency is responsible for meeting its needs of working capital and of capital for development expenditure. Some undertakings have been sold in which the Agency has for the time being retained some prior-charge securities and to one of which it has remained liable, up to a given amount, to finance future development. The Agency's cash surpluses are credited from time to time to the Iron and Steel Realization Account[2] on which it can draw for its capital outgoings. The balance on this Account is lent temporarily to the Exchequer through the Paymaster-General in Ways and Means Advances. (When it is clear that some part of the balance will never be required in future, that part can be transferred permanently to the Exchequer.)

(g) The *Exchange Equalization Account* has already been described in Chapter VII. Its significance for the present chapter lies in the movements of its holdings of sterling. When the country's gold and foreign currency reserves are falling, the Account is selling them for

---

[1] It is arguable whether the Issue Department should be included among 'extra-Budgetary funds'. It is certainly convenient to do so and there is some justification for this course in the very close relations between the Department and the Exchequer in the day-to-day management of the latter.

[2] This Account is presented annually to Parliament. The Agency also publishes an Annual Report on its operations and a volume which contains the annual accounts of all the iron and steel undertakings still vested in it.

sterling; its sterling balance increases and it can therefore lend more sterling back to the Exchequer. Conversely, when the reserves are rising, the Account is buying gold and foreign currencies and paying for them in sterling; to provide itself with the sterling it must call in some of its loans to the Exchequer. The Treasury's reaction to such movements in the sterling holdings of the Account, will depend to some extent on the circumstances of the time; but, as has already been pointed out, their aim will be, with the help of the Bank of England, so to arrange their borrowing policy as to minimize, as far as possible, the effects of such movements on the money market. If the Account is drawing in large amounts of sterling for the foreign exchange it is selling, money will tend to be short in the market and the Treasury will try to borrow as much as possible elsewhere. Conversely if the Account is paying out sterling because it is buying foreign exchange, money will tend to be plentiful in the market and the Treasury will try to increase its borrowings there. The vehicle for these operations is the Issue Department of the Bank of England and the mechanism is as described in paragraph (e) above.

The transactions between the Account and the Exchequer referred to above involve significantly large movements in the Account's holding of sterling, which either enable it to lend its acquisitions of sterling to the Exchequer on Treasury Bills or require it to let such Bills run off without renewal in order to meet its sterling outgoings. The Account, however, always maintains a working balance of sterling which is held for it by the Paymaster-General and which it lends to the Exchequer, through the Paymaster-General, on a day-to-day basis in interest-free Ways and Means Advances.

(h) *Special external transactions.* Occasionally the Government borrows (or otherwise draws) foreign currencies abroad. From the Exchequer point of view the process is rather complicated but perhaps it will be made clear by setting out exactly what happend on two such occasions in recent times.

(i) When the Government borrowed dollars (say, £X million worth) under the United States 'Line of Credit' in 1946 to 1948,[1] the dollars were received in the first place for the account of the Exchequer; but, as the proper home for dollars is the Exchange Equalization Account, they had to be transferred to that Account, which was done by the Exchequer selling them to the Account for sterling. To provide itself with the sterling purchase price the Account first obtained repayment from the Exchequer of £X million of the Treasury Bills in which its sterling balance was invested. It then paid this

[1] See page 199.

sterling back to the Exchequer as the purchase money and got the dollars. The net effect of these transactions was that the Account's total assets were unchanged: it had acquired £X million worth of dollars but had run down its holdings of Treasury Bills by £X million. The Exchequer finished up with neither more nor less cash, either in dollars or sterling: it owed £X million less on Treasury Bills to the Account but against this it owed £X million (in dollars) to the United States Government.[1]

(ii) In 1956 the Government 'drew' dollars from the International Monetary Fund: it actually purchased the dollars for sterling. In this case the procedure was as follows. The dollars (say, £Y million worth) were received by the Exchequer and sold to the Exchange Equalization Account exactly as in (i) above. The Exchequer had to pay £Y million in sterling to the Fund and, under the general arrangements constituting the Fund, the latter immediately lent that sterling back to the Exchequer in return for non-interest-bearing Notes. The net effect of all these transactions on the Exchange Equalization Account was the same as under (i), with Y substituted for X. The Exchequer again finished up with neither more nor less cash, in dollars or sterling: it owed £Y million less on Treasury Bills to the Account, but against this it owed £Y million more on its Notes to the Fund. (Within a certain period the Government is liable to repurchase with dollars the £Y million of sterling that it paid to the Fund. As and when that happens the effect will be to reverse all the transactions described above.)

It will be noticed that neither the borrowing of dollars under (i) nor the drawing of dollars under (ii) provides the Exchequer, at the moment when the borrowing or drawing takes place, with any additional sterling which it can use to meet its day-to-day commitments. But the Exchange Equalization Account has in each case more dollars than it had before and, as and when it sells them to private purchasers for sterling, the Exchequer will be able to borrow so much more sterling from the Account than it otherwise could have done, under the general procedure already described on page 163. If, however, any of the additional dollars are required for Government payments abroad the Exchequer acquires no extra cash from the whole transaction because it will have to pay the Account the sterling equivalent of the dollars it needs.

---

[1] A drawing of dollars under a line of credit from the Export-Import Bank of Washington involves the same processes as drawings under the United States line of credit of 1945–8.

SMALL SAVINGS SECURITIES

Now we come to possible ways of borrowing from the public.

First are the 'small savings' securities which are, except for rare occasions when there is a gap between two issues of the same security, continuously on tap in unlimited amounts—such limitations of amount as do exist relate to individual holdings and not to each issue as a whole. These securities are: National Savings Certificates, Defence Bonds, Premium Savings Bonds and deposits in the Post Office Savings Bank and the Ordinary Departments of Trustee Savings Banks. New money is continuously flowing into the Exchequer through these channels. At the same time money is equally continuously having to be found to pay off existing holders who have asked for repayment. The balance between the inflow and the outflow will vary from day to day and from season to season and is subject over longer periods to public sentiment about saving based on general economic and political factors. To some, at any rate, of the potential subscribers, 'small savings' securities may be in competition, as regards the rates of interest they offer, with other opportunities for investing savings, such as Building Societies, deposit accounts with the banks, small, mortgage loans to Local Authorities, and deposits with hire-purchase finance companies. The contribution which the 'small savings' group of sources will make day by day towards the financing of the Exchequer is clearly very difficult to estimate for any length of time ahead.

TAX RESERVE CERTIFICATES

Another continuous source of borrowing is through Tax Reserve Certificates. These Certificates, which are on tap to an unlimited amount, are designed to enable taxpayers to set aside, anything up to two years in advance, the money with which to pay their direct taxes when they eventually become due. In effect, but not in form, they moderate to a small extent the unevenness which we have already noticed in the flow of revenue to the Exchequer. They are subscribed for pretty regularly throughout the financial year but are heavily redeemed when the big tax payments have to be made in the fourth quarter. Only experience can be the guide to what is likely to come in from, or go out to, this source in the days and weeks ahead.

TREASURY BILLS

After all the preceding sources of borrowing have been explored, the next major sources to which the Treasury can turn involve specific and limited offers of securities to the public. First, there are Treasury Bills. Some of these, known as 'tap' Bills, are issued as and when needed to those lenders 'in the family' who are able to lend in that form and among whom we have already noticed, as being the most important, the National Debt Commissioners, the Issue Department and the Exchange Equalization Account. These Bills are in the same form as those issued to the public; but the rate of interest may be reduced to a purely nominal figure in certain cases. The proportion which their total bears to that of all Treasury Bills outstanding varies a good deal from year to year, but in the late 1950s it has been very roughly about one-third. The balance represents those Bills which have been sold through the weekly offer of Bills by tender, and which are subscribed for by the discount houses, overseas Central Banks, domestic financial institutions and large industrial undertakings.[1] (The commercial banks in this country do not apply for Bills on their own account at the weekly tender but buy what Bills they need from the money market.)[2]

The amount of the weekly offer of 'tender' Bills is determined primarily by the needs of the Exchequer for all its purposes, including movements in the gold and dollar reserves as reflected in the transactions of the Exchange Equalization Account. At the same time, in deciding the amount to be offered, some regard will be had to the state of the money market generally. Seasonal factors will, of course, play a large part. Since tax payments are always made in large volume in January and February, the banks and the money market like to have more rather than less Bills maturing then; and accordingly the offers of Bills at the weekly tenders three months or two months[3] earlier will probably be higher than average in order to make the tax transfers easier when they arise. In view of the various factors involved it is not surprising that the size of the weekly offer of 'tender' Bills varies a good deal. At present it varies between something like £200 million and £300 million a month. (Since the Bills are mostly for ninety-one days, so that thirteen weeks' issues are outstanding at any one time, the total of 'tender' Bills outstanding fluctuates around a figure of just over £3,000 million.)

[1] But the actual tender on behalf of any subscriber is required to be made through a London Bank, Discount House or Broker.

[2] The commercial banks, in fact, hold a large part of the total issue of 'tender' Bills and the volume of such Bills outstanding will, other things being equal, affect the banks' ability to grant credit. It should be noted, however, that no such effect flows from the issue of 'tap' Bills. The latter are merely a convenient channel for intra-family transfers and have no influence on monetary conditions outside the family.

[3] On the periods of Treasury Bills, see page 195.

The rate of interest at which the Government can borrow through the Treasury Bill tender is another matter. It will depend, of course, on the state of the money market generally and on the market's desire to make sure, in the face of competition from other potential subscribers, of getting as many as possible of the Bills which it wants. Feelings about current events, domestic and international, may also play a part. Among these, feelings about the Government's borrowing programme generally might affect the rate. The market understands the normal seasonal deficits on the Exchequer; but it may take a different view if the Government is working on a Revenue deficit or a large overall Budget deficit and financing it very largely through the Floating Debt. Obviously, if the amount of Bills in the market is thought to be excessive, the Government may well have to pay a higher price than would otherwise be the case when it seeks to issue more of them.

On the question of increasing the Floating Debt, two points should be made. First, from one point of view this can never be a satisfactory procedure. All the Floating Debt, whether it be Treasury Bills or Ways and Means Advances, is very short-term debt; in anything from a day to three months the Treasury is under the necessity of repaying some of it or reborrowing, if it can, what has fallen due for repayment. Obviously, the smaller the amount of debt of that kind, the better it will be for the reputation and the peace of mind of any Government.

On the second point to be added one must be less dogmatic and beware of universal rules: it relates to the effect of the Floating Debt on the general economy of the country. From this wider point of view we need consider only that part of the Debt which is in the form of Treasury Bills held in this country outside the Government system.[1] The biggest holders of such Bills are always the commercial banks, for whom they are the most important part of the liquid assets held against their deposits. It may not be the case that a given increase in the total of Treasury Bills held by the public always leads to any particular consequential increase in the banks' holdings. Still, the tendency will certainly be for an increase in the total to lead to an increase in those holdings. Now, if the banks' holdings (and therefore their liquid assets) are increased, the greater is their 'liquidity ratio' which can be restored, if the banks so wish, to its former lower figure by their increasing their other assets, that is, by increasing their advances or buying securities in the market. Either of these last two courses means that the banks create additional

---

[1] Since recourse to Ways and Means Advances from the Bank of England is so small and infrequent (see page 171) we can ignore them here.

deposits and so increase the money supply in the country generally.[1] Conversely, if their holdings of Treasury Bills are reduced, the money supply also is likely to be reduced. Clearly, therefore, any policy of increasing the volume of Treasury Bills held outside the Government system must be judged in the light of current economic conditions in the country. If those conditions are inflationary, such a policy would be quite contrary to what are certain to be the main objectives of the Government and the Bank, namely, to restrict credit and immediate spending power. But if conditions are deflationary—when, as we have already seen, the overall Budget deficit is likely to be larger—the opposite objectives may be the right ones and an increase in the Floating Debt, through an increase in Treasury Bills held by the public, may be justifiable.

STOCK EXCHANGE SECURITIES

After the issue of Treasury Bills we come to the possibility of borrowing by the sale of market securities which are longer-dated than Treasury Bills—let us call them Stock Exchange securities, whether short, medium or long. This, of course, is not a day-to-day matter like most of the borrowing operations already listed, although, once decided upon, it will have its effects on the day-to-day operations. The scene for this type of borrowing can be set by various circumstances. We cannot pretend to forecast all possibilities, but a few comments on the more obvious ones may be useful.

The final maturity of some security may be looming ahead, at some months' distance, and it will have to be paid off in cash or converted into some new security. Or the prospect may be that over a period ahead it is clear that the Exchequer will need to borrow to balance the overall Budget and that it ought not to rely on temporary or very short borrowings like those we have already discussed. Or, if it does not need to borrow on those grounds, it may be that there is a general case for a funding operation to reduce the Floating Debt and replace some of it by Stock Exchange securities. In all these cases—even in the first case, which involves the compelling circumstance of an inescapable maturity—the first question is always: is this a good time to issue a Stock Exchange security of any kind? On this the state of the gilt-edged market will be the primary consideration: is there any demand for a new security of any kind; is the market congested or otherwise? Would it be better to wait and—if it

[1] If the effective supplier of the securities bought by the banks is the Issue Department, the banks' liquid assets are reduced and there is no increase in the money supply in the country generally.

is a question of a maturity—meet immediate needs by increasing the Floating Debt? The answer to those questions may well depend on the answer to another: if a new security were to be issued, what would its term best be; in particular, should it be a short-dated, medium-dated or long-dated one? That answer in turn would depend to a large extent on 'what the market wants'. If it is a question of a new stock to be offered for the conversion of an impending maturity, much will depend on where it is believed the bulk of that maturity is held: is it held by the banks or by other financial institutions or by the general public? A long stock may be as unacceptable to the banks as a short one would be to the general public. But even that consideration is not final. It may be that while a long stock would be unattractive as an immediate conversion offer there is a prospect that it would be in demand in the market over a period ahead: so the stock might be issued now (with the help of the Issue Department and other official sources having funds to invest), the proceeds or part of them used to repay the maturing stock, and the new stock sold gradually to the public over a period.

What part do interest rates play in all this? If current interest rates are high, potential lenders—assuming they have no particular reason to avoid capital fluctuations in the meantime—will try to get the benefits of the high rates for as long as possible by lending long. Private borrowers, on the other hand, will wish to pay such rates for as short a time as possible and, hoping that rates will sooner or later come down, they will try to borrow as short as possible. The Government, however, cannot always act as a private borrower would do. It has a duty to avoid piling up short-term debt which, when it has to be redeemed in large quantities at dates very close together, could become a cause of embarrassment. (The Treasury has in any case to watch carefully the natural course of events by which stocks, originally issued for medium or long periods, approach their maturity dates and are in due course bought up by the banks and the money market. Every effort must be made to replace them by new medium or long stocks, and not by shorts.) Again, if interest rates are high it is probably in circumstances in which saving and lending should be encouraged, and the offer of a stock at a high interest rate for as long a period as possible is one way of encouraging saving. If interest rates are low, the positions of our potential lender and private borrower are the converse of the above. Will the Government want to borrow long for the same reasons as before? The first reason (avoidance of increases in short-term debt) is clearly operative again. The second (encouragement of saving) is probably less strong than before. If interest rates are low, that probably reflects conditions in

which there is no special check on the supply of credit and no
special need for the Government to try to stimulate saving by offering
the long-term rate of interest rather than the short-term. (When interest rates generally are high, the short, medium and long rates tend
to come together; but when rates generally are low, they tend to
separate at relatively larger intervals, the shortest rates being definitely the lowest.)

There are clearly no universally applicable rules in all this—except,
perhaps, one. Broader policy of some kind will almost always prevent
the Government from letting decisions on the terms of an issue turn
solely on a desire to minimize the cost of interest, present and
prospective, to the Exchequer. The Government must not hesitate
to accept for the Exchequer the consequences of whatever general
level of interest rates has been called for by current economic
conditions.

BORROWING FROM THE BANK

The Treasury cannot command any of the potential lenders discussed
above—whether it is an 'extra-Budgetary fund' or the public—to
lend it any given sum at any given time. Suppose, however, that they
have all been called upon as far as practicable and that the Exchequer
still, for the time being, requires cash to meet all its obligations. Where
does the Treasury turn then with any certainty that its needs will be
met? Who is its lender of last resort? By long tradition it is the Bank
of England.[1] As the Governor of the Bank wrote to the then Chancellor of the Exchequer in 1885: 'We have always felt absolutely
bound to respond to a request for a loan. . . . We are ready to act at
any moment.'[2] And, of course, it is true that there could be no lender
of last resort, other than the Bank, to whom the Treasury could turn
with confidence in fair weather or in foul. Such loans by the Bank are
always in the form of day-to-day Ways and Means Advances and are
formally made under the annual Consolidated Fund Acts and Appropriation Acts. Each of these Acts states that 'the Bank of England
and the Bank of Ireland may advance to the Treasury' on the credit
of the amount of Ways and Means which the Act has provided any
amount which, with the issue of Treasury Bills also authorized by the
Act, does not exceed the total of Ways and Means provided. Like

[1] But the Bank's powers in this matter are closely circumscribed by statute.
See page 194 (note 8) and Appendix G.
[2] Sir John Clapham, *The Bank of England* (1944), Vol. II, p. 317. The occasion
was a hint that the Treasury might have offers of Ways and Means Advances
from other banks. The Bank retained its monopoly of such Advances, both
before and after nationalization.

all other Ways and Means Advances, those from the Bank must be repaid not later than the end of the quarter after that in which the money was borrowed.

But the Exchequer finances would truly be in a very bad way if it ever had to borrow from the Bank any measurable fraction of the large amounts which the annual statutes allow. In fact, Bank advances are avoided whenever possible, they are kept to the absolute minimum and, when resorted to, they are seldom outstanding for more than a day or so. There are two reasons for this. First, such advances are made by the Banking Department of the Bank. When made, they swell the total of 'Government Securities' among the assets of the Department. Equally—since the whole purpose of the Advances is to enable the Exchequer to pay out cash to meet its liabilities—they swell the total of 'Bankers' Deposits' on the other side of the Bank Return; and that means that they increase the amount of cash or its equivalent in the hands of the banks and therefore increase the ability of the banks to give credit. It is clearly undesirable that by such means the cash necessities of the Exchequer should give rise to a situation which may be at variance with a general policy requiring the restriction of such credit. The second objection to Bank advances is a more general one. If resorted to in any significant volume they cannot be good for any Government's credit, since they suggest that it is either relying too much on borrowing to meet its liabilities or is unable to borrow from its public through more normal and non-inflationary channels. The very small use made of Bank Advances by the United Kingdom Exchequer is shown by the weekly Exchequer Returns. During the financial year 1957–8 they were used on less than a dozen occasions and only once did the amount exceed £5 million.

A PRESCRIPTION FOR SUCCESSFUL FINANCING

That completes the list of sources from which the Exchequer can borrow, if it needs to do so, to finance its commitments. One point stands out clearly. Given the Budget pattern of receipts and payments, above- and below-the-line, the extent to which the Exchequer can call on most of the sources at any given time of the year is outside its control. The broad flow of revenue and expenditure is settled for it by the Budget. The ability of all but one of the 'extra-budgetary funds' to lend depends on their own position and prospects: the one exception—the Issue Department—will be referred to in a moment. The assistance given by 'Small Savings' and Tax Reserve Certificates is settled by the public. Indeed, in any or all of these cases it is possible for the Exchequer to be under the necessity on any particular day of repaying old debt rather than borrowing new money. The amount of Treasury Bills to be offered to the market at any weekly tender is, in form, directly controlled, but many factors may limit the Treasury's freedom of action and the Bills allotted at any tender are not actually taken up and paid for until some day in the following week. (The same objective of adjusting the amount of Bills offered to the market can be secured through the more flexible procedure of the purchase and sale of Bills by the Issue Department. These two procedures—the weekly tender and the Department's transactions in Bills—must be regarded as one for the purpose of assessing how far the Exchequer can finance itself by issuing Treasury Bills to the public.) So far as financing through Stock Exchange securities is concerned, the decision is entirely in the hands of the Treasury, although, as we have seen, the practicability of issuing a new security at any given amoment is another matter. Finally, as a matter of practical politics, the Treasury can always rely, in the last resort, on getting what it needs in the form of advances by the Bank of England.

With such limitations and qualifications to what the Treasury can hope to borrow from most of its potential leaders, and bearing in mind the constant desire to have only minimal recourse to the lender of last resort, what is the prescription for a sound state of the Exchequer's health? Assume for the moment economic conditions in which inflation is either actively present or dangerously near. The prescription has three main elements. First, the Chancellor of the Exchequer, at Budget time, must take an informed, prescient and cautious view of the total expenditure which he is likely to be able to finance from revenue and from non-inflationary types of borrowing over the year as a whole. Secondly, the Treasury, with the help of the Bank of England, must throughout the year take views of the Exchequer's liabilities and probable resources over shorter periods so that its borrowing programme can be planned ahead wherever that is possible. Thirdly, the policy of the Bank, with the willing assent of the Government, must be one that gives it such control over the monetary and financial system outside the public sector as will enable it, by its day-to-day operations, to ensure that the agreed Budget policy is carried out with the minimum disturbance to that system or to the general economic health of the country.

What happens to our prescription if economic conditions are deflationary rather than inflationary? The second and third elements in it are still apt and necessary. The first is obviously subject to some qualification because part of the answer to the deflation may be some inflationary borrowing by the Government. But there will still be room for caution and for a controlled process of trial and error. The country has had no experience of serious deflation in the industrial, commercial and financial structure which has developed since the Second World War and there has therefore been nothing to guide 'the authorities' as to the effect on that structure, in conditions of incipient or active deflation, or particular types of Treasury borrowing in given volumes. They may well take a more lenient view of borrowing through the Floating Debt; but they must assuredly watch carefully the state of the nation's economic and financial health which, having swung from fever to lethargy, may, through excess of stimulants, swing back again.

DISPOSAL OF TEMPORARY SURPLUSES

In the first part of this chapter we said that the financing of the Exchequer involved problems not only of financing overall deficits over the whole of the year or day-by-day but also of disposing of similar surpluses. The disposal of a surplus over the year as a whole is bound up with the statutes governing the National Debt and can be dealt with more conveniently in the next chapter. The disposal of a temporary surplus on any given day or a series of days is a matter of technical management between the Treasury and the Bank of England which needs but few words of explanation. It has already been mentioned that their daily objective is to keep the Exchequer balance at about £2 million at the Bank of England and at rather over £1 million at the Bank of Ireland. Some such figures are necessary as working balances. If, on any day's transactions, an excess over those amounts arises, an endeavour is made to employ the excess by, for example, buying Treasury Bills of suitable date for the Issue Department, either from the market or from the Banking Department of the Bank of England. The Bills so purchased are held by the Issue Department until maturity. By this means, the Issue, Department will have cash available for lending to the Exchequer on future dates when the latter is short of funds.

CHAPTER IX

The National Debt

(1) SOME GENERAL QUESTIONS

REASONS FOR BORROWING

THE National Debt is the epitaph which History writes afresh each year on the long succession of past Budgets and on all the various reasons, good, indifferent and bad, for which Governments have borrowed in the past. But among all these reasons the waging of war has been the most potent in carrying the total of the National Debt to the almost incomprehensible level at which it now stands—£27,000 million. We need not trouble to look for figures for years around the Napoleonic, Crimean and Boer Wars; those around the First and Second World Wars are sufficiently eloquent. Consider the following:

At March 31st	Total National Debt[1] £ million	Of Which Floating Debt £ million
1913	656	10
1919	7,435	1,412
1939	7,131	920
1945	21,366	6,116
1958	27,232	4,848

When, as in the Second World War, the Government's annual expenditure on current account rises in the space of five years to more than fourfold, the main question is, not whether there shall be any recourse to borrowing, but at what point the balance should be struck between increased taxation and borrowing. Then follow the subsidiary, but still vitally important questions, to find the just and prudent ways of spreading the extra taxation and to find the soundest ways of borrowing in face of the inflationary pressure inseparable from a major war effort. This is not the place to pursue these ques-

[1] The figures for 1919 include, but those for the later years exclude, the External Debt arising out of the First World War.

tions. They have already been acutely analysed by the historian of financial policy during the last war.[1] But we mention them here as a reminder that, as to about half its total nominal amount (and as to three-quarters of the Floating Debt) the reasons why we have to deal today with a National Debt of £27,000 million, and in its present form, lie in the huge expenditure during the Second World War and in the day-to-day decisions on financial policy and technique which it entailed.

The process of borrowing in wartime is sometimes spoken of as a means of shifting part of the burden of the war from the present to future generations; but this (except in one particular, mentioned below) is an illusion. The war must be carried on with the then current resources of manpower and materials and this can only be done if the wartime generation give up some of the demands they would otherwise have made on those resources. In real terms there is no doubt that it is they who bear the burden of the war effort, as, surely, our 1939–45 population knew to their cost. Of course, future generations may be the poorer for all the waste of war; but that is another matter. The illusion has arisen from the financial aspects of the process of borrowing. War borrowing—like any other borrowing —means that various members of the public lend to the State, directly or indirectly, the unspent portions of their incomes in return for some form of claim on the State in the future; and that claim is satisfied out of the taxation or borrowing of future years. But all this amounts to is that, in those future years, value is being transferred within the country from one set of people to another of the same generation. There is no shifting of the real burden of war from one generation to another.[2] There is only one sense in which such a shift occurs. That is when the country borrows abroad during the war to meet the cost of imports of essential supplies. Such borrowings must be repaid later through exports or some equivalent transfer of value from this country to the foreign lender and that undoubtedly means sacrifice here over the years of repayment instead of at the time of the borrowing.

The Debt has gone on increasing since 1945—in all by more than a quarter—but for the years since 1945 the story is a very different one from that between 1939 and 1945. The wartime borrowing helped to finance expenditure which from the economic point of view was largely nugatory and indeed positively wasteful. But, while the total of the Debt increased by £5,600 million between 1945 and 1957, the

---

[1] R. S. Sayers, *Financial Policy, 1939–45* (1956), especially Chapter I ('The Problems of War Finance').

[2] See Sayers, *op. cit.*, page 14.

Finance Accounts[1] show that in the same period the estimated assets of the State increased by £5,200 million. In other words, against the great bulk of the new net borrowing the State had something new, tangible and valuable to show. The assets here covered are financial assets in the sense that they represent claims to the repayment of money which the State has lent to others: but it made the loans to enable those others to construct or acquire tangible assets. For example, £2,808 million net was lent to local authorities for new houses, schools and other capital works: £284 million net was lent to the nationalized industries for capital development (i.e. excluding the railways deficits); £170 million net was invested in the construction of new towns; £557 million was contributed as this country's share of the working assets of the International Monetary Fund and the International Bank for Reconstruction and Development. Such objects are highly praiseworthy and, in principle, for the Government to borrow for them is certainly no cause for criticism. But that does not amount to *carte blanche*; clearly the amount of any such borrowing in any given year must depend on the economic circumstances of the moment. At the same time, we must remember that the finance for the State's capital purposes need not be, and in recent years has not been, provided entirely by borrowing. We have already seen[2] that a large Budget surplus above-the-line helps to mitigate the risks inherent in trying to carry out large capital programmes in highly inflationary conditions.

In duscussions and statistics about the National Debt use has often been made of the phrase 'Deadweight Debt'.[3] The Shorter Oxford English Dictionary defines 'deadweight' as 'the heavy, unrelieved weight of an inert body'. The National Debt is certainly not inert: but the point of the phrase lies in the wood 'unrelieved.' The Deadweight Debt was generally intended to means that part of the debt which was not offset by useful assets to which it had given rise. In fact the official National Debt Return used to employ the phrase to cover all the Debt other than certain 'Capital Borrowings under various Acts', being almost entirely borrowings under the Post Office and Telegraph (Money) Acts. This use of the phrase would now seem to be too restricted and outmoded. As we have seen, quite a lot of what the Return called 'Deadweight Debt' represented debt

[1] Finance Accounts, 1956–7, pages 62–3.

[2] Page 52.

[3] Not to be confused with 'The Deadweight'—Cobbett's nickname for the annuity which the Government in 1823 persuaded the Bank of England to buy from them in order that they might use the capital purchase-moneys to meet naval and military pensions arising out of the Napoleonic Wars! (See Sir John Clapham, *The Bank of England* (1944), Vol. II, pages 88–9.)

incurred in order to finance the creation of valuable, and largely revenue-producing, assets; and this is a process which in future is likely to increase rather than diminish. The use of the term 'Dead-weight Debt' was, in fact, dropped from the National Debt Return for 1956–7.

We have already noted[1] that in an incipient depression a future Chancellor of the Exchequer might regard it as being in the best interests of the country if he relaxed his Budgetary standards to the point, if necessary, of an above-the-line deficit to be covered by borrowing. For such borrowing specific parliamentary authority would be required. Under Section 48 of the Finance Act, 1930 (as amended by the Finance Act, 1954, Fifth Schedule), if a deficit occurs above-the-line in any year, an equivalent sum must be issued out of revenue in the following year and applied to the redemption of debt. In fact, on every occasion since 1931 when such a deficit has occurred —the last being in 1946–7—Parliament has legislated in the Finance Act of the following year to set aside the 1930 requirement and has allowed the increase in the National Debt to remain. Similar or equivalent legislation would be required on future occasions of an above-the-line deficit, deliberate or otherwise.

STATUTORY AUTHORITIES

The sanction of Parliament, in one form or another, is necessary for every act of borrowing by the Government. For every security that is issued, such sanction is not only the Treasury's authority for issuing it but also the holder's guarantee that the full resources of the Consolidated Fund are behind it. But, just as the occasions for borrowing are various, so are the authorities which Parliament has given. They may be classified as follows:

(i) We have seen that Budget revenue is received, and (to a less extent) expenditure has to be met, unevenly over the financial year, so that for long periods of the year the Exchequer cannot meet its commitments out of the revenue. The first and essential borrowing power which the Treasury must have, therefore, is one which will enable it to borrow temporarily in order to cover such seasonal deficits. Parliament grants such powers in respect of each financial year and does so in the Consolidated Fund Act and the Appropriation Act which it passes each Session. The purposes and terms of these Acts are explained in Chapter XI. The points to notice here are that the only (and very ample!) limit placed on this seasonal borrowing is the amount of Supply voted by Parliament for the financial year;

[1] Page 53.

that the Treasury may borrow from any person by Treasury Bills or otherwise, and the Bank of England and the Bank of Ireland may lend to the Treasury; that any Treasury Bills issued under this authority must be repaid by the end of the financial year in question and cannot be renewed; and that borrowings in any other form—which means, in practice, Ways and Means Advances—must be repaid by the end of the quarter after that in which the borrowing took place. (In fact the power here given to borrow on Treasury Bills is never used now; the borrowing is wholly through Ways and Means Advances.)

Borrowing under this authority can therefore be only temporary, to meet seasonal needs. We have already seen[1] that specific authority would be required to enable a Budget deficit above-the-line over the year as a whole to be financed by borrowing.

(ii) Next in importance and urgency is the need to borrow to redeem existing debts. This power is needed, for example, when a market loan is issued either to provide funds with which to repay an existing loan falling due or to fund a part of the Floating Debt. But it also needed every day to support the continuous process by which new Treasury Bills are issued to replace those falling due. This power is given by the National Loans Act, 1939. This Act was primarily required to authorize the borrowing necessary in 1939–40 for the prosecution of the Second World War. In that respect it was followed by similar authorities each year during the war. But the main interest now of the Act of 1939 is that it also empowered the Treasury to issue such securities as they think fit for the purpose of redeeming maturing debt.[2] Since the power is confined to the redemption of debt, there is no occasion for any new money limit to the use of it. A very important feature of the Act is that it leaves the Treasury with complete discretion as to the type and terms of the securities to be issued. (So, if it wished to do so, the Treasury could provide funds to repay a maturing stock entirely by an increase in the issue of Treasury Bills.) The Act also charged on the Consolidated Fund the service of any securities issued under it.

(iii) In one or two cases where the public have rights against the Exchequer—e.g. for war damage, post-war credits—Parliament has agreed, at the time the rights were given or later, that the Treasury should have power to borrow to meet these commitments. (The Miscellaneous Financial Provisions Act, 1946, gave the power for war-damage payments; the Finance Acts of 1946, 1947 and 1954 did the same for post-war credits.) A different type of case is the power

[1] Page 177.
[2] In both respects it continued powers given by the War Loans Acts, 1914–19.

given by the Finance Act, 1932, to borrow to make issues of capital to the Exchange Equalization Account, which was described in Chapter VII. In all these cases the Treasury is empowered to borrow in any manner in which it is authorized to borrow under the National Loans Act, 1939 : that is, it has complete discretion as to the securities to be issued. Moreover, these borrowing powers are not limited in money terms : such limits are inappropriate where the sums to be issued are limited by the terms and conditions of the statutes giving rise to them, or where, as with the Exchange Equalization Account, the Account must have whatever funds are necessary to enable it to carry out the functions for which it was set up.

(iv) As we have seen in Chapter VI, there is a long list of statutes in which Parliament has enabled the Government to carry out new functions of a capital character and has agreed that it may raise the necessary funds by borrowing. Examples are loans through the Local Loans Fund to local authorities ; the provision of capital to the Post Office and to the nationalized industries ; and the financing of expenditure on New Towns. The legislation governing such cases normally provides that the Treasury may borrow the necessary funds in any manner in which it is authorized to borrow under the National Loans Act, 1939; this means that the Treasury has complete discretion as to the form and terms of the borrowing. But, unlike that under (iii) above, this type of legislation always limits the Treasury advances, and therefore the amount to be borrowed, to a stated sum. Further, it usually provides that interest and repayments of principal received from those to whom the Treasury has lent money shall be paid into the Exchequer ; that so much as represents principal shall be issued out of the Consolidated Fund and applied in redeeming or paying off such debt as the Treasury thinks fit; and that so much as represents interest shall be similarly issued and applied towards meeting interest charges on the National Debt. We have already seen that this last operation is carried out below-the-line.[1]

(v) In another type of case Parliament authorizes, not the borrowing of cash, but the issue of securities. This was done when the Bank of England and the Coal Industry were nationalized, the new securities being issued in exchange for securities or assets of the bodies concerned.

(vi) Finally, there are one or two statutes which have been necessary for international purposes and which have been wholly or partly concerned with borrowing. Examples are the United States of America (Financial Agreement) Act, 1946, which confirmed the Agreement about the 'Line of Credit' opened by the United States

[1] Page 106.

and the arrangements for its repayment; the Bretton Woods Agreement Act, 1945, which, among other things, empowered the Treasury to borrow to pay this country's subscriptions to the International Monetary Fund and the International Bank; and the European Payments Union (Financial Provisions) Act, 1950, which authorized payments in respect of any United Kingdom debts to the Union.

THE FORM OF THE DEBT

In the last chapter, when discussing the financing of the Exchequer, we saw that the Government's ability to borrow, when it wishes to do so, from any of the varied field of potential lenders, and the form in which it can borrow, depend on a very great variety of circumstances. It is therefore not surprising that the list of Government securities which constitute the National Debt displays a corresponding variety. There are some fifty securities that are repayable in sterling. Some are repayable on demand, others only when the Government so desires. Between those extremes, some are repayable after three months: one not until the year 2004 and another, 2016. One carries interest at 2 per cent; others, $5\frac{1}{2}$ per cent. We shall shortly look at some of them more closely; but we might here look at once aspect of them which is, perhaps, of more serious and continuous concern to the Treasury than any other: that is, the spread over the years of the maturity dates of the Stock Exchange securities issued by the Government. In arranging terms of borrowing it is a cardinal objective to avoid the bunching of maturities and so to minimize the amount of debt to be repaid or reborrowed within any one year. It is an extension of this principle of debt management to try, on every occasion when the facts make it possible, to borrow for a medium or long term, so as to avoid piling up short-term debt which will have to be repaid on maturity within, say, five years.[1,2]

[1] Most stocks allow the Government a short period with which to choose the repayment date. E.g. the dates in $3\frac{1}{2}$ per cent Funding Stock, 1999–2004, mean that the Government *can* redeem it, if it wishes, from 1999 onwards but *must* redeem it by 2004. This allows the Government some latitude in choosing a convenient time for redemption. But it may be deterred from using this option if interest rates are high during the years of the option or if those years already contain heavy final maturities. The market does not like long spreads during which uncertainty about the date of redemption is overhanging it. Probably five years is the maximum desirable spread for a long stock and one year for a short stock.

[2] In theory there may be occasions when there is a case for saying that conditions call for greater liquidity in the economy generally and that the Government should help to meet this need by using short-term rather than long-term securities. Any such argument, however, would be as likely as not to be overborne by the practical necessities of debt management.

But the principle is a hard one to follow. The following figures show the amount of Stock Exchange securities issued by the Government for which the final maturity dates fall in each of the next ten (calendar) years. Except in 1959, 1960 and 1963, when two securities mature, only one security falls due finally each year.

	£ million		£ million
1959	894	1964	274
1960	648	1965	713
1961	796	1966	500
1962	758	1967	752
1963	694	1968	540

The programme over the first five years is not an easy one, but, given the amount falling due over the five years as a whole, the spread between the years might certainly have been worse. That leads on to the second point: the amount falling due in the five years in proportion to the total amount of the Stock Exchange securities issued by the Government and outstanding. The following figures, showing the distribution of the maturity dates for each of four years suggest that this is a point which needs careful watching.[1]

	(At March 31st)							
Final Maturity Date	1939		1945		1948		1958	
	£ m.	%	£ m.	%	£ m.	%	£ m.	%
Not more than 5 years	100	4	1,672	22	2,023	24	3,773	33
More than 5 years and not more than 15 years	961	43	3,072	41	2,160	26	4,766	42
More than 15 years and not more than 25 years	382	17	1,276	17	2,823	33	1,818	16
More than 25 years	811	36	1,523	20	1,440	17	1,049	9
Total	2,254	100	7,543	100	8,446	100	11,406	100

The trend cannot be regarded as wholly satisfactory, in that, over the ten years 1948 to 1958 the proportion of this part of the Debt falling due within five years has increased quite significantly.

All the foregoing figures relate only to the Stock Exchange securities which form part of the National Debt. They exclude the Floating Debt, as well as 'Small Savings'. This makes it all the more important that the task of dealing with the maturities in the early years ahead should be facilitated as far as possible by a continuous reduction of the total of the Floating Debt.

[1] The figures exclude 4 per cent Victory Bonds redeemable by annual drawings up to September 1976. The figures for 1948 and 1958 include, under 'more than twenty-five years', £78 million of 2½ per cent Treasury Stock, 1986–2016, which is wholly held by the National Debt Commissioners and not quoted on the Stock Exchange.

THE WEIGHT OF THE INTEREST CHARGE

During any year the maturities we have just been discussing may complicate the Chancellor's task of raising new loans to finance the capital expenditure he contemplates. But for the purposes of his main Budget policy it is the total amount of the year's interest charge above-the-line (including management) which really matters. In 1957–8 it represented no less than 13 per cent of the total Budget expenditure above-the-line; but there is little that the Chancellor can do about it. The proportions vary from year to year, but in 1957–8 77 per cent of the total charge (above- and below-the-line) for interest and management represented the contractual interest on securities already issued, other than Treasury Bills and Ways and Means Advances, and cannot be touched. The balance—the interest on Treasury Bills and Ways and Means Advances—depends primarily on the level of Bank Rate and this will have been fixed for broad reasons of economic policy, of which the consequences, for this item of the Budget, must be accepted. Short of breaking faith with the State's creditor's there is no prospect of any material reduction in the total interest charge until economic conditions permit a substantial reduction of interest rates generally, which will in turn permit a reduction not only in the total of Treasury Bill interest but also, as and when maturities allow, in the cost of that part of the Debt which is represented by Stock Exchange securities.

The interest on the National Debt is classed by statisticians as a 'transfer payment.'[1] 'Having arisen almost exclusively from financing abnormal current expenditures (mainly in war) it cannot, without straining language, be regarded as corresponding with any currently produced goods and services.'[2] Nevertheless, the interest is abstracted by taxation from the incomes of the taxpayers in order to be passed on by the Government to the holders of its securities. Thus, it is one of the factors that determine the necessary level of taxation and for that reason, if for no other, a reduction in the interest charge is something gained.[4]

Although there is little to be gained from the figures by way of

---

[1] See page 36.

[2] Central Statistical Office, *National Income Statistics: Sources and Methods* (1956), page 2.

[3] We have already seen (page 106) that part of the total interest charge is covered by interest received from those—including local authorities and the nationalized industries—to whom the Government has re-lent the moneys it has borrowed. This part of the interest is therefore not a factor in the level of taxation; and its size depends entirely on the extent to which the Government is prepared to borrow and re-lend for various capital purposes.

useful information or practical guidance, the following are the approximate average rates of interest being paid on the whole of the Internal Debt at certain dates:

	Average Rate%
March 31, 1939	3·1
March 31, 1945	2·1
March 31, 1948	2·1
March 31, 1958	3·4

Details showing the amount of interest paid in any year on each security forming part of the National Debt are given in the Finance Accounts and in the National Debt Return.

THE DISTRIBUTION OF HOLDINGS OF THE INTERNAL DEBT

There is no need to discuss here the distribution of External Debt (that is, the debt payable in external currencies) since that is plain from the published list of creditors, who are referred to below. As to the Internal Debt, we have already seen[1] that, when dealing with the maturity of a particular stock, it is very relevant for the Treasury to know broadly in what types of quarters that stock is held. Its action is likely to be different according to whether the stock is held by banks or by other financial institutions or by the general public. Knowledge of the situation can never be detailed or precise; but some information about where a stock is held can be obtained, in very general terms, from those who are expert in the market for the stock.

How far is it necessary or desirable or indeed practicable to know at any given time how the whole of the Internal Debt is held? At present, while partial information is published—as in the official accounts of many Government funds[2] or in the balance sheets of banks and other financial institutions or some other public companies—no complete official figures or estimates exist, although private estimates have been made from time to time.[3] It would be difficult to say that such information is ever necessary to the Treasury

[1] Page 169.

[2] A footnote to Part I of the National Debt Return gives the current total for the amounts held by Government Departments, excluding the Exchange Equalization Account and certain Trustees. It also excludes the Issue Department of the Bank of England.

[3] The latest estimates appear to be those of E. G. Jones and E. Nevin in *Economica*, Vol XXIV, Nos. 95 and 96 (August and November 1957). This reference must not be taken to mean that the present writer agrees with all their criticisms of the official attitude to this question!

or to the Bank of England or that it is ever very relevant to their policies.[1] Such pleas as have been made that the publication of comprehensive figures of distribution is desirable have been made by economists and statisticians. One can appreciate their desire tha an attempt should be made to fill an obvious gap in public knowledge of this subject; and it may be that, from some of their points of view, information about changes from time to time in the distribution of the Debt and therefore in the direction of the flow of interest, would be welcome. Sometime, no doubt, the authorities will consider the matter, including the practicability of producing reasonably accurate information of the kind suggested. It is by no means clear that even the registers of the Bank of England themselves could yield it. Wide margins of possible error may be permissible in private estimates, but to admit them to official estimates is another matter.

CHANGES IN THE DEBT IN RELATION TO A BUDGET SURPLUS OR DEFICIT

The change in the total nominal amount of the Debt during any financial year bears no direct or necessary relation to the overall cash surplus or deficit on the Budget for the year in the form presented by the Chancellor of the Exchequer at the beginning of the year. There will always be factors making for a difference. We have already seen[2] that the Chancellor's Budget estimates make no provision for maturing debt, for new borrowings to meet the maturities, or for changes in the capital of the Exchange Equalization Account. Examples of other possible factors are: the issue of securities at a discount[3] or the repayment of debt at a premium[4]; the issue of direct Government stocks for non-Budgetary purposes such as the acquisition of undertakings to be nationalized (as with the Bank of England and the coal industry); the cancellation in 1957 of securities held by the National Land Fund; the periodical adjustment of the sterling subscriptions to the International Monetary Fund and the International Bank. The effect of such factors in any year can only be evaluated after a study of the details of the changes in the Debt given in the current annual National Debt Return and the Finance Accounts.

[1] That is probably true even of the figures for overseas holdings of the debt. A good deal is known about this and used for the purposes of the half-yearly White Papers on the Balance of Payments but the information is admittedly incomplete. (See Cmnd 273 of October 1957, page 26.)

[2] Page 43.

[3] See page 190.

[4] e.g., Defence Bonds.

OFFICIAL PUBLICATIONS ABOUT THE DEBT

Figures for the Debt as a whole, and for the securities constituting it, are made up at the end of the financial year, on March 31st each year. Three documents contain such figures and, in the order of their appearance, they are:

(i) The *Financial Statement* issued as soon as the Chancellor has made his Budget speech about the next year. This contains a table giving the approximate figures for the constituent securities and the total of the Debt on March 31st, alongside the figures for a year earlier.

(ii) The *Finance Accounts*, appearing in September or October, give the figures again for each stock or other item at March 31st and at the preceding March 31st and the reasons for any changes during the year. Statements are added for each of the 'specific' Sinking Funds (referred to below), showing the amount issued from the Consolidated Fund for each of them and the amount applied to the purpose of the Sinking Fund, which except in one instance—that of the Victory Bonds—is normally the whole amount so issued. An account is added of the Victory Bonds and 4 per cent Funding Loan transferred for Death Duties, Finally, a statement is given of the Estimated Assets at March 31st.

(iii) The *National Debt Return* is issued (as a Command Paper) in the following November. Its most interesting new tables are those which give, for years going back to 1939, the totals of the various parts of the debt, the cash applied to debt redemption and that raised by borrowing, and the debt created and redeemed through cash transactions and conversion operations. Particulars of cash and conversion operations and of the Debt affected by them are given in greater detail for the last financial year. A final Appendix contains notes on Acts of Parliament affecting the Treasury's borrowing powers each year back to 1939.

Incidentally, the weekly Exchequer Return gives the totals of Treasury Bills and Ways and Means Advances outstanding at the end of each week.

(2) THE COMPOSITION OF THE DEBT

In order not to overload the following notes, which are already long, figures will not normally be given. It is assumed that the reader will have before him, sooner or later, one of the publications just mentioned. But to show the magnitude of the broad headings under which the Debt is classified, the following were the figures for March 31, 1958:

Internal Debt	£ *million*
Funded Debt	3,768
Terminable Annuities	10
Unfunded Debt:	
Stock Exchange Securities	11,612
Terminable Annuities[1]	1,067
Small Savings Securities	2,734
Tax Reserve Certificates	346
Treasury Bills	4,571
Ways and Means Advances	277
Other Debt	765
	25,150
Less—Victory Bonds, etc., purchased but not yet cancelled	82
Total Internal Debt (net)	25,068
Debt payable in external currencies	2,163
Total National Debt (net)	27,231

(*a*) FUNDED DEBT

This means that part of the debt which, in the following sense, has been made permanent. Each stock under this head gives the Government the option to repay it on or after a certain date, but the stockholder himself has no right to repayment. He is entitled only to the due payment of interest at the stipulated rate and dates. Apart from the Government's right to repay, the debts are in fact perpetual annuities. The roots of some of them go deep into the past, notably to the middle of the eighteenth century when the first partial attempt was made by the issue of 'Consolidated Annuities' to consolidate a variety of annuities by which the Government had in the past raised money for many different purposes and which were charged on many separate funds. The present 2½ per cent Consols (short for 'Consolidated Stock') are descended from this first consolidation, having been issued in 1888 in conversion of some Consolidated and other Annuities and carrying 2¾ per cent interest at first, reduced to 2½ per cent from 1903. The original issue was for £549 million which with various additions grew to £591 million in 1903. After a large conversion into one of the loans of the First World War and subsequent

[1] Due to National Debt Commissioners.

purchases and cancellations the total in March 1958 was £276 million.

But there have been some important additions to the Funded Debt since the First World War. The $3\frac{1}{2}$ per cent Conversion Loan, 1961 or after, now about £624 million, dates originally from four conversion operations in 1921 and 1922 and was issued for cash by tender three times in 1925. It has subsequently been reduced by the operation of the Sinking Fund described on page 108. The biggest of all the new arrivals, at over £1,900 million, is the $3\frac{1}{2}$ per cent War Loan, 1952 or after, which was the result of the massive conversion in 1932 of the 5 per cent War Loan, 1929–1947, issued during the First World War. The smallest new arrival, 3 per cent Treasury Stock, 1966 or after, amounting to £58 million, was issued to the holders of the Capital Stock of the Bank of England when the latter stock was transferred to the ownership of the Treasury in 1946.

While it is always rash to make guesses in such matters, it seems likely that Governments will in future be very chary of borrowings by means of 'funded' or 'undated' issues. Having no final date of redemption to which, however slowly, the market price must steadily appreciate, they are completely at the mercy of changes in interest levels and therefore liable to big fluctuations in value. Thus, $2\frac{1}{2}$ per cent Consols have fluctuated between just under par (in 1946 and 1947) and $43\frac{5}{8}$ (in 1920); and $2\frac{1}{2}$ per cent Treasury Stock, 1975 or after, having been issued at par in 1946 was down to $43\frac{1}{2}$ in September 1957.

Included in the Funded Debt are also the debts to the Bank of England and the Bank of Ireland. These debts, which have been unchanged since 1834 and 1840 respectively, are perpetual annuities in the form of interest at $2\frac{1}{2}$ per cent. The debts represent the consolidation of amounts lent to the Government for various purposes and at different times, beginning with the loans made by each Bank when it was first incorporated.

(b) TERMINABLE ANNUITIES

These Annuities are not to be confused with the very much larger Terminable Annuities referred to below under 'Unfunded Debt' and all issued to the National Debt Commissioners. The Annuities here in question have been sold to private individuals by the National Debt Commissioners. Under Government schemes originating in 1808, since amended, and now consolidated in the Government Annuities Act, 1929, the Commissioners can sell life annuities (payable until the holder dies)[1] in return for cash or for Government Stock. The price in cash or the amount of stock to be transferred at any given date depends on the price of 2½ per cent Consols at that date, which is another way of saying that it depends broadly on the then current yield in interest on undated Government stocks. The cash received by the Commissioners is used to purchase Government stock in the market and this stock, together with any stock transferred to them by purchasers of annuities, is then cancelled. The results, for the Debt, are as follows. When an annuity is purchased, a certain amount of existing stock or stocks is cancelled, which reduces the total of the nominal Debt at once. On the other hand, a new item must be added to the Debt representing the capital element in the annuities to be paid, which must be estimated according to the mortality tables. As the annuities are paid the interest element, which is large to begin with but tapers off, is charged to the Exchequer under the heading 'Interest of the National Debt', while the capital element, which grows annually from small beginnings, is charged to the item 'Sinking Funds', since like any sinking fund it extinguishes each year a part of the total capital liability inherent in the annuity. For one reason or another, this scheme does not seem to have attracted much business in recent years. The total capital liability in respect of all outstanding annuities fell from £14·7 million in 1941 to £10·7 million in 1957; which means that the sale of new annuities is not keeping pace with the expiry of the old ones.

Life annuities are charged direct on the Consolidated Fund. Deferred annuities and insurances are charged on the Government Annuities Investment Fund, into which the sums received for the annuities and insurances were paid, and any deficiency in this Fund is charged on the Consolidated Fund: there has, in fact, been such a deficiency for the last twenty years or so. An annual account of the Commissioner's transactions under all heads is presented annually to Parliament—the National Debt Annuities and Insurances Account. An annual account of the Government Annuities Investment Fund is likewise presented—the Government Annuities and Insurances Account. But neither of these Accounts is published.

(c) THE UNFUNDED DEBT

This consists of nearly thirty different securities marketable on the Stock Exchange; Terminable Annuities issued to the National Debt

---

[1] The Commissioners also have powers to issue deferred annuities and to do life insurance business but (apart from variation of existing insurances) business under these heads, which was always small, has been discontinued.

Commissioners; the 'Small Savings' securities—National Savings Certificates, Defence Bonds and Premium Savings Bonds; Tax Reserve Certificates; the Floating Debt—Treasury Bills and Ways and Means Advances; certain 'other debt' payable in sterling to creditors abroad; and a number of other items also payable to creditors abroad but in external currencies.

(i) The great variety of the Stock Exchange securities has already been referred to and it would be tedious to go through them in detail. All the published lists give the full name, and therefore the essential details of, each security. Thus, '3 per cent Savings Bonds, 1960–70—£1,024 million' means that £1,024 million of this security is outstanding and must in due course be paid out to redeem it; that while it is outstanding the security carries 3 per cent interest; that the Government have the right to redeem it at any time from a certain date in 1960, but that the Government must redeem it by a certain date in 1970.

One question which must occur to anyone looking down the list is, how have the names of the different securities been selected? There are Conversion Stocks, Exchequer Stocks, Funding Loans and Funding Stocks, Savings Bonds and Treasury Stocks. Conversion stocks explain themselves: for the greater part they have been issued in exchange for maturing earlier issues. Any security with the word 'Exchequer' in its title is generally a fairly short one, the word having the flavour of financing the Exchequer over a short period rather than of a long-term adjustment of the Debt. Funding Loans and Funding Stocks show their purpose of substituting longer term securities for Treasury Bills or securities shortly maturing. (There is no particular difference here between 'Loan' and 'Stock'.) Savings Bonds were issued during the Second World War, when saving was important as a means both of combating inflation and financing the war. The title 'Treasury Stock' attaches to really long stocks—there are two in the Funded Debt: as a matter of recent history the title has in fact been used for issues connected, in one form or another, with nationalization operations.

One point to notice about Stock Exchange securities generally is that when a given security has once been issued there is normally no objection to the issue of a further amount of the same security in connection with some subsequent debt operation. The new 'tranche',[1] as it is called, will, of course, have to be issued at a valuation which is more or less the same as the current market value of the original issue; and the whole proceeding depends on the suitability of the terms of the stock for the operation contemplated.

[1] French word for 'slice'.

Finally, the figures included in the total of the National Debt for these Stock Exchange securities are the nominal amounts of the securities outstanding: that is, except in special cases, they are the amounts the Treasury will have to repay when it redeems them. Securities are often issued at a small discount, and in these cases the nominal amounts to not represent the amounts of cash the Treasury received when it issued the securities. (Thus the $5\frac{1}{2}$ per cent Exchequer Stock, 1966, issued in January 1958 was issued at £99½ for each £100 nominal.) The reason for a small discount of this kind is that it is not convenient for the interest to be expressed in multiples of less than a quarter of 1 per cent; that the Government may nevertheless want to make the annual yield on a new security (that is, the annual interest *plus* the annual equivalent of the appreciation to par by maturity) correspond broadly to the yield on similar existing market securities, which may include odd amounts of shillings and pence; and that this can best be achieved by issuing at a small discount. Thus, if it is desired to issue a 5 per cent twenty-year security at a price which will yield, altogether, about £5 7s 6d per cent per annum, this can be done by issuing it at £95½ per £100 nominal instead of at £100. (If it were desired to adjust the same security to a yield of under 5 per cent this could only be done by issuing at a premium which is done very rarely.) Big discounts in issue prices raise other considerations. Is it right to issue at £80 or £70 per £100 nominal? It has been argued that such a low price might be regarded by the ill-informed as suggesting that Government credit is very low. Another objection has been that it presents the holder with a large tax-free capital appreciation. Neither objection is quite watertight; and if the Treasury needs cash and the market is in the mood to seek capital appreciation, the Treasury may have to give the market what it wants. In 1956, £250 million of $3\frac{1}{2}$ per cent Treasury Stock 1979–81 was issued at a price of £80 per £100 nominal.

(ii) After the Stock Exchange securities come three groups of *Terminable Annuities* issued to the National Debt Commissioners, the groups carrying interest at $2\frac{1}{2}$ per cent, 3 per cent and $3\frac{1}{2}$ per cent respectively. They served two purposes at once: the purchase moneys provided the Treasury with cash needed for its capital operations; and the Annuities themselves provided the Commissioners with a remunerative investment for the funds of the Post Office Savings Bank and other moneys which they were responsible for investing. The $2\frac{1}{2}$ per cent Annuities (for thirty years) were issued in 1946 in return for an advance of £250 million; the 3 per cent Annuities (for twenty-seven, thirty or thirty-one years) in the years from 1943 to 1949 in return for £1,300 million; and the $3\frac{1}{2}$ per cent Annuities (for thirty years) in 1950 in return for £50 million. By March 31, 1958, the capital liability in the outstanding annuity payments had been reduced to £1,067 million. This type of borrowing could not, of course, be continued indefinitely because the Commissioners could not prudently lock up an undue proportion of their funds for long periods in non-marketable securities.[1]

(iii) Next come the '*Small Savings*' securities. National Savings Certificates have been on issue more or less continuously since 1916, when they were invented as a means of encouraging small savings during the First World War. Defence Bonds were first issued in 1939 and their issue also has, for practical purposes, been continuous. Premium Savings Bonds are a late arrival, having been first put on sale in November 1956. The general nature of each of the first two securities has been the same throughout, but new Series of Certificates and Bonds have been issued from time to time, mainly to take account of changes in the prevalent level of interest rates. The common distinguishing features of all three securities are that they can be bought in small amounts; they are continuously 'on tap' not only through the Post Office and the Savings Banks but through the very numerous voluntary local representatives of the National Savings Movement; and they can be cashed on demand (in the case of National Savings Certificates and Premium Savings Bonds) or on a few months' notice (in the case of Defence Bonds) without any risk of capital depreciation in the meantime. As to interest, that on National Savings Certificates is not paid currently but accumulates on the agreed terms until repayment is demanded, when it is paid free of income tax and surtax; that on Defence Bonds is paid in the ordinary way half-yearly and is subject to tax; while that on Premium Savings Bonds is not paid as such but is set aside to form a fund to be distributed as prizes on the results of monthly drawings. It is not the policy to try to adjust rates of interest on these securities to current market rates at all finely. In fact, allowing for the tax exemption, the rate on National Savings Certificates if held for a few years is generous by any standards; and the yield of Defence Bonds, allowing for the tax-free premium if the Bonds are held to maturity, is generous too. It is intended that (apart from the chance of a prize on the Premium Savings Bonds) the attraction of all three shall rest on a combination of the yield, the ease of repayment and the absence of any risk of capital depreciation. At the same time not even those attractions will always be able to resist seasonal urges to spend or the pressure of rising prices on incomes; and so the extent to which

[1] The assets of the Post Office Savings Bank also include similar annuities arising out of advances for the capital expenditure of the Post Office. See page 129.

these securities have been taken up has varied considerably from time to time. The following figures of the amounts outstanding at certain dates are interesting—those for National Savings Certificates represent only the issue price and exclude all accrued interest:

	National Savings Certificates £ m.	Defence Bonds £ m.	Premium Savings Bonds £ m.	Total £ m.
March 31, 1919	227	—	—	227
March 31, 1939	381	—	—	381
March 31, 1945	1,511	762	—	2,273
March 31, 1955	1,814	805	—	2,619
March 31, 1956	1,833	777	—	2,610
March 31, 1957	1,907	742	65	2,714
March 31, 1958	1,886[1]	702	146	2,734

Figures connected with the National Debt are not usually matters of satisfaction because of their mere size. These are an exception. Despite their ups and downs, they are an impressive tribute to the work of the thousands of voluntary workers of the National Savings Movement who have devoted themselves, over more than forty years, to the cause of encouraging small private savings. Indeed, the figures would be more impressive still if they included deposits in the Post Office Savings Bank and the Trustee Savings Banks[2] which are partners in the Movement. Such deposits are not included above only because they have not come directly into the Exchequer and are not included in tha National Debt. But they have helped the Exchequer in other ways. The accumulated funds in the Post Office Savings Bank have been invested in Government securities or in the Post Office; those in the Ordinary Departments of the Trustee Savings Banks have been invested in Government Securities; while those in the Special Departments of the latter Banks have been invested partly in Government securities and partly in loans to Local Authorities who might otherwise have gone to the Government. To round off this picture, then, we would add that this deposits in the Post Office Savings Bank amounted to £1,677 million at December 31, 1957, and those in the Trustee Savings Banks (Ordinary Departments) to £834 million at November 20, 1957.

(iv) *Tax Reserve Certificates* were first issued during the Second World War, in December 1941.[3] The main reasons for their introduction still hold good today. Owing primarily to the date at which

---

[1] In addition, approximately £515 million had accrued in interest at this date.

[2] See page 205.

[3] See Sayers, *op. cit.*, pages 210–18.

Income Tax Schedule D is payable (January 1st), the Inland Revenue flows into the Exchequer very unevenly and piles up in the early part of the last quarter of the financial year. But most business undertakings set aside at least some part of their ultimate tax liability as the profits on which it will be levied accrue, and the sums so set aside generally remain as deposits at their banks. If they can be attracted to the Exchequer instead of the banks they will halp to finance the Exchequer during the periods of the year when revenue receipts are at their lowest; and will, in effect, help to spread receipts a little less unevenly over the year. Tax Reserve Certificates are designed to do that. They can be subscribed for in cash at any time and can be surrendered in payment of certain taxes[1] at any time after two months. They carry interest which is free of all taxes. (The rate of interest offered for new subscriptions is varied from time to time. The first Certificates carried 1 per cent: on August 20, 1958, the rate was $2\frac{1}{4}$ per cent.) As inducements to use the Certificates in payment of taxes and not as continuing investments, there are two restrictive conditions. First, interest is not paid for more than two years however long the Certificates are held. Secondly, holders can ask for repayment in cash at par at any time, but in that case they get no interest at all. The Certificates are not negotiable. The rate at which they have been taken up has varied a good deal from time to time. They have, of course, to compete with other uses to which undertakings can put their money temporarily, such as deposit accounts with the banks; and they have clearly only covered a minor part of the whole tax field for which they are available. But, so far as they have gone, they have been a useful and interesting development of Exchequer borrowing. The outstanding at March 31, 1958, was £346 million. In 1957–8 £367 million of new Certificates were subscribed for: £371 million were surrendered in payment of taxes and £13 million were encashed without interest. (When a holder surrenders a Certificate in payment of tax, the Treasury pays the principal and accumulated interest to the Inland Revenue, charging the interest above-the-line with other interest on the Debt and charging the principal below-the-line under 'Redemption of Debt'. The Inland Revenue then pay in both amounts to the Exchequer as revenue under the appropriate heading. When a Certificate is cashed without interest, the repayment is charged below-the-line under 'Redemption of Debt'.)

(v) The *Floating Debt* consists of Treasury Bills and Ways and

[1] Income tax (other than Schedules C and E and a minor case under Schedule D), surtax, profits tax and excess profits tax. Death Duties are excluded because they would require a much longer life for the Certificates.

G

Means Advances. The nature of the latter and the occasions when they are used are described elsewhere[1] and we need not add anything more here.

Treasury Bills play a more active and important part than any other Government security not only in Exchequer finance but in monetary policy in the widest sense. They are the maid-of-all-work on the financial side of the Government's household. They are available, if other means fail, to raise money quickly when the Exchequer needs it. They are, as we have seen, a ready and easy channel for a host of essential transactions between Government funds,[2] between the Government and the Bank,[3] between the Government and the market,[4] and between the Bank and the market.[5] In their own field they have abundantly yielded all the advantages of the commercial Bill of Exchange, from which, at the suggestion of Walter Bagehot,[6] the Treasury Bill was copied.[7] That suggestion led to the passing of the Treasury Bills Act, 1877, and Bagehot lived just long enough to hear the results of the first tender.

The Act of 1877 does not itself confer any borrowing powers on the Treasury: for these the Treasury must look, according to the occasion, to one or other of the types of statutory authority referred to on pages 177–180 above. The Act simply provides machinery for borrowing by means of Treasury Bills. The only important points on which the Act itself gives categorical directions are that the currency of a Bill must not be longer than twelve months; that Bills shall be issued by the Bank of England under the authority of a warrant from the Treasury countersigned by the Comptroller and Auditor-General; and that the Bank may 'lend to Her Majesty upon the credit of Treasury Bills any sum or sums not exceeding in the whole the principal sums named in such Bills'.[8] For the rest, the Treasury was given power to regulate the form of a Bill, the rate of interest to be paid and the manner of paying it, and the preparation, issue, etc., of the Bills.

Under the Treasury regulations now in force, practice is as follows.

[1] See pages 161–2, 178 and 240.
[2] E.g. the Exchequer and the Exchange Equalization Account.
[3] E.g. the Exchequer and the Issue Department.
[4] At the weekly tender.
[5] E.g. in regulating the supply of funds in the market.
[6] Born 1826, died 1877. Editor of *The Economist*, 1860–77.
[7] 'Treasury Bills' had existed in Ireland since 1779 but the name was simply a local one for Exchequer Bills (see below).
[8] Specific authority of this kind was necessary because, from the date of its incorporation, the power of the Bank of England to make advances to the Government has been very jealously circumscribed by Parliament. Some details are given in Appendix G.

In form a Treasury Bill simply states (over the signature of a Permanent Secretary to the Treasury) that 'This Treasury Bill entitles (X.Y.Z.) or order to payment of £A at the Bank of England out of the Consolidated Fund of the United Kingdom on the [date]'. If no payee's name is inserted in the Bill it will be paid to bearer. Bills are issued in two ways—by weekly 'tender' and through the 'tap'. For the tender, a notice is inserted in the *London Gazette* every Friday specifying the total nominal amounts of Bills of a given currency (normally ninety-one days)[1] offered for tender on the following Friday. The tenders received on the Friday are opened at the Bank on that day in the presence of a Treasury representative and must be for a nominal amount or not less than £50,000.[2] A tender means that the person tendering offers to take a certain nominal amount of Bills on the terms that he pays the Exchequer £X for every £100 of that amount on a day or days, which he chooses, in the following week, in return for which he will get £100 ninety-one days afterwards. The difference between the £X and the £100 represents the interest which he requires on each £X for the ninety-one-day period and will vary from time to time according to current levels of interest rates and market conditions. Thus, if he wants 6 per cent interest he will tender a price of £98 10s 6d for every £100 nominal of the Bills he would like to take up, since interest at 6 per cent on that sum for ninety-one days equals £1 9s 6d. This means that if he wants Bills to a total nominal amount of £100,000 he will have to pay £98,526 for them.[3] Other people may tender a higher or a lower price, which means that they will be content with a lower rate of interest or that they want a higher rate, as the case may be. The highest tenders are accepted, then the next highest, the next highest after that, and so on, until the desired total amount of Bills has been allotted. The amount actually allotted will never be higher than the total advertised, but it

[1] Bills used to be offered for three (calendar) months but 'ninety-one days' was substituted in 1950 as being more convenient, in that it means that Bills mature on the same day of the week as that on which they are paid for. In addition, since 1955, sixty-three-day Bills have been offered during November and December each year in order to provide the market with funds in January and February when large tax payments are being transferred to the Exchequer.

[2] Individual 'tender' Bills are issued in denominations of £5,000, £10,000, £50,000 or £100,000.

[3] The way these transactions appear in the Exchequer account is as follows. If the offer of £98,526 for £100,000 of Bills is accepted for a given day, the Treasury pays the Bank £1,474 and charges it to the Echequer under 'National Debt Interest'. The Bank immediately pays that sum and the £98,526 into the Exchequer as 'Money raised by the creation of debt'. Thus the Treasury has raised and will ultimately have to repay £100,000 on the Bills and has prepaid the interest on it.

may be less if, on any occasion, the Bank and the Treasury feel that the prices offered are lower than they like or if the Exchequer's needs have changed in the meantime. The current practice is that firms in the Discount Market always, between them, tender for the full amount of Bills on offer. But there are always other tenders from banks on behalf of customers[1] and tenders through London Houses which represent the needs of overseas institutions like Cnetral Banks; and the market generally has to be content with less than half the Bills allotted because many of the outside tenders are more favourable to the Exchequer.

'Tap' Bills are issued as and when required to Government funds and accounts and to the Issue Department of the Bank of England, in circumstances which have already been described in previous chapters. The rates of interest are fixed by the Treasury. Where the Bills are required as a liquid investment by the funds concerned—as with some of the funds whose assets the National Debt Commissioners are responsible for investing—the rate of interest in any week is the average at which 'tender' Bills were allotted for that week, rounded down to the sixteenth of 1 per cent next below. In other cases, where the Bills are really used as channels for frequent cash transactions with the Exchequer, the rate is purely a nominal one. 'Tap' Bills have, in practice, a currency of anything up to ninety-one days. Individual Bills are issued for whatever nominal amounts—which may be very large—are most convenient for the operation being carried out.

We have already seen[2] that 'tap' Bills, when originally issued, have no effect on the supply of money outside the Government financial system: the only Bill having such effect at any given time are the Bills then held outside the system, namely, 'tender' Bills and any 'tap' Bills which may have been sold by the departmental holders.

Before leaving the Floating Debt it may be useful to mention three forms of that Debt which, though very important in their (widely differing) times, are no longer with us. First, from the end of the seventeenth century onwards *Exchequer Bills*, which had currencies up to five years, formed the whole of the Floating Debt; each series of Bills was issued under a special Act of Parliament and (until the advent of the Consolidated Fund) was secured upon specific annual taxes. But for various reasons these Bills in time fell out of favour;

---

[1] It is the practice of the larger banks not to tender on their own account: when they want Bills they buy them in the market. This is because the purchase and sale of Bills form an essential part of their daily transactions with the Discount Market when they adjust their cash and liquidity positions.

[2] Page 166 (note 2).

new issues were confined to renewals from 1861 onwards and the last issue of any kind was made in 1892. Secondly, under Section 12 of the Exchequer and Audit Departments Act, 1866, which confirmed a practice started early in the nineteenth century, the Bank of England was authorized to advance any deficiency between a quarter's income of the Consolidated Fund and the quarter's charges upon it. The last of such *Deficiency Advances* was made in January 1914, when Consolidated Fund Services had shrunk in size in proportion to the total Budget, and they were formally abolished by the Finance Act, 1954. Finally, and more recently, there was the system of borrowing from the banks on *Treasury Deposit Receipts* which was introduced in 1940 and continued throughout the Second World War and until February 1952.[1] This security was devised to prevent such an increase in Treasury Bills as would have had undesirable reactions on the banking system and on the Discount Market. It was a flexible, residual form of borrowing by which each week a proportion of the Government's large war expenditure was borrowed back from the banks and was to that extent self-financing. Treasury Deposit Receipts had a currency of six months and carried interest at a shade above the Treasury Bill rate. They were non-negotiable, but they could be used by the banks to cover subscriptions to Government loans on their own account or on that of their customers.

(vi) The last part of the Internal Debt, that headed '*Other (Internal) Debt*', covers a number of sterling debts to overseas institutions and governments. First, when the International Monetary Fund and the International Bank for Reconstruction and Development were set up in 1944 under the Bretton Woods Agreement,[2] the United Kingdom, like other member countries, had to subscribe to each of them a certain amount of capital. The United Kingdom subscriptions were made partly in gold but mostly in sterling. Until the Fund or Bank requires the sterling for credits or loans to other members it is lent back to the United Kingdom by the two institutions on *Interest-free Notes*, which are the securities included under this head of the Debt. When the United Kingdom drew dollars from the Fund in December 1956 it paid sterling for them and this sterling also was lent back to us in that way. '*Bank of England—Interest-free Notes*' is a residual item connected with United States dollar aid and does not now justify our spending time on the complicated transactions lying behind it. The debt to the *European Payments Union* represents the use which the United Kingdom has made of the credit facilities

[1] See Sayers, *op. cit.*, pages 218–25.
[2] United Kingdom participation was confirmed by the Bretton Woods Agreement Act, 1945.

of the Union to cover past deficits with other members of the Union and has already been described on page 156. Payments due in gold or currencies other than sterling under bilateral agreements with certain individual member countries are included under 'Debt payable in external currencies' below. The debt to the *Government of Portugal* represents sterling balances accumulated by Portugal during the Second World War which are being repaid by instalments. The debts to the *Governments of India and Pakistan* are the present capital elements in sterling annuities which the United Kingdom undertook to pay to those two countries in return for capital advances in 1948. India and Pakistan have used the greater part of the annuities to meet their liabilities for pensions to British members of the Indian Civil Service. Under the Pensions (India, Pakistan and Burma) Act, 1955, the United Kingdom Government took over India's liabilities as from April 1, 1955, and the debt transactions are being adjusted accordingly. The remaining items under this head of 'Other Internal Debt' include a debt to the Government of Northern Ireland for the proceeds of *Ulster Savings Certificates* lent to the United Kingdom during the Second World War; some loans free-of-interest still outstanding from that war; and two sterling loans made to the United Kingdom by the United States Government in 1951 and 1953 in order that the former might re-lend the sterling for the development, in the first case, of the Rhodesian Railway and, in the second case, of the ports of Mombasa and Tanga.

(vii) That completes the story of the Internal Debt, subject to one qualification. Two of the Stock Exchange securities—the 4 per cent Funding Loan, 1960–90, and the 4 per cent Victory Bonds—were issued in 1919 with the condition that they would be accepted at time in satisfaction of Death Duties, in the case of Funding Loan at a price of 80 and in the case of Victory Bonds at par. The Funding Loan carries a Sinking Fund, referred to below; the Victory Bonds are repaid by means of annual drawings, which should repay them all by 1976. When any of these securities are tendered for Death Duties they are transferred to the National Debt Commissioners who pay the value at which they were accepted to the Inland Revenue to be credited by the latter to the Exchequer as revenue. The National Debt Commissioners continue to hold the Funding Loan until it is redeemed and the Victory Bonds until they are redeemed by the annual drawing. (When Victory Bonds are drawn and paid off the Commissioners pay the redemption money into the Exchequer.)[1]

---

[1] An account of the Commissioners' transactions in Funding Loan and Victory Bonds transferred for Death Duties is included in the annual Finance Accounts: see page 61 of the Finance Accounts, 1956–7.

The securities held by the National Debt Commissioners constitute an asset which has for a long time been shown as a deduction from the total of the Debt. At March 31, 1958, they amounted to £82 million.[1]

(d) DEBT PAYABLE IN EXTERNAL CURRENCIES

Much the biggest item under this head is the loan (or 'line of credit') which the *United States Government* granted to the United Kingdom for reconstruction purposes in 1945 and which was taken up over the years 1946 to 1948. It was to be repaid by an annuity for fifty years, beginning in December 1951, the interest rate being 2 per cent; but, in certain circumstances relating to the state of this country's gold reserves and trade balance and other matters, the United Kingdom Government had the right to ask for the waiver of the interest element in any annuity payment. The interpretation of the conditions of the waiver was never very clear and in 1956 the United States Government agreed to the substitution of a new arrangement under which the United Kingdom Government has the right to ask for the postponement (not waiver) of the annuity on not more than seven occasions. When the United Kingdom exercises that right, the post-poned annuity becomes due after the remainder of the loan has been repaid, interest being paid on it in the meantime at 2 per cent. The original annuity payments were made in full from 1951 to 1955. both inclusive; interest was postponed in 1956 and the whole annuity in 1957. The original loan was for $3,750 million and the annuity is payable in dollars. At March 31, 1958, the principal outstanding had been reduced to $3,470 million.[2] The full annuity is $119 million (£43 million), of which, at December 1958, $68 million (£25 million) will be interest and $51 million (£18 million) will be principal.

Next in size is the liability on a loan from the *Canadian Government* (the 'Canadian Credit') which was made in 1946 on terms exactly similar to those of the United States loan of the previous year. The Canadian Government also agreed in 1957 to the same new arrangements for postponements. This loan was originally for Canadian

[1] The Financial Statement deducts this asset from the Internal Debt. The Finance Accounts and the National Debt Return deduct from the total Debt, including the External Debt.

[2] For the purpose of the National Debt figures the dollar liability is converted into sterling at the current rate of exchange. This meant that when sterling was devalued from $4.03 to $2.80 in 1949, the sterling equivalent had to be written up by 44 per cent. On the same principle the sterling equivalent of the Canadian Government loan next mentioned fluctuates in the Debt figures according to changes in the rate between sterling and the Canadian dollar.

$1,250 million, of which only $1,185 million was actually drawn. At March 31, 1958, it had been reduced to Canadian $1,097 million. The full annuity is Canadian $38 million (£14 million), of which, at December 1958, Canadian $22 million (£8 million) will be interest and Canadian $16 million (£6 million) will be principal.[1]

The remainder of the debt payable in external currencies consists mainly of that portion of the United States Aid which took the form of loan rather than grant; the repayment to the United States of the value of Lend-Lease goods 'in the pipe-line' in 1945; an interest-free debt to the Canadian Government for loans made to this country during the Second World War; and the debts to certain members of the European Payments Union (mainly Germany, Belgium and the Netherlands) which have already been mentioned.

(e) This is a convenient place at which to mention two groups of liabilities which, although not included in the total of the National Debt, are akin to it in that they are capital liabilities. In some cases they include liability for interest as well. The only lists of these are to be found, with short explanations, in the annual Finance Accounts.

First is a group of 'Contingent or Nominal Liabilities' of varied character and amounts. They include contingent or nominal liabilities of the Consolidated Fund in respect of certain funds deposited by suitors in the Supreme Court and the County Courts; of the funds of bankrupts' estates; and of the liabilities of the Public Trustee. They also include the Consolidated Fund guarantee of the claims of depositors in the Post Office Savings Bank and the Trustee Savings Banks. Largest of all the items included is a charge on the Consolidated Fund to fulfil guarantees given by the Export Credits Guarantee Department if for any reason the necessary funds are not provided in the usual Supply Vote for that service.

Secondly, there is a long list of Loans Guaranteed by the British Government. These loans are all charged in the first instance on the revenues of the Governments or authorities raising them or on special funds allocated to their service. The guarantee means that if the due payments of principal and interest (or sometimes interest only) are not met from those sources, the British Government will meet the payments out of the Consolidated Fund. In that event the Government normally has an equivalent claim against the debtor. In each case, of course, the giving of the guarantee has been authorized by some specific or general statute. The earlier entries in the list—apart from stocks issued in connection with Irish Land Purchase—relate to loans issued by overseas governments (including those of some

---

[1] Conversions are here made at £1=Canadian $2.74⅜, the middle closing rate on March 31, 1958.

Colonies and Mandated Territories) going back to a Turkish loan during the Crimean War. But the later entries relate to the very large amounts of the stocks issued by the nationalized industries (other than coal) since the Second World War either in compensation for the privately-owned assets they took over or to raise funds for subsequent capital development before 1956, when the Exchequer began to provide such funds. (In the case of coal, the previous owners were compensated by the issue of a Treasury stock, which is included in the National Debt, and the National Coal Board has always drawn from the Exchequer funds needed for development.) The list of guarantees also includes that of the Redemption Stock which was issued as compensation for Tithe rent-charge and which is charged in the first instance on the redemption annuities payable to the State by tithe-payers in lieu of the former rent-charge.[1]

(3) SINKING FUNDS

The history of Sinking Funds for the reduction of the Debt is long and tortuous and we can notice only a few of the milestones on the way.[2] Curiously enough the first systematic attempt to provide for such reduction—Sir Robert Walpole's Sinking Fund of 1716—was based on the one principle which is clearly the right one and on which many subsequent experiments have vainly tried to improve. The principle is that the only real Sinking Fund is a surplus of current revenue over current expenditure. The attempted improvements have generally taken the form of directing that specified sums should be set aside annually to be applied to the reduction of the Debt by purchase or redemption; but time after time the flesh has been weak and either the money has been diverted to other uses or a reduction of old debt has been offset by new borrowings. The right principle, however, emerged again in the Sinking Fund Act of 1829 and was re-enacted in Section 16 of the Exchequer and Audit Departments Act, 1866. Under that section, an account was to be prepared each quarter of Exchequer income and expenditure for the preceding twelve months and, if it showed a surplus of income, one-quarter of that surplus was to be issued in the following quarter of the National Debt Commisioners and applied by them to the reduction of debt.

[2] See page 127.
[1] For the detailed history up to 1869 see the memorandum by H. W. Chisholm attached as Appendix No. 13 to the Return of Public Income and Expenditure (House of Commons Paper, No. 366, 1869). The Sinking Fund is dealt with on pages 710–30 of the memorandum. This remarkable memorandum is a mine of information about our financial system up to 1869.

These last provisions, however, were soon superseded by the Sinking Fund Act, 1875. This Act maintained the principle of 1829 and 1866 but substituted an annual assessment of the surplus over the financial year and provided that any surplus should be applied to the reduction of the debt in the following year. For this purpose the Act provided that the Treasury should for every financial year present to Parliament an account, certified by the Comptroller and Auditor-General, of the public income and expenditure showing the amount of any surplus of income or excess of expenditure. The Act called the amount of any surplus the 'Old Sinking Fund' to distinguish it from the 'New Sinking Fund' which the Act introduced. For the latter purpose it established a 'permanent annual charge for the National Debt' which was fixed at a figure sufficient to cover the interest and management of the Debt and leave a margin to be applied for the reduction of the Debt. This margin was the 'New Sinking Fund' and it varied not only with the amounts fixed from time to time in later years for the whole permanent annual charge but also with the extent to which the charge had first to be devoted to interest. The whole charge was, of course, reckoned as expenditure for the purpose of calculating the Old Sinking Fund: so the process of debt reduction was intended to be two-fold—first through the margin in the permanent annual charge and secondly through the 'Old Sinking Fund. Both the Old and New Sinking Funds were to be issued by the Treasury from the Consolidated Fund to the National Debt Commissioners who were to apply them to purchasing or redeeming debt. The Commissioners were to prepare accounts of the application of both funds which, after audit, were to be presented to Parliament.

The 1875 arrangements lasted until the increase in the debt due to the First World War made a review necessary. As a result the idea of a permanent annual charge was abandoned in 1923 and was superseded by the 'New Sinking Fund, 1923', under which, after the first two years, £50 million was to be set aside out of revenue every year for the reduction of debt. But this new plan did not last long. In 1928 there was a reversion to the idea of a permanent annual charge to cover interest and a margin for certain Sinking Funds attached to particular stocks and then for debt reduction generally. The annual charge was fixed at £369 million for 1928–9 and at £355 million annually thereafter, which it was calculated could extinguish the then Debt in fifty years. But, of course, that was a vain hope. Year after year, as the debt and the cost of interest increased, the amount of the permanent debt charge had to be increased by a section in each year's Finance Act and the great increase in the Debt during the Second World War finally showed up the hollowness of the whole idea. But it was not until the Finance Act of 1954 that the permanent annual charge was abolished. The year's cost of the Debt service—that is, interest, management and the five contractual and 'specific' Sinking Funds referred to on page 108—now falls on the Budget as a Consolidated Fund Service without trappings of any kind. The 'Old Sinking Fund', however, remains, although with a rather important change of technique. Between the wars it came to be realized that if the Exchequer was going to show a surplus in any year there was no good reason why the surplus should not be applied to debt reduction during the year as it arose instead of being accumulated and issued for that purpose in the following year. It accordingly became an annual habit for Parliament to provide that sums applied during the year to debt reduction should be regarded as 'expenditure' for the purpose of calculating the Old Sinking Fund, for which the surplus available would then be correspondihgly reduced or might, indeed, be reduced to nil. In the Finance Act, 1954, this annual practice was made permanent. So, while the principle of applying a revenue surplus to debt redemption remains, and the form of the Old Sinking Fund also remains, the principle will apply through the use of the surplus as it arises over the financial year. The amount so used is shown in the annual 'Public Income and Expenditure' Account under the item: 'Issued from Revenue to redeem debt and directed by the Finance Act, 1954, S.34(2), to be included as Expenditure.'

One may hazard a guess that any policy of legislating years ahead for the reduction of the National Debt by any kind of predetermined Sinking Fund other than a revenue surplus, when there is one, will now generally be regarded as outmoded and discredited. The reason for this is not only that experience has shown the vanity of such legislation. It is rather that some fundamental conceptions have changed. Any kind of fixed Sinking Fund is incompatible with the idea that the need for a revenue surplus or deficit, and the amount of either, must depend on broad economics considerations. Again, a large element in any future borrowings is likely to be due to the Exchequer's commitments to finance the capital developments programmes of the nationalized industries and other official bodies; and, so far as the Exchequer is concerned, borrowings for this purpose, or an equivalent amount of other kinds of debt, will be gradually repaid out of the repayments which it receives form those to whom it has lent the money. Altogether, therefore, the day of legislation to reduce the National Debt by predetermined annual Sinking Funds other than revenue surpluses would seem to have gone for ever.

There is another aspect of this question. We said in Chapter III that a revenue surplus above-the-line reduces the increase in the total of the Debt which would otherwise result from borrowings necessary to meet below-the-line issues. Now the idea of the Old Sinking Fund —that is, the application of a revenue surplus to debt redemption— was conceived long before the capital outgoings below-the-line attained their present variety and importance and before the steady annual increase in the debt which they involve. It may be that in due course the Old Sinking Fund will itself come up for review and a question be raised whether some more direct way of linking an above-the-line surplus with below-the-line outgoings is desirable. Since the future volume of such outgoings cannot be foreseen, it may still be found better to retain the present system. In the meantime, the system works perfectly smoothly. The daily turnover in Treasury Bills alone is sufficient to accommodate any likely above-the-line surplus available for debt redemption; during the year the Exchequer borrows the full amount required to finance below-the-line issues for which it has power to borrow; and the result is that, at the end of the year and apart from any other transactions, the outstanding debt is increased by the below-the-line issues but reduced by the surplus above-the-line.

(4) THE NATIONAL DEBT COMMISSIONERS

The Commissioners for the Reduction of the National Debt—to give them their full title—were first appointed under the National Debt Reduction Act, 1786. Minor changes have been made in their constitution since that date and they now consist of the Speaker of the House of Commons, the Chancellor of the Exchequer, the Master of the Rolls, the Lord Chief Justice, the Accountant-General of the Supreme Court, and the Governor and Deputy Governor of the Bank of England. There are, in fact, no recorded meetings of this distinguished body as a Board since 1860 and their day-to-day functions are exercised by the Comptroller General of the National Debt Office, who is a permanent Civil Servant. In carrying out his duties the Comptroller General maintains close relations with the Treasury and he has direct access, when occasion arises, to the Commissioners most closely concerned with his work, namely the Chancellor of the Exchequer and the Governor and Deputy Governor of the Bank of England.

FUNCTIONS

From what has already been said earlier in this chapter, it will have been seen that the Commissioners are not responsible for the general management of the National Debt, which is performed by the Bank of England; but they manage the business of Government Life Annuities and they effect purchases and sales of Government securities on the Registers of the Post Office and the Trustee Savings Banks. The Commissioners' primary function has always been to administer whatever provisions have been made from time to time for the reduction of the National Debt through Sinking Funds or other means. But since 1786 many other duties have been laid upon them, in no less than a hundred different statutes. Broadly, however, their functions now fall into three groups—first, the application of moneys set aside through Sinking Funds, etc., for the reduction of the National Debt; secondly, the investment and management of the assets of various capital funds; and, thirdly, certain ancillary management duties, all of which are, in one way or another, connected with some aspects of public capital funds.

SINKING FUNDS, ETC.

Under existing procedure[1] the Commissioners have no responsibilities in relation to the Old Sinking Fund, and the only active operations now under their control are those arising from the Specific Sinking Funds described on page 108 and certain other similar operations of a relatively minor character. The Comptroller General is one of the Trustees for two of the three private funds for the reduction of the National Debt referred to at the end of this chapter.

INVESTMENT OF CERTAIN CAPITAL FUNDS

At March 31, 1957, the Commissioners held, over all their various accounts, securities to a nominal amount of about £4,800 million. Of this sum, about a fifth represented securities guaranteed by the Government; the rest were direct Government obligations of all kinds. Of the total, something like 90 per cent represents assets of the following Funds.

Funds for the Banks for Savings, that is, the Trustee Savings Banks
These Banks, the pioneers of 'small savings', are local institutions under the voluntary management of honorary Trustees, whose proceedings are governed by the Trustee Savings Banks Act, 1954 (a consolidating Act), since amended by the Trustee Savings Banks Act

[1] See page 203.

1958. Legislation about the Banks dates from 1817—seven years after the formation of the first Bank—when the chief problem was to find safe and remunerative investment for depositors' moneys. The Act of 1817 (which the Act of 1954 now follows) accordingly entrusted the custody and investment of deposits to the National Debt Commissioners who account for them through this Fund.[1] Other important provisions of the Act of 1954 are a charge on the Consolidated Fund of any amount by which the assets of the Fund are insufficient to meet its liabilities to the banks; a fixed rate of interest to depositors; a charge on the Consolidated Fund for any deficiency of income on the Fund and the transfer to the Exchequer of a proportion of any surplus—there has been a surplus every year since 1909; an Inspection Committee[2]; and extensive powers of control by the National Debt Commissioners over the administration of the Banks.[3]

An annual account of the liabilities of the Commissioners to the Banks is published under the title 'Trustee Savings Banks', as a non-parliamentary paper. (At November 20, 1957, the amount of deposits lodged with the Commisioners was £834 million.) A separate account of the income of the Fund is published (along with a similar account for the Post Office Savings Banks) under the title 'Savings Banks Funds', which is also a non-parliamentary paper.

The Post Office Savings Banks Fund
This is the largest Fund under the Commissioner's control. It was in 1861 that the Postmaster-General was first authorized to receive and repay deposits and to pay interest at $2\frac{1}{2}$ per cent per annum—a rate which has never since been altered. Deposits were to be paid over to the National Debt Commisioners for investment and at December 31, 1957, the total amount due to depositors was £1,677 million.[4]

[1] Under the Finance Act, 1956, this custody has been extended to deposits in the Depositors' Department No. 2 of the Birmingham Municipal Bank.

[2] This Committee presents an Annual Report which is published as a non-parliamentary publication and contains a wide range of statistics about the Trustee Savings Banks.

[3] The deposits invested with the National Debt Commissioners are those in the 'Ordinary Departments' of the Banks. The Banks may also establish 'Special Investments Departments' in which depositors with a qualifying deposit in the Ordinary Departments can earn higher rates of interest and in which the Trustees can, with the Commissioners' approval, themselves invest the deposits in various ways set out in the Act of 1958. For a full account of the Trustee Savings Banks, see H. Oliver Horne, *A History of Savings Banks* (1947).

[4] Deposits were strikingly increased during and just after the Second World War. They were at their maximum in 1946 (£1,982 million), since then they have gradually, and almost continuously, decreased.

The business of the Bank is now regulated by the Post Office Savings Bank Act, 1954—another consolidating Act—and the financial provisions governing the Fund are similar to those in the case of Trustee Savings Banks. On Income Account, any deficiency is to be met out of the Consolidated Fund and a proportion of any surplus is payable to the Exchequer—there has been a surplus every year from 1911. On Capital Account, the Consolidated Fund is liable to provide any amount by which the assets of the Post Office Savings Banks Fund may at any time be insufficient to meet depositor's claims. (Owing to the depreciation in the market value of the securities held there is a deficiency on Capital Account but there has, of course, been no occasion to call on the Consolidated Fund guarantee.) An annual Account is published as a non-parliamentary paper under the title 'Post Office Savings Banks' showing the deposits received and paid in the year, the aggregate liabilities to depositors outstanding and the securities held by the National Debt Commissioners. An annual in come account is also published in the paper 'Savings Banks Funds' referred to in the previous paragraph.

National Insurance Fund, National Insurance (Reserve) Fund and Industrial Injuries Fund

These Funds are described in Appendix D. The annual Accounts of the Funds, there referred to, include statements of the securities held for them by the National Debt Commissioners. For the three Funds together at March 31, 1957, the Commissioners held securities of a total nominal value of £1,788 million, representing the investment of about £1,670 million of cash.

In addition to the Funds mentioned above, the National Debt Commisioners are entrusted with the investment of other capital funds for various Government departments. Prominent among these are moneys paid into Courts by suitors in the Supreme Court and the County Courts: in so far as such moneys are not required to meet current demands they are handed over to the National Debt Commissioners for investment until they are needed.[1] There are Consolidated Fund guarantees in respect of these Funds. Other Funds, carrying no such guarantee, are the Hospital Endowments Fund, the Crown Estate Investment Fund and the Ironstone Restoration Fund,

---

[1] Accounts of the National Debt Commissioners in respect of these two sets of moneys are published annually as House of Commons Papers: 'Supreme Court of Judicature—Account of the Receipts and Expenditure of the Accountant-General of the Supreme Court, in respect of the Funds of Suitors of the Court' and 'County Courts—Account of the transactions of the Accountant-General of the Supreme Court under the County Court Funds Rules'.

accounts of all which are published annually as House of Commons Papers.

INVESTMENT POLICY

It is important to be clear about the nature of the duties and responsibilities which the National Debt Commissioners have assumed in connection with the investment of the assets of these Funds. In form it varies according to the statutory provisions governing the several cases, which fall into two main classes according as the capital and/or income liability of the fund is or is not guaranteed by the Consolidated Fund. If it is, the function of the Commissioners is to try to see that the fund does its work without a call on the Consolidated Fund being necessary: their duty is towards the Exchequer rather than the beneficiaries of the fund. If there is no Consolidated Fund guarantee, their duty is directly towards the public department which has entrusted them with the money, and so indirectly towards the ultimate beneficiaries. The National Insurance Fund may be used as an illustration to make clear the latter relationship and the principles by which it is carried out. The National Insurance Act, 1946, Section 35(1), states that the Fund is to be 'under the control and management of the Minister'. The next subsection but one then goes on to say that 'any moneys forming part of the National Insurance Fund may from time to time be paid over to the National Debt Commissioners and by them invested . . .'. What, then, is the relation between the Minister and the Commissioners in this matter of investment? Shortly, it is as follows. The Minister, being in general charge of the National Insurance system and its policies and being in control, in particular, of the Fund, is the person who (with the help of Government Actuary) is responsible, from time to time, for forming a view of the future course of the Fund and for deciding on the amount of cash to be handed over for investment. In handing over that cash, he should (and does) give the Commissioners the fullest possible information as to the future prospects of the Fund, as to when capital is likely to be required, and as to the relative importance, in the meantime, of earning the maximum income on the new investments or of preserving the capital intact. It is then for the Commissioners, armed with this information and in the light of the existing assets of the Fund, to select the particular investments which will best serve the purposes of the Fund and to invest accordingly.

The Savings Banks funds, and the smaller guaranteed funds, present a rather different management problem. The changes in capital liability can be more or less foreseen, in the short term at least, as well as the outgoings from income, and so long as prudence is exercised in preserving capital and maintaining income at the required level, the investment operations can be adjusted to suit the broader policy of the Government which, through the Consolidated Fund, is the only loser if anything goes wrong. Historically, the Savings Banks funds played a significant part in Government financial operations in the last century.

That last point brings us to the other aspect of the matter. The National Debt Commissioners are responsible for operations on a corpus of marketable Government securities which is of the order of £2,500 million and on which their transactions involve hundreds of millions in a year. It is therefore inevitable that there should be the fullest collaboration between the Commissioners on the one hand and the Treasury and the Bank of England on the other, since the latter two are, between them, responsible for current general financial policy and in particular for current borrowing and 'funding'[1] programmes.

Formal expression is given to this by the fact that the Chancellor of the Exchequer and the Governor and Deputy Governor of the Bank not only are Commissioners individually but together form the effective quorum of the Commissioners. The day-to-day collaboration takes place, of course, at lower levels. Now the Commissioners, when taking decisions themselves or when decisions are taken on their behalf by their Comptroller General, are completely independent. They cannot be dictated to in any way by the Treasury or the Bank. Yet it is obviously desirable, if it is at all possible, not only that they should not act contrary to Government financial policy but that they should positively assist that policy. They can, for example, give assistance by investing in a new market issue of a Government stock, or by lending to the Government in other ways,[2] or by refraining from purchasing in the market when the Treasury and the Bank are 'funding' by selling stock; or, when the Commissioners have to sell, they may be able to help to avoid disturbance to the market by offering securities to, for instance, the Issue Department of the Bank. It is perfectly right and proper for the Treasury or the Bank, when it judges it desirable and with due explanations of its policies, to make suggestions to the Commissioners in such matters. But the final decision must always rest with the Commissioners and in taking the decision they must have primary regard to the interests of the Funds whose money would be concerned, as

[1] See page 150.
[2] Such as on the terminable annuities described on page 190.

described to them by the responsible departments. This is, of course, fully recognized by the Treasury and the Bank.[1]

ADMINISTRATIVE FUNCTIONS

Principal among these are the statutory supervision of the Trustee Savings Banks; purchases and sales of Government stocks on the Post Office Register; conduct of the business of Government Life Annuities, which is described on page 187; the holding of unclaimed Government stock and dividends and redemption moneys; the management of the Local Loans Fund, described in Appendix E; the management of the Funds relating to Land Purchase in Ireland; and the calculation and certification of the allowances to the Banks of England and Ireland for management of the National Debt.

(5) BEQUESTS FOR THE REDUCTION OF THE NATIONAL DEBT

As the tailpiece to this chapter, mention must be made of three Funds left in trust for the reduction of the National Debt. They are:

(a) *The National Fund.* This started with a gift of approximately £500,000 in 1927 on the condition that it should be retained and accumulated until either alone or with other funds it was sufficient to discharge the National Debt. A firm of merchant bankers were named as Trustees by the donor and they have complete freedom to invest the Fund in any kind of investments whatever or in trade or business. The value of the Fund at March 31, 1957, was about £2¼ million.

(b) *The Elsie Mackay Fund.* This also was started with a gift of about £500,000 in 1929 and was to be accumulated for not less than forty-five and not more than fifty years and then applied to the reduction of the National Debt. The Trustees are the Chancellor of the Exchequer, the Governor of the Bank of England and the Comptroller General of the National Debt Office with the Treasury Solicitor as Custodian Trustee, and they have discretion to invest the Fund in any Trustee Securities. The value of the Fund at March 31, 1957, was just under £1½ million.

[1] Since the Second World War, the Public Accounts Committee of the House of Commons has on several occasions taken evidence about the relations between the National Debt Commissioners, the Treasury and the Bank. The most interesting occasion was on June 19, 1952: Reports of the Committee of Public Accounts, Session 1951–2, Evidence, Questions 5697–5821.

(c) *The John Buchanan Fund*. The donor left the residue of his estate, subject to certain annuities, to be accumulated for fifty years beginning two years after his death and then to be applied in reduction of the National Debt. The Trustees are the same as under (b). The sums so far received from the estate amount to about £8,000 and on March 31, 1957, the value of the Fund was about £11,700.

Audited statements of these three Funds are presented annually to Parliament as a Command Paper under the title—'National Debt: paper relative to the position as at March 31, 19—, of certain Funds left in Trust for the Reduction of the National Debt'.

CHAPTER X

The Control of Supply Expenditure
(1) *Preparation and Form of Estimates*

'SUPPLY' expenditure for any year means the sums necessary in that year to carry out those public services which are maintained by annual votes of the House of Commons, as distinct from the 'Consolidated Fund Services', which Parliament has once-and-for-all authorized to be met from the Consolidated Fund for so long as the services shall continue. When a statute authorizes expenditure to be met out of annual Supply votes it says that is shall be met 'out of moneys provided by Parliament'. For a Consolidated Fund Service it says that it shall be 'charged on the Consolidated Fund' or 'issued out of the Consolidated Fund'. As we have already seen, Supply expenditure is over five times as large as the Consolidated Fund Services.

The procedure by which Parliament provides for Supply expenditure involves four distinct stages. First, the Crown (that is, the executive Government) makes its needs known by means of the annual Estimates.[1] Secondly, the House of Commons, after deliberating in Committee of Supply,[2] grants, in the form of Votes, the sums demanded (or possibly reduced sums) to be spent on the purposes indicated in the Estimates. Thirdly, the House, again in Committee—this time in Committee of Ways and Means[2]—sanctions the issue from the Consolidated Fund of the sum necessary to meet the agreed expenditure. Finally, in order to give the necessary statutory authority to these grants and to ensure that the sums thus put at the disposal of the Crown are not diverted to purposes other than those for which they have been specifically granted, the grants are legally 'appropriated' to such purposes, and the authority to issue

[1] Note the distinction between an 'Estimate' and a 'Vote'. An Estimate is the document which the Government presents to Parliament by way of asking for a given sum for a particular service and showing in some detail how it is proposed to spend that sum. A Vote is the deed by which Parliament actually grants and appropriates that sum for the stated service. Consequently, the word 'Vote' is commonly used to denote the sum granted, as when we speak of 'meeting a payment out of a Vote' or of a department 'accounting for a Vote'.

[2] See page 22.

funds to meet the grants is confirmed, by a statute (the Appropriation Act) which is passed at the end of each session. By reason of their privilege in financial matters[1] the Commons alone debate and grant Supply; but the Lords must assent to the Appropriation Act before it is passed, as to any other Act of Parliament.

Underlying the parliamentary procedure on Supply is a rule of the House of Commons which is of fundamental importance. It is enshrined in a Standing Order which, in its earliest form, was passed in 1706 and which now (as Standing Order No. 78) provides as follows: 'This House will receive no petition for any sum relating to public service or proceed upon any motion for a grant or charge upon the public revenue, whether payable out of the Consolidated Fund or out of money to be provided by Parliament, unless recommended from the Crown.' This Order has been described as a 'measure of protection against the easy extravagance of a large assembly'[2] as shown in the large number of grants petitioned for, and often secured, by private members before the eighteenth century. Only the Crown, therefore, can initiate proposals for expenditure and in the House the Crown's right and responsibility in this respect are exercised by Ministers in the Government of the day. No private member, on either side of the House, can exercise such initiative or move for an increase in any grant above the sum proposed by the Government.[3] The contribution which this Standing Order makes to the reasonable control of public expenditure is so obvious as to require no further emphasis.

THE NATURE OF TREASURY CONTROL

Standing Order No. 78 applies *par excellence* to the annual Estimates and the responsibility for deciding the amounts and details of them lies primarily with the Chancellor of the Exchequer, who has at his command for this purpose a large part of the staff of the Treasury. This affords at least a formal basis of what is known as 'Treasury control', which extends not only to the amount to be spent on any given service but also to the precise purposes of the expenditure and to the terms and conditions on which the money may be paid out. This aspect of Treasury control is emphasized by the fact that the

[1] See page 29.

[2] Redlich, *Procedure of the House of Commons* (1908), Vol. III, page 122.

[3] A private Member can propose a resolution advocating expenditure for a given purpose provided it is framed in general terms. Such a resolution has no operative effect and no grant or charge is imposed by its adoption. Only the Government can introduce the measures (e.g. a Bill or an Estimate) necessary to give effect to the proposals.

Estimates for all civil departments are presented to Parliament by the Financial Secretary to the Treasury. Treasury controls extends, as we shall see, to the Defence Estimates also; but in these cases—partly for historical reasons and partly, no doubt, because of the special professional responsibilities of the Fighting Services—the Estimates are presented to Parliament by the Board of Admiralty, the Army Council and the Air Council as the case may be. The approved defence expenditure of the Ministry of Supply is included in that Ministry's general Estimate which is presented with the Civil Estimates. The Estimates for the Ministry of Defence, also after approval by the Treasury, is presented by the Minister of Defence.

Muc has been written elsewhere about the origins, nature and extent of Treasury control,[1] but a few words—necessarily of a general and summary character—by way of explanation of the Treasury's position may be useful here.

Neither in relation to the Estimates nor in its wider aspects does Treasury control of expenditure (except in certain limited cases) rest on any statutory authority. It is the inevitable and accepted result partly of historical and constitutional cuases and partly of the Treasury's responsibility for co-ordinating the economic and financial policies of the Government. Historically, as we have already seen,[2] the early Treasury, as part of the Lower Exhcequer, was very close to the Throne, collecting the Sovereign's revenue and acquiring, over the years, an increasing responsibility for advising how it should be spent. This gradually gave the Treasury such a position of prestige, influence and control that, as relations between the Crown and Parliament evolved to their present form and Parliament insisted on more rigid, public control over the Government's expenditure, it was not unnatural that responsibility for such control within the Government should be put on the shoulders of the Treasury. This position was confirmed in 1861, when the Public Accounts Committee of the House of Commons,[3] then first appointed in its present form, insisted—as it has always done since—that no expenditure should be provided for in the Estimates, or be actually incurred, which has not received Treasury sanction.[4] It was again confirmed in 1866 through

---

[1] Cf. Lord Bridge's Stamp Memorial Lecture, 'Treasury Control' (1950); S. H. Beer, *Treasury Control* (1956). The (Sixth) Report from the Select Committee on Estimates, Session 1957–8, on 'Treasury Control of Expenditure' has been published just as this book is going to press and it is therefore not possible to give any considered account of it here.

[2] See pages 13–14.

[3] See page 262.

[4] Subject to the practice by which the Treasury may delegate to a department a limited degree of financial authority in specified matters.

the responsibilities and powers which the Exchequer and Audit Departments Act of that year assigned to the Treasury. But apart from history, it is only logical that the department which is responsible for the national finances and for advising the Government on broad financial and economic policy should have the right and duty to control the objects and amounts of the public expenditure.

In carrying out this function, the Treasury does not attempt to pose as expert on all the many and various proposals involving expenditure which are put forward by Government departments. It possesses a traditional *expertise* in criticism and cross-examination, born of long experience but continuously brought up to date. Subject to that its attitude is somewhat that of the intelligent layman who asks such questions as: does this proposal seem sensible on merits; does it accord with Government policies elsewhere; has it the sort of priority to justify spending the sum proposed in the financial and economic circumstances of the time; if it is a continuing service, is the cost likely to increase in the future; and are the conditions on which the money will be spent satisfactory, so that the country shall get value for its money? The Treasury's task therefore is to see that the proposals are reasonable as to purpose, amount and method in the light of current conditions and policies and—so far as this can be done in advance—that the purpose can be achieved without waste or extravagance. But, on the latter point, it must be realized that, once Treasury sanction has been given and Parliament has provided the funds, the responsibility for seeing that the funds are expended properly and prudently lies with the spending department.[1] In exercising its control, therefore, the Treasury will as far as possible avoid intervention in the details of administration, which are the spending department's responsibility. And, throughout its examination of a case, it will be in close consultation with that department.

It is important to realize that neither the Treasury nor the Chancellor of the Exchequer is a dictator in these matters. The Minister in charge of a spending department will desire to press his own policies and proposals, expensive though they may be, and he may be unwilling to take 'No' from the Treasury or the Chancellor. In that case he can appeal to the Cabinet where he and the Chancellor must argue the matter out. The decision of the Cabinet will be a joint decision by which all its individual members will be bound, and if either the Minister concerned or the Chancellor feels strongly that he cannot be a party to the decision his natural course is to resign. But, even though decisions on expenditure can thus be taken out of the Chancellor's hands by the Cabinet, the Chancellor's position in

[1] See Chapter XII.

the Cabinet is (or should be) a strong one. He has eventually—in his Budgets—to take responsibility for the resulting level of taxation and other consequences; so the Cabinet are likely to attach special weight to his views, at any rate where the expenditure at stake is of any significant size.

Although Treasury control of expenditure is primarily of importance in connection with the Estimates, it goes on all the year round. At any time of the year, any department may wish to embark on a new policy involving expenditure, or to alter the terms, or increase the cost, of some policy which has already received Treasury sanction. In all such cases it may submit proposals accordingly direct to the Treasury, where they will be examined and sanction will be given or withheld as the case may be. If it is withheld the Minister concerned has the right of appeal to the Cabinet, as has already been described above. In some cases, where he judges the policy to be of special importance, the Minister may submit his proposals direct to the Cabinet; but such cases are subject to a long-standing rule that due notice must first be given to the Treasury, so that the financial implication of the proposals may be properly examined before the Cabinet takes its decision on them.[1]

SETTLING THE CIVIL ESTIMATES

Let us now return to the Treasury's responsibilities in connection with the Estimates. There are differences of procedure between the Civil and Defence Estimates, and we will begin with the Civil Estimates. On these, the Treasury's responsibilities commence well before the threshold of the financial year to which they relate. Take the Estimates for the year X. Two years before—that is, just before the beginning of the year $X-2$—the departments provide the Treasury with forecasts of these Estimates. These are necessarily provisional and approximate, but they are nevertheless very useful—indeed they are essential—as a guide to how the financial costs of existing policies are working out and to the likely total of Civil expenditure in the years immediately ahead. Costs have a habit (apart from the effects of inflation) of providing more expensive than was anticipated when the Governments concerned embarked upon the

---

[1] Between 1919 and 1922 an outpost of the Treasury, consisting of a high-ranking Treasury Officer and his staff, was established in the Ministry of Transport. This was done primarily to facilitate Treasury control of capital expenditure on the railways while the wartime Government control of the latter continued and until the amalgamations of 1921. The case was exceptional and no such outpost has ever been created since.

various policies. It is easy to say that they should have looked as far ahead as possible—and that the Treasury should have prompetd them to do so—for any signs that expenditure was likely to increase significantly in the future: it is not always easy for mortals to see very far in such matters. However, whether a past Government deliberately accepted the fact that a given service would cost much more in the future than at its inception, or whether it simply was not aware of the full possibilities of such an increase, the courses open to the Government of the day, when a bigger bill is about to come in than it can afford on the basis of the general Budget policy it desires to follow, are quite clear: either the service must be cut or some other service must be cut to leave room for it or taxation must be increased. In any event the choice is an unenviable one; and when such situations are likely to arise it is as well to have a long warning of them as possible. So the practice of making forecast estimates some time ahead is very desirable; although, to be of use as a guide to practical policy it is doubtful if they would be reliable enough if made more than two years ahead, or three years at the most.

To return to the forecast Estimates for the year X, it is relevant even to the Budget for year X−2, and certainly to that for year X−1, to know what the figures may look like two years and one year ahead: a proposed cut in a department's demands may look harsh considered by itself, but may look very different in the light of probable large increases in those demands in the following two years. And if important, and possibly unpleasant, changes of policy have to be made in order to accommodate an otherwise rapidly growing expenditure over a period of years, it is as well that they should, if possible, be put in hand gradually. The forecasts made at the beginning of year X−2 are revised at six-monthly intervals. Very soon after Budget Day for year X−1 is over, the revised forecasts for the year X must be examined more closely; and, with less than a year to spare, the Chancellor must begin to consider whether he must take any special steps ahead of the formal Estimates procedure to keep the total within reasonable bounds having regard to current conditions and policies. If the prospect is serious enough from this point of view, he may have to ask his ministerial colleagues, individually or collectively, to join with him in a special effort to get the total down. Since significant reductions can only be secured by changes of policy, such a proceeding involves many inter-ministerial battles and most probably references to the Cabinet. Parliament and the public know nothing, of course, of the first bids of departments for the totals of their Estimates and they are therefore normally unaware of the details of the Chancellor's struggle until some public announcement has to be made of whatever changes of policies have been agreed to secure the necessary economies.

These battles on the Forecast Estimates overlap the first formal stages in the preparation of the actual Estimates to be presented to Parliament. These begin on or about October 1st every year, when the Treasury send out its 'Estimates Circular'. This is an official invitation to departments to submit formal Estimates by December 1st, unless some later date is agreed. The circular gives a variety of technical instructions about the basis on which Estimates should be prepared and usually contains a passage in which the attention of departments is drawn to current economic and financial conditions and—for one reason or another the need is always there—the need for the strictest economy in their plans for expenditure. No doubt this passage hardly ever conveys anything which, at October 1st, is new to the departments, but there is some virtue in putting on official record the general attitude which the Chancellor must take towards the total of Government expenditure in the year ahead.

As each department's draft Estimate comes in it is examined by the 'Supply' division of the Treasury which deals with the department's policies and expenditure generally. The division subjects it to a very rigorous scrutiny from such angles as : whether everything in the Estimate is in accordance with sanctions previously given by the Treasury ; if there is anything not so sanctioned, should it be challenged ; are the department's estimates of what it will spend during the year on its various agreed policies reasonable or do they look inflated or contain provision for contingencies not very likely to occur? Even if everything is in order from those points of view, should the department be asked to forgo this or that item, or reduce the provision made for it, either because the scale of the expenditure is running well beyond what was contemplated at its inception or as a practicable contribution towards any given reduction which the Chancellor desires to make in the total of all the Estimates? Any matters appearing in the Estimates which have already been taken up by the Chancellor on the earlier 'Forecast' Estimates will, of course, be reserved by the division pending a final ministerial decision thereon. At the same time, duplicates of most of the draft Estimates are examined by the appropriate division on the Establishment side of the Treasury to see that the number of staff and their salaries and wages are in accordance with existing instructions. Of necessity there is close collaboration between the Supply and Establishments divisions, since the organization and number of a department's staff depend primarily on its current policies. As many as possible out of all these various questions are taken up with the departments by the Treasury divisions at official level. Major matters on which there is disagreement are reserved for consideration by Treasury Ministers: some of them may already be engaging the chancellor's attention. When the examination and criticism of a draft Estimate have been carried as far as they can be at official level the draft is formally submitted to the Financial Secretary to the Treasury either with a recommendation that it should be approved or with notes on points which the division suggests should be taken up with the department. The Financial Secretary may then deal with the estimate himself or he may submit it with his own recommendation to the Chancellor. Not until the Financial Secretary, or he and the Chancellor, as the case may be, are satisfied on all outstanding points are the total and details of the Estimate finally agreed by the Treasury.

SETTLING THE DEFENCE ESTIMATES

The above procedure relates, as stated, to the Civil Estimates. The Defence Estimates are handled rather differently. In the first place the Government, in deciding what it shall spend on Defence from year to year, considers all the three Fighting Services as a whole. This follows from the fact that in the defence of the country each of the Services, though charged with its own specific tasks, plays a part in one integrated plan. That plan must be designed as a whole in the light of the Government's appreciation of international political and strategic conditions, as well as of economic and financial conditions at home. (One important financial consideration will always be the outstanding commitments of the Services under contracts already place or on projects already started.) The final design, at any one time, will therefore have to be a balance of different factors, often pulling different ways, and the only rational approach to the financial problem is to assess what must, or can be, spent on all aspects of defence taken together. Also, from a broad economic point of view, each Service makes the same kind of demand on the national resources—on productive capacity for weapons and equipment and on manpower for their personnel. These demands should clearly be considered as a whole. For these reasons the Chancellor and the Minister of Defence[1] in the first place will normally consider many months before the beginning of each financial year what the overall expenditure should be in that year. At the outset of their discussion their

---

[1] For the respective responsibilities, in relation to defence, of the Prime Minister, the Cabinet, the Defence Committee of the Cabinet, the Minister of Defence and the Service Ministers, see the White Paper, 'Central Organization for Defence' (Cmnd 476), issued in July 1958.

ideas may well differ greatly and much argument and consideration of alternative plans may take place. High policy may be involved and the question at issue may often have to be put to the Cabinet or to its Defence Committee. But sooner or later agreement is reached on the total and the agreed figure is then divided, again on an agreed basis, between the three Fighting Services, the defence activities of the Ministry of Supply, and the Ministry of Defence. Each department then splits up its allocation between its own various purposes and prepares its Estimates accordingly. The Treasury is in continuous contact with all the departments during this procedure. Moreover, even though it has been agreed that a particular department may spend in total a certain sum, that sum is not necessarily a final figure from which no departure may be made. Treasury sanction is still necessary for the amounts to be spent on different purposes within the total—such as particular weapons or equipment or stores or buildings—and the Treasury may try to get the final result within the agreed figure. On the other hand, detailed examination may lead a Defence Department to press for more. (Sometimes it may not be physically possible for agreement to be reached on all these details with the Treasury before the Estimates have been presented; in that case the department is allowed to show in its Estimates items not yet sanctioned but is under obligation not to spend the money until Treasury sanction has been obtained.)

As soon as the Defence total has been settled, divided between the Services and allocated by each of the Services to its various Estimates, the Government publishes the White Papers on Defence Policy and Defence Statistics, which have already been referred to.[1] Shortly after their presentation these papers are debated in Parliament, thus giving an opportunity for discussion of broad defence policy before the House of Commons is asked to consider the Services' individual Estimates.

VOTES 'ON ACCOUNT'

In the preparation of both Civil and Defence Estimates the Government has to work to a rigorous time-table, which obliges us to antici-pate one point in the parliamentary procedure discussed in the next chapter. Parliament grants Supply for a given year, beginning on April 1st and ending on March 31st and departments cannot carry over any of this Supply into the following year. At the same time it has always been found impracticable for Parliament to go through all the procedure of granting Supply for any year before that year

[1] Page 59.

begins. Interim arrangements must therefore be made to enable departments to carry on after March 31st until all the Supply for the new year can be voted and appropriated. Here again the procedure differs between the Civil and the Defence departments. In the case of the Civil departments, Parliament is asked to grant an aggregate sum 'on account'. For this purpose an Estimate is presented by the Treasury in February showing the total of every Estimate which will later be presented and against it how much will be required to cover the first four or five months of the new year, that is, until the middle of August, by which time Parliament has normally granted all Supply and appropriated it.[1] The individual requirements of departments on account are then added up and Parliament is asked to vote this total in one lump sum as the Civil 'Vote on Account'; but the resolution by which it is voted allocates it to the different services and that allocation is binding on the departments. In the past Parliament has sometimes shown anxiety about the period for which it voted money on account, lest the Government of the day should be enabled to carry on too long without coming to Parliament with its full Estimates and so disclosing its policies. Happily, the understanding between modern Governments and Parliaments is sufficiently close to make such anxieties unnecessary. Moreover, there is a rule thet funds thus voted on account can only be spent on services already sanctioned by Parliament either in the previous year's Estimates or by specific legislation; so the Government itself, which is generally anxious to get ahead with some new policy or other, will, in its own interest, not wish to delay the presentation and discussion of the full Estimates. The Estimate for the Civil Vote on Account is normally presented to Parliament about the middle of February and debated shortly afterwards. (The debate does not range over the whole field of expenditure but is normally limited to some one subject chosen by the Opposition.) The full detailed Estimates are then normally presented over the following period to March 31st, so that they are available, even though they are not debated, before the new financial year begins. This procedure means, of course, that the total of each and every Estimate for the new year must be agreed between the Treasury and departments by about the middle of February.

The three Defence Services also need funds to carry on after March 31st, but their funds are provided in a different way. The normal rule is that each of the Services presents its full Estimates late in February or early in March and Parliament is then asked to vote

[1] This Estimate for the Vote on Account is the first public disclosure of the total and constituent items of the Civil Estimates for the coming year.

money on two or three Estimates for each Service, which is allowed
to be used to finance the whole of that Service during the early
months of the new financial year. This different procedure is due to
the fact that, while money voted on one Civil Estimate can in no
circumstances be used to finance any other Civil Vote, money which
has been granted for one Navy, Army or Air Vote can be used *ad
interim* for any other Vote of the same Service. While this is the
normal procedure for providing the Defence Services with funds, it
may happen that, for one reason or another, the Estimates of one
or all of the Services may not be ready in time to allow that procedure
to be followed. In that event the Civil procedure is adopted and
Parliament is asked to provide one sum on account for the Navy or
the Army or the Air Force. This was done in 1957 when not even the
total figure for any of the Services had been settled in time and it was
necessary to take Votes on Account for all three Services. For the
reassurance of Parliament, the Government, in asking for the Votes
on Account, then announced that the total estimated cost of Defence
in 1957–8 would not exceed that in the Estimates for 1956–7.

THE FORM OF AN ESTIMATE

Let us now see what the Estimates look like, taking the Civil Estimates first.[1] There are about a hundred and fifty of them, for which
some eighty departments, large and small, are responsible. Thus some
departments have more than one Estimate to account for. For
example, the Board of Trade has four Estimates—one for the expenses
of the department, one for Assistance to Industry and Trading
Services, one for Strategic Reserves and one for Services in Development Areas. The Ministry of Agriculture, Fisheries and Food has
five—one for the expenses of the department, one for Agricultural
and Food Grants and Subsidies, one for Agricultural and Food
Services, one for Food (Strategic Reserves) and one for Fishery
Grants and Services.[2] The number of separate Estimates is a balance

---

[1] The Treasury is generally responsible for the form of the Estimates subject
to consultation, as may be appropriate, with the Public Accounts Committee
and the Select Committee on Estimates. This responsibility flows from the
Treasury's power to prescribe the manner in which departments shall keep their
accounts. See page 251.

[2] Sometimes a Minister answers in Parliament for matters arising on an
Estimate, and the corresponding Vote, where the Vote is accounted for, not by
his own Department, but by another Department which has no separate Ministerial Head. As examples, Treasury Ministers may have to answer in a variety
of cases, including the Exchequer and Audit Department, the Public Works Loan
Board, the British Museum and the National Gallery.

between conflicting considerations. On the one hand, it is undesirable to multiply the number of separate Parliamentary resolutions, the number of accounts to be audited and the number of separate margins for contingencies. On the other hand, if the scope of an Estimate is widened to reduce the number, Parliament's control over the spending of the grant is weakened because, as we shall see later,[1] money can be transferred, under Treasury authority, between the services included in one Vote.

All Estimates are divided into three parts:

Part I specifies the services and purposes for which the Estimate is presented (what is known as the 'ambit' of the Vote) and the net amount of the grant required.

Part II classifies under 'subheads' the expenditure and receipts (if any) which go to make up the net amount specified in Part I, and names the department which will account for expenditure of the grant under those subheads.

Part III explains in such detail as is considered necessary the nature of the expenditure and receipts provided for under each of the subheads in Part II. (Where but little more information can be given than is apparent from the title of a subhead in Part II, detailed explanation is sometimes omitted in Part III, and where the Estimate is a very simple one Part III is sometimes omitted altogether.)[2]

Each of these Parts has its own special purpose. Part I, which alone is reproduced in the statute which finally appropriates the grants, is of supreme importance as providing the description in that statute of the purpose for which Parliament grants the money. Part II shows the subheads under which the Treasury, as laid down by Parliament,[3] requires the expenditure to be accounted for. Since the authority ultimately given by Parliament depends on Part I only, the distribution of the total grant among the subheads in Part II has no statutory significance; and, as we shall see later, the Treasury— not the department concerned—may by 'virement' sanction the use of savings under one subhead to meet an excess under another, provided, however, that neither the gross total nor the net total voted by Parliament is exceeded.[4] The details given in Part III are merely

---

[1] Page 235.

[2] The number of printed pages occupied by one Estimate and its appendices varies from one to over thirty according to the complexity of the service concerned and the amount of detail given. But the basic structure of all Estimates is the same. One of the simplest and smallest—that for the National Maritime Museum, 1956–7—is reproduced in Appendix H.

[3] Exchequer and Audit Departments Act, 1866, section 23.

[4] See page 235. Such sanction is only given after the Treasury has considered the nature of each case.

for the additional information of Parliament. They are not binding on the spending department or the Treasury; but if they had set out the conditions on which it was proposed to spend the money asked for, and it was desired later in the year to make a material change in those conditions without increasing the grant already made, it would generally be held right to inform Parliament and this might be done by presenting a Supplementary Estimate indicating the change and asking only for a token sum (£10).[1]

The Defence Estimates are issued in three booklets, one each for the Navy, Army and Air. The provision for each Service is divided into a number of Estimates according to the object of the expenditure. The Army and Air Estimates follow the same pattern, with separate Estimates for Pay of the Army (or Air Force), Reserve, etc., Services, the War Office (or Air Ministry), Civilians at outstations, Movements, Supplies (of food, fuel, etc.), war-like and general Stores, Works and Lands, Miscellaneous Effects Services, Non-Effective Services and a token Estimate for Additional Married Quarters (which are financed out of borrowed moneys). The Navy Estimates include one for Shipbuilding, Repairs, Maintenance, etc.,; but unlike the Army and Air Estimates they also include separate Estimates for certain services such as the medical, educational and scientific services. All the Estimates for each of the Services follow the same form as the Civil Estimates in being divided into Parts I, II and III. The Parts serve the same purpose as in the Civil Estimates subject to the important difference we have already noted. Whereas money appropriated to one Civil Vote is in no circumstances applicable to another such Vote, so that the power of virement can only be exercised between subheads of the same Vote, money appropriated to one Navy, Army or Air Vote is applicable, on certain conditions, to any other Vote of the same service. This difference is no doubt due primarily to the fact that grants for the Army and Navy were originally made in the form of one lump sum for each service because (in the words of an early Parliamentary Committee) of 'the impossibility of providing specially in the Estimates for every contingency which may arise in carrying on those great services in every part of the world'. It is also justifiable in that, while the Civil Votes cover a heterogeneous collection of grants to many different departments, all

[1] E.g. the Estimate for Colonial Services, 1957–8, included contributions towards the cost of internal security measures in certain African territories, and Part III of the Estimate set out the channels through which they would be paid. It was later desired to pay through other channels and parliamentary authority for the alteration was sought by a token addition of £10 to the relevant subhead (with appropriate explanations) in a Supplementary Estimate for Colonial Services in February 1958.

Navy or Army or Air Votes are under the same control and relate to the different requirements of one service.

CASH BASIS OF THE ESTIMATES

The Estimates, both Civil and Defence, show only the sums which are expected actually to come in course of payment during the year to which the Estimates relate. They include, but do not distinguish between, cash required to meet liabilities outstanding (but not then due to be met) at the end of the previous year and cash required to meet new liabilities incurred in the current year: they do not provide for liabilities which may be incurred in the current year but which do not mature for payment until a later year.[1] The Estimates are thus drawn up on a strictly cash basis which is the basis of all our Exchequer accounting, on both the revenue and expenditure sides above-and-below-the-line. In this respect our system differs radically from some foreign systems where—apart from any other arrangements that may be made for the control of the expenditure—the legislature is asked to appropriate—their equivalent to our 'Vote'— sufficient funds to cover all liabilities to be incurred in a given year irrespective of the time when they will mature for payment. The latter system may be thought more logical; but this country has preferred practical advantage to logic. Payments under departmental liabilities may go on for years so that, under the foreign system, it may be a very long time before the accounts of any given year's appropriations can be closed and audited. When opening his Budget, the Chancellor could have no clear, satisfactory picture to give of the past year which could be used as a starting point for the discussion of the coming year's finance. Moreover in normal peacetime circumstances—that is when the level of Budget expenditure is not greatly changing from one year to the next—the British system works well enough because there is not likely to be any significant difference between the unpaid liabilities outstanding at the beginning and end of any given year.

THE ESTIMATES AND LEGISLATION

The expenditure provided for in the Estimates flows in many cases from past legislation in which Parliament has authorized a service and may have put a limit to the amount which may be spent on it, either in any one year or in total. Suppose that a department includes

[1] In some cases (e.g. for works and buildings) particulars of eventual total cost may be included, but this is purely for the information of Parliament.

H

in its Estimates sums for such a service which carry it beyond the previous statutory authority or limit; can it rely on the Appropriation Act (which finally sanctions the expenditure asked for) to override the earlier statute? This matter has been debated between the Public Accounts Committee and the Treasury at intervals over many years, the outcome of which is agreement that, while it is competent for the Appropriation Act to be used in that way, constitutional property requires that such extensions of the earlier legislation should be regularized at the earliest possible date by amending legislation, unless they are of a purely emergency or non-continuing character. But when the latter type of case arises, a clear statement of the facts must appear on the face of the Estimate so that Parliament may be fully aware of the position.[1]

'ALLIED' AND 'AGENCY' SERVICES

The Estimate for any department or service does not include the whole cost of the activities to which it relates. The department concerned requires to be provided with certain services which are common needs of all departments, such as accommodation, lighting and heating, stationery, postage, etc. The cost of such services, known as 'allied services', is included in the Estimates of the departments whose function it is to provide them; for example, the Ministry of Works, the Stationery Office and the Post Office. On the whole it makes for economical control of the 'allied services' if the cost of building or renting offices or buying stationery is borne on the votes accounted for by the departments which are the experts in such services. But in order that Parliament may be aware of the total estimated cost of any given department or service, including the 'allied services', a note is appended to—though not forming part of—the Estimate for that department or service showing all the costs borne by other departments for services rendered to it.

Another case to be noticed is where one department may be asked by another department, on grounds of economy or convenience, to render a service outside the functions which the first department

[1] Some examples of this matter will be found in the 'Epitome of the Reports of the Public Accounts Committee, 1857–1937'. Thus, the Committee of 1930 (pages 711–12) drew attention to a case where a Ministry incurred expenditure out of its Vote on various schemes which did not appear to be within its powers as defined by the statutes regulating its functions. In 1936 (page 761) it drew attention to a case where the salaries of certain officials, which were laid down by statute and payable out of the Consolidated Fund, were increased by supplements paid out of the relevant Vote. In each of these cases the matter was regularized by subsequent legislation.

primarily exists to perform. In such cases the first department performs an 'agency service' for the second department and—except when separation of the cost would be difficult—is paid in cash by the latter department which bears the final charge on its own vote. The second department (as principal) is responsible for the policy necessitating the expenditure; the first department (as agent) is responsible for exercising efficiency and economy in administering the service which it is providing. As an example of this, the Air Ministry is paid for works and other services carried out for the Ministry of Transport and Civil Aviation and other departments.

DEPARTMENTAL RECEIPTS—APPROPRIATIONS-IN-AID

The last matter we must notice about the form of the Estimates is the treatment of departmental receipts—not major items like the taxes shown on the Revenue side of the Budget, but receipts incidental to the ordinary course of a department's business, such as fees, proceeds of the sale of products, etc. These, where they arise, are shown in the final subhead of Part II of an Estimate; and the sum specified in Part I of the Estimate is a net sum, being the difference between the total gross expenditure shown under the other subheads in Part II and any receipts shown in the final subhead. If the full gross expenditure were to be voted by Parliament and the receipts were to be paid direct into the Exchequer substantial sums would appear on both sides of the Exchequer account which would be unduly inflated. It is accordingly the practice of the Treasury[1] to allow a department concerned, instead of paying such receipts into the Exchequer, to use them to defray part of its expenditure. Such receipts are then said to be appropriated in aid of the department's vote and are known as 'appropriations-in-aid'. When the Committee of Supply debates an Estimate it cannot discuss the application of these appropriations-in-aid or reduce them, because they are not sums which the Crown is demanding from Parliament but sums which the Crown has available from other sources. Nevertheless this does not mean that the disposal of large sums of public money escapes the formal control of Parliament, because the final Appropriation Act authorizes the expenditure on a given service not only of the net sum specified in Part I of the Estimate but also the precise amount (and not more than that amount) of the receipts shown in

[1] Acting under the Public Accounts and Charges Act, 1891, Section 2. In this respect Parliament has sanctioned a breach of the principle that all public revenue must be paid into the Exchequer Account. But as shown below, Parliament still controls the extent of the breach in each case.

Part II as being appropriated-in-aid. If more receipts come in than can be so appropriated they are surrendered direct to the Exchequer as 'Exchequer Extra Receipts'. Some types of receipts—mostly of a capital nature, such as repayments of loans, proceeds of sale of land, building, surplus war stores and so on—are not allowed to be appropriated in aid and must in any case be surrendered as Extra Receipts.[1]

LIMITS TO GROSS AND NET EXPENDITURE

The result of this system is that, on any Estimate, Parliament is asked (a) to vote a net sum of £X (the amount in Part I of the Estimate) and (b) to authorize in addition the use of receipts of £Y (the amount in the Appropriation-in-aid subhead). In effect, there-fore, Parliament is also asked (c) to authorize a *gross* expenditure of £(X+Y), which is the total of all the expenditure subheads of the Estimate before the appropriations-in-aid are deducted. If Parlia-ment does, in fact, vote a grant in precise accordance with the Estimate, the department concerned cannot exceed *any* of the sums authorized under (a) or (b) or (c).

THE ESTIMATES IN WARTIME—VOTES OF CREDIT

During the war something more flexible than the ordinary Estimates procedure is required. The amount of expenditure to be incurred and the rate at which it will be spent cannot be estimated in advance with any precision; security reasons often prevent some details being given; new services may arise at any time and the necessary authori-ties to finance them must be available without delay. Estimates are therefore presented from time to time for 'Votes of Credit' in very large sums (e.g. £2,000 million) and with a Part I in very wide terms. Thus, in the Second World War Votes of Credit were obtained to cover expenses to be incurred 'for general Navy, Army and Air

---

[1] The above is the normal practice. Exceptionally an Estimate may contain a 'net subhead'. This device is used where expenditure under the subhead is offset by receipts attributable to the same service, the total of both expenditure and receipts being set out under the subhead. The device avoids the inflation of the gross total of the Estimate that would result from full gross accounting. Net sub-heads are used where the receipts represent, wholly or mainly, funds provided on other votes (e.g. the subhead for services rendered to other departments on repayment terms in the Estimate for Public Buildings, United Kingdom—see also page 121) or where the expenditure and receipts relate to trading services (e.g. the subhead for Trading Services (Food) in the estimate for Agricultural and food Services).

services and supplies in so far as specific provision is not made therefore by Parliament; for securing the public safety, the defence of the realm, the maintenance of public order and the efficient prosecution of the war; for maintaining supplies and services essential to the life of the community; and generally for all expenses, beyond those provided for in the ordinary Grants of Parliament, arising out of the existence of a state of war'. This wide wording covered not only military expenditure but a host of civil measures like the management of food supplies and food subsidies, economic warfare, public information services, security measures and so on. The Estimates for Votes of Credit gave no analysis or details corresponding to Parts II and III of an ordinary Estimate. But, at an early stage in each financial year a White Paper was issued showing, where considerations of public policy allowed, the various services for which it was proposed to make provision during the year through Votes of Credit. Figures were given—some of a global character—but it was emphasized that these were merely an indication of the probable scale of expenditure, that they were entirely provisional and that they were liable to wide variations during the course of the year.

Votes of Credit are accounted for by the Treasury, which makes issues therefrom to the departments concerned according to their requirements. During the Second World War, the ordinary Estimates of the Defence Services were confined to nominal sums and substantive provision under each of their Votes was drawn, as required, from a Vote of Credit. A similar procedure was followed with the new departments like the Ministry of Supply and the Ministry of Food, for which only token Estimates were presented. Ordinary expenditure on normal peacetime services of the Civil departments was provided for by normal Estimates and Votes, and a Vote of Credit was not applicable to meet any deficiency on such expenditure. But to the extent that excess expenditure on an ordinary Vote arose out of services to which a Vote of Credit was applicable issues could be made from the latter to the Vote in question. Votes of Credit conform to the ordinary Supply procedure in the Committees of Supply and Ways and Means and require to be covered by Consolidated Fund Acts and Appropriation Acts in the usual way.

CHAPTER XI

The Control of Supply Expenditure
(2) The Estimates in Parliament

SUPPLY 'ALLOTTED DAYS'

NOW we must see what the House of Commons does with the Estimates when they are presented to it by the Government. The Committee of Supply is set up early in each session as soon as the debate on the Speech from the Throne is ended and the Estimates are formally referred to the Committee as soon as they are presented. The amount of time which should be given each session to Supply business has been much discussed in the Commons over the last hundred years or so. On the one hand the Government of the day is always anxious to find as much time as possible for other business such as new legislation. On the other hand, the Opposition, who choose the Estimates which are to be discussed, will be equally anxious to have as many days as possible on which they can use the Estimates to challenge or probe the policies and administration of different Ministers and their departments. The result is that Standing Order No. 16 now provides that twenty-six days shall be allotted to the business of supply before August 5th in each session. (This date was fixed in 1896, when Mr Balfour suggested that 'the House is not in its best parliamentary form' after the August Bank Holiday.) The parliamentary 'session' has, of course, no relation to the financial year and commonly runs from one autumn to the next. In any one session, therefore, the House of Commons may have to consider Supply relating to more than one financial year. Hence, for the purpose of the Standing Order, 'the business of Supply' includes not only the main Estimates for the current or the coming financial year but also supplementary or additional estimates, excess votes, votes on account and consideration of reports from the Public Accounts Committee and the Select Committee on Estimates. It does not include Votes of Credit or supplementary or additional votes on other estimates for war expenditure.

IN COMMITTEE OF SUPPLY

On any allotted day Supply is put down as the first order of business; but that does not mean that on such a day the Speaker always and automatically leaves the Chair so that the House may go into Committee of Supply. In recognition of the old constitutional doctrine that redress of grievances should precede the grant of supplies, provision is made for occasions on which the motion 'that Mr Speaker do now leave the Chair' can be debated and amendments moved to it relating to 'grievances', and these amendments and the motion must be disposed of before the House can go into Committee. On such occasions the debate can range over any subject covered by the Estimates which are about to be discussed in Committee, and the rules of debate are in some particulars less strict than in the Committee of Supply itself. In practice such debates are held on any Navy, Army, Air Force or Civil topic on the first occasion in each session on which the House is to go into Committee on the Army, Navy, Air or Civil Estimates respectively; on these occasions the right to open the debate and choose its subject is conferred by ballots among members. In addition any Minister may propose such a debate on any allotted day, but this is done more rarely: it is done by arrangement with the Opposition who choose the subject and move the amendment accordingly.

The number of allotted days is not expected to be sufficient to allow all the Estimates to be debated before August 5th. Further, as we have already seen, some Estimates for the coming year must be dealt with before April 1st; and any Supplementary Estimates for the year just closing must be voted in time to allow departments to make use of them by March 31st. The Standing Order therefore provides a system of closures or 'guillotines' to ensure that all necessary votes are obtained by the requisite dates. First, at the end of the Supply on some day before March 31st but not earlier than the seventh allotted day, the Committee of Supply is required to vote, without further debate, on the Estimate for any Vote on Account for the coming year, on any Defence Estimate which has already been put down for debate and (provided they have been presented seven days previously) on any outstanding Supplementary Estimates for the current year. All these votes are at once 'reported' to the House itself for, as it were, ratification and on a subsequent allotted day—still before March 31st and not earlier than the eighth such day—the House is required to vote on them. Similarly, towards the end of July, on the last but one of the allotted days the Committee of Supply is required to vote, without further debate, on all Estimates then outstanding;

and on the next, the last, allotted day the Estimates are reported to the House and the House itself votes on them.

The debate in Committee of supply can range over all matters relating to the particular services set out in the Estimates before the Committee and over the administration of the department concerned. But the need for legislation of any kind or matters involving legislation cannot be discussed, since legislation is a function of the House itself and of its other Committees but not of the Committee of Supply. The Committee can only grant, refuse or reduce the sum demanded: it cannot attach new conditions. As we have seen, it cannot discuss the receipts appropriated-in-aid in the Estimates. No increase in the sum specified in the Estimate can be proposed in Committee of Supply, even by the Government. If the Government wishes to make such an increase, it must present a Revised or Supplementary Estimate to the House, which can then be referred to the Committee. If a private member desires an increase, his only course is to move a reduction of the Estimate with such explanation that, if his motion is accepted by the Committee, the Government will treat it as a demand that the Estimate be withdrawn and an increased Estimate be presented to the House. Although the debates in Committee of Supply are thus hedged round with many formalities restricting the amounts which can be voted, it cannot be said that the debates now serve the cause of economy to any noticeable degree. Occasionally some example of waste or extravagance may be unearthed; but the debates have become occasions on which members with special knowledge of or interest in the subject of an Estimate press views on the Minister concerned which are often likely to involve increased rather then reduced, expenditure. When the House itself receives the report of a Vote from the Committee of Supply, the Vote may, if the Opposition so choose, be debated again—this debate counting against the number of allotted days.

There is no compulsion on either the Committee of Supply or the House to come to a decision at the end of a day's debate on an Estimate or Vote. Very often the subject is one on which the Opposition wish to keep up pressure on the Government and will almost certainly want to revert to it later in the session. In such cases the Estimate or Vote is 'left open'—that is, the debate is simply adjourned until a future allotted day.

What happens if, by an adverse vote, the Committee of Supply or the House rejects a Government demand for Supply? Only the Government concerned can decide its course of action in the light of all the circumstances of the time and it would be idle for us to speculate about what they would do. Clearly much would depend on the actual occasion itself. If the Estimate or Vote concerned, or the grounds for rejecting it, related to some relativity unimportant matter the Government would no doubt merely think again and come forward, if they thought fit, with a Revised Estimate. On the other hand, if the occasion involved the finance for a major policy of the Government it might well be that at least the Minister concerned, if not indeed the whole Government, would decide to resign. But we cannot pursue such intriguing possibilities further.

THE SELECT COMMITTEE ON ESTIMATES

This is perhaps the point at which to notice the work of the Select Committee on Estimates. Dating from about the beginning of the last century, many attempts were made to have the Estimates examined by some smaller parliamentary body which could study the Estimates in more detail, and with more time available, than was possible in the Committee of Supply. For this purpose Select Committees of the House of Commons were appointed at infrequent intervals; but it was not until 1921 that the practice began of appointing a Select Committee on Estimates every session. This Committee's terms of reference are now as follows: 'To examine such of the Estimates presented to this House as may seem fit to the Committee, and to suggest the form in which the Estimates shall be presented for examination, and to report what, if any, economies consistent with the policies implied in those Estimates may be effected therein.' The Select Committee, which consists of thirty-six members, operates through a series of sub-committees, each examining a particular group of the Estimates or a general subject. A sub-committee will normally take, and publish, evidence from officials of the department concerned and of the Treasury, and it may also take evidence from non-official witnesses who are concerned or interested in the subject under examination. Some of the sub-committees, when so authorized by special resolution of the House, have gone overseas to take evidence. A report is issued as each particular investigation is completed.[1] When, as is usual, a report makes criticisms or positive suggestions, the department concerned submits its observations in a memorandum direct to the Committee which is later published by the Committee. The treasury comments on reports of a general character.

[1] E.g. the Select Committee of the Session 1956–7 took evidence and issued separate Reports on HM Stationery Office; the supply of military aircraft; stores and Ordnance Depots of the Service Departments; Customs and Excise; the Meteorological Services and the Royal Greenwich Observatory; the running costs of hospitals; the Youth Employment Service and Youth Service grants; and War Histories.

This annually appointed Select Committee is now an established feature of the system of parliamentary control of expenditure. Over the years it has undoubtedly performed a useful service in bringing outside criticism to bear on departmental administrations. Possibly it has also had the converse advantage of bringing Members of Parliament into closer touch with the practical problems of departments. Sometimes, however, doubts may have been raised whether so small a body as one of its sub-committees—often consisting of some half-a-dozen members—is not liable to be unduly influenced by some one or two of its members who have special interest in a subject and particular points of view to press. The most important point in the Committee's terms of reference is that the policy implied in any Estimate is outside its competence. It could not deal with major matters of policy without encroaching on the powers of the executive government. It ought not in fact to attempt to examine policy without calling Ministers, rather than officials, as witnesses and the proper place for Ministers to explain and justify policy is in the House itself.

ADJUSTMENTS OF THE ESTIMATES

If the future always conformed to departmental assumptions and expectations, the Estimates presented in February and March, on which the Budget is based, and the corresponding grants made by Parliament, would finance the Government's activities until the end of the financial year to which they relate. But matters never turn out like that. It must be remembered that the Estimates are, in the main, submitted to the Treasury between three and five months before the beginning of the financial year. In many cases the figures in the Estimates depend on factors which can be forecast but cannot be controlled, so that estimating for a period ending fifteen months ahead can sometimes be a hazardous operation. Again, as the financial year passes the Government may be faced with new situations at home and abroad demanding new decisions, new objects of expenditure and increased expenditure on existing services. It is not surprising therefore that, in every year, some original Estimates are falsified by the course of events. This situation can be met, according to circumstances, in a variety of ways.

REVISED ESTIMATES

Suppose that some new factor has arisen which involves a radical change in an Estimate before it has been voted on in Committee of

Supply. If the change involves a reduction in the Estimate it would be wrong to ask Parliament to vote an unnecessarily large sum; so the original Estimate is withdrawn and a 'Revised Estimate' is substituted. If the change involves an increase in the Estimate, the same procedure could be followed and would probably be the right course of it were necessary to widen the governing words in Part I of the Estimates. But the increase may also be met by presenting a Supplementary Estimate and, in fact, modern practice rather leans to this latter course.

'VIREMENT'

The next case to consider is where Parliament has actually granted the sum asked for in some original Civil Estimate, and that sum is still sufficient to meet the requirements of the service as a whole, but the department wishes to spend more under some subhead or subheads, and less under others, than is provided in the Estimate. We have already seen that the figures shown under the different subheads of the original Estimate do not bind anyone and in fact the Crown— that is the Government of the day—has discretion (subject to what follows below) to vary the allocation of the total grant between the subheads. This discretion is exercised by the Treasury, not by the spending department concerned. The Treasury alone can sanction the use of savings under one subhead to meet excess expenditure under another subhead—a process which is known as 'virement'.[1] It does not give such sanction automatically or lightly but considers each case carefully in the light of circumstances and considers in particular whether excess expenditure under a given subhead should not, after all, be submitted for parliamentary approval. The Treasury has always been jealous of its discretion in this matter and has deprecated any attempt to draw up a precise code of rules laying down when virement should or should not be exercised. But it has agreed with the view of the Public Accounts Committee that 'services which are large or novel or contentious or which, while small at the outset, involve heavy liabilities in future years, ought not, save in very exceptional circumstances, to be undertaken without previous authority of Parliament' and therefore ought not to be financed by the exercise of virement.

There are two qualifications to these Treasury powers of virement. First, in no circumstances can savings on any subhead be used to increase the provision under another subhead in the form of what is

[1] This French word for 'transfer' appears to have been adopted by the Treasury about 1900 and brought into public use very shortly afterwards.

known as a 'grant-in-aid'. A 'grant-in-aid' is exempt from the normal rule that unspent balances of Supply grants must be surrendered to the Exchequer at the end of the year; and it is frequently subject to special or less rigid audit than ordinary Supply grants. Parliament therefore requires to know precisely when, and in what amounts, it is voting money on such unusual conditions, and the services and amounts involved are set out separately in the Estimates. It would be inconsistent with all this for the Treasury to increase by virement the amount shown for a grant-in-aid in the original Estimate. Any increase in the amount must be submitted to Parliament in a Supplementary Estimate. Examples of grants-in-aid are: grants by way of subscriptions to scientific and similar societies; grants to museums or galleries for the purchase of pictures or *objets d'art*; certain grants to Colonial governments; grants to certain bodies carrying out public functions but with a measure of independence of government control, like the Arts Council and the British Council.

The second qualification to the Treasury's powers of virement is that they cannot be used to apply an excess of receipts under the appropriations-in-aid subhead to meet excesses under any of the expenditure subheads. Only Parliament can sanction such transfers and its authority must be obtained by means of a Supplementary Estimate. The need for this procedure follows from the fact that the amount of appropriations-in-aid which may be applied to meet expenditure under any Vote is fixed by the Appropriation Act.[1]

The exercise of virement by the Treasury takes a different form in the case of Defence Votes. We have already seen (page 224) that money appropriated to one Navy, Army or Air Vote is applicable, to certain conditions, to any other Vote of the same service. The procedure by which this can be done is as follows. The Appropriation Act of each session[1] authorizes the Treasury, so long as the aggregate sums appropriated by the Act to Navy, Army and Air services respectively are not exceeded, to sanction the temporary application of a surplus on any Vote for those services to meet a deficiency in receipts on any other Vote for the same service or to provide for excess expenditure (again, for the same service) which cannot, without detriment to the public service, be postponed until Parliament can provide for it in the ordinary course. This power is described as temporary because, where the Treasury uses it, Minutes stating what has been done must be laid before Parliament, and, after the accounts of the year have been audited, and if the Public Accounts Committee so recommends, resolutions of the House of Commons must

[1] See page 241.

confirm the application of surpluses to which the Treasury has temporarily agreed. These resolutions form the basis of statutory confirmation in the Appropriation Act of the second year after that in which the Treasury authority was given.

SUPPLEMENTARY ESTIMATES

Now we come to the case where a department desires to incur additional expenditure on some service or services which cannot be met by savings on other subheads (or, in the case of the Defence departments, on other Votes) and is therefore faced with an increase of the total sum which Parliament has granted. The Treasury has never been willing to agree that in such circumstances the department has an automatic right to ask Parliament to provide the necessary additional funds. The inauguration of some major new policy by the Government, or a falsification of the conditions assumed when the original Estimate for some essential service was drawn up, may make the presentation of a Supplementary Estimate unavoidable. But minor new services, however desirable, must whenever possible wait until the next financial year; and any excess expenditure on any existing service must, as far as possible, be met by reductions of expenditure elsewhere. Any easy or widespread recourse to Supplementary Estimates would clearly be liable to upset Budget forecasts and policies materially. The Treasury always therefore seeks to satisfy itself not only about the desirability of the additional expenditure proposed but about any claim that it is impossible to postpone it or finance it otherwise than by a new demand to Parliament. If the Treasury is satisfied on such points, it will agree to the presentation of a Supplementary Estimate requesting a stated addition, with suitable supporting detail, to the sum already granted by Parliament on the original Estimate. In essentials, a Supplementary Estimate takes the same form as the original Estimate: in particular, Part I shows the total net sum requested. It is a net sum because the Estimate will show not only the additional provision required under any existing subhead or possibly under a new subhead but also (subhead by subhead) any savings which can be made on the amounts provided in the original Estimate under other subheads. The net sum required is the difference between the total additions and the total savings. Supplementary Estimates which involve new services are generally presented in June or July and, if agreed to, the votes are appropriated with the votes on the original Estimates in the Summer Appropriation Act. Supplementary Estimates due to additional expenditure on existing services are generally not presented until February when the probable out-turn of the votes concerned will be more accurately known.

The Supplementary Estimate procedure is also used as a matter of convenience in three special cases not involving any additional cash requirement. The first case is where expenditure on some new service can be met out of savings on existing services but the new service is not within the ambit of Part I of the original Estimate and therefore not within the purposes to which the original Vote has been or will be appropriated in the Appropriation Act. In such cases the necessary Parliamentary authority is obtained by presenting a Supplementary Estimate for a token sum (£10) and with a suitably expanded Part I: against the cost of the new service under a new subhead there are shown savings on other subheads sufficient in total to cover that cost all but £10. The second case is where expenditure in excess of the total of the original Estimate and within its Part I can be met out of an excess of receipts over the amount shown as appropriated-in-aid in that Estimate. Only Parliament can sanction the used of additional receipts in this way and a token Supplementary Estimate is presented to secure authority for the new arrangements. Thirdly, even though no additional money is required it may be desired to make a material change in the conditions of a grant set out in the original estimate: as we have already seen,[1] it is proper to inform Parliament what is proposed and a token Supplementary Estimate is presented for the purpose.

EXCESS VOTES

The last method by which Supply grants can be adjusted is that of Excess Votes. It is, of course, the duty of every department to plan and watch its expenditure in such a way that it does not exceed the total amount voted by Parliament on the original Estimate and any Supplementary Estimates. If an excess seems probable it should make every effort to avoid it by postponements of expenditure in all practicable directions. It must not do this by delaying payments which are due and fully matured but by postponing new commitments. Even so there are usually one or two cases each year in which a department does overspend. This may be due to miscalculation; but very often it is due to some change of circumstances arising very near the end of the financial year when it is too late to present a Supplementary Estimate and secure the completion of all the necessary parliamentary Supply procedure on it. No action is taken about such an excess until the department completes its accounts and the exact amount of the excess is disclosed: that will be in the autumn

[1] Page 224.

or winter following the end of the financial year concerned. It is then brought to the notice of the Public Accounts Committee of the House of Commons by the Comptroller and Auditor-General in his Report on the accounts. The Committee examines the department on the causes of the excess and makes a first report to the House, in the following March if possible. If the Committee reports that it sees no objection to Parliament authorizing the excess expenditure, the Treasury presents to the House a 'Statement of Excesses' setting out for each of the cases the additional sum to be voted and the reason for it. This Statement is then referred to the Committee of Supply and subsequent procedure follows that for ordinary Supply grants.

IN COMMITTEE OF WAYS AND MEANS

Having noticed the different types of Supply grants which Parliament may be asked to make and the circumstances in which they arise, we come to the point where, at least twice a year, the procedure collects together the grants voted on all types of Estimates.

We have already seen that when Supply has been voted by the Committee of Supply and confirmed by the House itself on report from that Committee, the House, sitting in Committee of Ways and Means, is asked to sanction the issue from the Consolidated Fund of the sums necessary to put such votes at the disposal of the departments. (It is interesting to note that, whereas Supply votes are granted to the Crown in response to the Crown's demands through the Estimates, Ways and Means are granted—as appears from the confirmatory legislation—in the form of an authority to the Treasury as the department in charge of the Consolidated Fund.) The process of granting Ways and Means is now merely a formal matter both in the Committee and, on Report, in the House. Action takes the form in each case of a resolution 'That, towards making good the Supply granted to Her Majesty for the service of the year ending (or ended) March 31, 19—, the sum of £X be granted out of the Consolidated Fund of the United Kingdom'. Such resolutions are necessary, normally, on two occasions in the parliamentary session. Shortly before the end of March there must be two, or possibly three, resolutions to authorize the issue of funds necessary to cover respectively: Excess Votes (if any) for the previous financial year: Supplementary Votes for the current year; and the Civil Vote on Account and the selected Defence Votes for the year to begin on April 1st. Before the summer recess, normally in July, there will be one resolution covering the whole of the Supply granted for the current year, Civil and Defence, since the March resolutions. The

Ways and Means authorized by any of these resolutions is not ear-marked to Navy, Army, Air or Civil expenditure; it is available, until exhausted or appropriated by the Appropriation Act, for any Supply belonging to the year quoted in the resolution whether that Supply has been already granted or is granted later in the same Session. But Ways and Means granted in one session is not available to meet any Supply voted in any other session. Formal though the Ways and Means procedure may be, the House of Commons of any session is not prepared to loosen its purse-strings for any purposes other than those it has explicitly approved in that session.

CONSOLIDATED FUND ACTS AND APPROPRIATION ACTS

The passing of the Ways and Means resolutions in March and July authorizes the Government, on each occasion, to bring in the legislation which will give statutory effect to what the House of Commons has so far done by way of authorizing expenditure and providing the Government with the necessary funds. But the legislation of March differs from that of July. In March, the Bill is called a Consolidated Fund Bill and consists of three clauses as follows:

Clause 1 confirms to the Treasury the authority to issue out of the Consolidated Fund the sums necessary to cover Excess Votes (if any) for the preceding financial year and Supplementary Estimates for the current year just closing.

Clause 2 does the same for the Civil Vote on Account and the selected Defence Votes for the coming year.

Clause 3 gives the Treasury temporary powers—known as 'Ways and Means borrowing powers'—to borrow within the total amount in the first two clauses in anticipation of revenue. If the borrowing is by Treasury Bills the Bills must be paid off by the end of the current financial year; sums raised by other methods of borrowing must be repaid by the end of the quarter after that in which they are borrowed.[1]

This Bill does not include any appropriation clauses: these are reserved for later legislation, normally in July or early August. Since the Bill covers supplementary grants for the year just closing the time of its passage through Parliament needs careful watching. It must receive Royal Assent in time to allow such grants to be made available to departments by March 31st; and if Easter falls round about that time it may be necessary to secure Royal Assent two or three days earlier.

[1] Nowadays all 'Ways and Means' borrowing under this Clause and under Clause 2 of an Appropriation Bill is effected by Ways and Means Advances. All Treasury Bills are issued under other powers.

The summer legislation is introduced as the Consolidated Fund (Appropriation) Bill, although when it is passed its title becomes simply the Appropriation Act. Formally it consists of six clauses and three schedules and its provisions are as follows:

Clause 1 confirms to the Treasury the authority to issue out of the Consolidated Fund, towards making good the Supply granted for the current year, a total amount equal to the further Supply granted in the current session for the current financial year since the March Consolidated Fund Bill. (This total is the sum of (i) the balance of the Civil Votes after deducting the sum voted on account; (ii) the outstanding Navy, Army and Air Votes not granted in March; and (iii) any Supplementary grants voted to date since the original Estimates were presented.)

Clause 2 gives the Treasury temporary borrowing powers of the same type as those given by Clause 3 of the March Consolidated Fund Bill.

Clause 3 appropriates to the particular services for which sums have been voted in Supply the Ways and Means granted by the present Bill (Clause 1) and all preceding Consolidated Fund Bills of the current session. It does this by reference to two Schedules, A and B. Schedule A sets out the total Ways and Means for each financial year concerned—for excess votes in the year next but one preceding; for supplementary votes in the preceding year; and the Vote on Account and the balance of all other grants for the current year. Schedule B sets out, Vote by Vote, the sums granted during the current session under the above heads and the purposes of each Vote in the terms of Part I of the respective Estimates. The Clause also authorizes the application as appropriations-in-aid of receipts of specified amounts which are set out in a separate column against the respective Votes in Schedule B.

Clause 4 authorizes the Treasury to exercise the power of virement between Defence Votes which has already been described on page 236.

Clause 5 confirms such applications of surpluses to meet deficits as may have been temporarily sanctioned by the Treasury under powers given by the section corresponding to Clause 4 in the Appropriation Act of two years previously. The surpluses and deficits in question are set out in detail in Schedule C.

Clause 6 provides for the making of declarations (that is, life certificates) by all persons receiving half-pay or pensions out of moneys appropriated by the Bill.

Debate on this Bill must be confined to the conduct of those who receive or administer grants specified in the Bill. In practice the debates on the second or third reading are allotted to general subjects which the Opposition or groups of members on either side of the House wish to discuss. The Committee stage is usually only formal. On being sent to the House of Lords, an Appropriation Bill is endorsed with the Speaker's certificate that it is a 'Money Bill' within the meaning of the Parliament Act, 1911; and, on being passed by the House of Lords, it receives Royal Assent in a special form and before all other Bills then awaiting Royal Assent.

We have just described the normal situation in which there is one Consolidated Fund Bill in March and one Consolidated Fund (Appropriation) Bill just before the summer recess. Sometimes more than one of either of these Bills may be necessary. For example, early in the session before the March Bill is due to be introduced, some departments may require a large supplementary vote for a purpose which is too urgent to wait to be covered by the normal Consolidated Fund Bill. It may then be necessary to introduce and pass a special Bill to cover that requirement alone, in which case the normal Bill comes along later at its usual time and is called the Consolidated Fund (No. 2) Bill. Or—and this is more rare—when the parliamentary session extends into the autumn and supplementary votes have to be asked for in the autumn, after the passing of the summer Appropriation Act, it will be necessary to introduce and pass a second Appropriation Act to cover the autumn Supply.

THE CIVIL CONTINGENCIES FUND

Parliament has recognized that occasions will often arise when the Government will wish to incur expenditure on some service, old or new, which is too urgent to wait until the necessary Supplementary Estimate can be voted and funds provided in the course of the normal Supply procedure. It has therefore set up by statute the Civil Contingencies Fund with a permanent capital on which the Treasury can draw to make advances to departments. Starting from very small beginnings in the nineteenth century the capital has been increased from time to time, with an exceptionally large temporary increase just after the Second World War. The present (1958) position is that the capital of the Fund is limited to £75 millions or such lower figure as the Treasury may by order direct.[1] The objects for which advances can be made are laid down in the Miscellaneous Financial Provisions Act, 1946, Section 3 (1). Advances may be made in respect of urgent services in anticipation of the provision made or to be made by Parliament for those services becoming available; in

---

[1] Miscellaneous Financial Provisions Act, 1955, Section 1 (3). No such Treasury order has yet been made.

anticipation of the realization of receipts in connection with any service for which provision is so made or to be made; or to any Government Department for the provision of any necessary working cash balances in connection with any such services.[1] Sometimes a department's need, however urgent, is too large to be financed from the free balance of this Fund; and sometimes its need is to finance a new service which is of such a nature—novel or possibly controversial—that it is right to seek the specific approval of Parliament before any expenditure is incurred. But, subject to such cases, the Treasury can make advances out of the Fund to meet the urgent needs of departments. No expenditure, however, can be finally charged to the Fund so that when the Treasury does make such an advance the department must repay the Fund by getting a vote from Parliament either on a Supplementary Estimate in the same year or in its original Estimate for the following year. In either case the Estimate must bear a note to show the amount already advanced from the Fund.[2]

The Fund is also used to meet a variety of small payments which do not fall conveniently into existing Estimates and are too small to justify separate Estimates. In these cases the Fund is repaid in the following year by means of a special omnibus vote for 'Repayments to the Civil Contingencies Fund'. Parliament, through the Public Accounts Committee, watches with some care what use the Treasury makes of this Fund since it means that Parliament is in due course asked to give *ex post facto* approval to whatever the department concerned has done with the money advanced to it. For the same reason, whenever legislation has been proposed to alter the size of the Fund Parliament has expected a reasoned justification from Treasury Ministers of the new figure which they propose.

THE TREASURY CHEST FUND

Formerly, when departments had payments to make abroad, the necessary exchange business was transacted by the Treasury Chest Fund. This Fund, which was originally established in 1833, had a

[1] Although the Fund is called the *Civil* Contingencies Fund, the Act of 1946 does not confine its use to Civil departments. It has in fact been used to finance end-of-the-year working balances of the Defence departments.

[2] The Supplementary Estimates of any year normally show one or two examples of this procedure. Among the 1957–8 cases, £2,200,000 was advanced to the Home Office to enable it to finance the Anglo-Egyptian Resettlement Board, which was assisting British subjects who had had to leave Egypt; and £12,000 was advanced to the National Gallery to enable it to acquire a picture which was for sale.

capital of £700,000. No expenditure could be finally charged to it: it was essentially an agency, whose capital was kept intact. Exchange profits over any year were paid into the Exchequer and exchange losses made good by Supply Votes. In course of time the business came to be handled more and more by the department's own financial organizations and the Fund became less necessary. It was finally wound up at the end of March 1958 by the Finance Act, 1958, which transferred the then balance on the Fund to the Exchequer.

MAKING SUPPLY GRANTS AVAILABLE TO DEPARTMENTS

To complete this account of the Supply procedure, we must notice how and when the funds so granted are made available to the departments by whom they are intended to be spent. When Parliament grants Supply it is, of course, granting to the Executive the right to spend money lying in the Consolidated Fund which is the proceeds of taxation and other sources of Budget revenue. Once those revenues have become part of the Consolidated Fund—as they must do under the law—it is only by Parliament's authority that they can be withdrawn and spent. Even when Parliament has gone through the whole process of granting Supply and Ways and Means and appropriating them there are still statutory formalities to be completed. These are laid down in the Exchequer and Audit Departments Act, 1866. The Crown places the grants at the disposal of the Treasury by a Royal Order under the sign-manual and Section 14 of the Act provides for the issue of such an Order 'when any sum or sums of money shall have been granted to Her Majesty by resolution of the House of Commons or by an Act of Parliament', the Order being limited to the amount of the sums so voted or granted. But in order that the Treasury, having the grants at its disposal, may issue them out of the Consolidated Fund, it is necessary for it to receive a credit on the Exchequer Account at the Bank of England from the Comptroller and Auditor-General. The latter officer is, by Section 15 of the Act of 1866, allowed to grant such a credit 'when any Ways and Means shall have been granted by Parliament to make good the supplies granted to Her Majesty by any Act of Parliament or resolution of the House of Commons', but the total credits must not exceed the amount of Ways and Means so granted. Accordingly, as soon as the Treasury has received the Royal Order it applies to the Comptroller and Auditor-General for a credit at the Bank of England for the same amount. If he is satisfied that the application is in order the Comptroller and Auditor-General informs the Bank that he grants the credit and the Treasury is then in a position to make the necessary issues from the Exchequer Account. The credits given by the Comptroller and Auditor-General, it should be noted, are credits in respect of Ways and Means and are given in large lump sums within the totals authorized by the relevant Consolidated Fund Act or Appropriation Act. He is not concerned at all, at this stage, with the way in which the sums covered by the credits are distributed to the spending departments.

It will also be noted that Section 14 allows the Treasury to meet expenditure on a service as soon as the corresponding Supply Vote has been agreed to on report by *the House*, but by reason of Section 15 the necesssary isues can only be made out of Ways and Means already granted by *Parliament*, that is by an earlier Consolidated Fund Act or Appropriation Act. These provisions are of importance in deciding how soon the Treasury can make funds available for urgent services included in Supplementary Estimates. As we have seen, Ways and Means is not appropriated to individual votes in the March Consolidated Fund Bill; but the Ways and Means then granted in respect of any financial year are available to cover any Supply granted for that year in the same session as that in which the Bill was passed. These provisions are unlikely to be of help in connection with Supplementary Votes granted in March because no spare Ways and Means are then likely to be available in repect of the financial year just closing: urgent cases must then be dealt with, as we have already seen, by recourse to the Civil Contingencies Fund or to a special Consolidated Fund Bill. But July supplementaries are in a better position. The Ways and Means granted by a March Consolidated Fund Act includes cover for the Civil Vote on Account and certain Defence Votes in the coming financial year and is not appropriated to individual votes. It is sufficient to cover all Government expenditure up to about the middle of August and so includes some margin which could be used if necessary to begin spending on any service covered by the July Supplementaries. This the Treasury can do, by virtue of the Section 14 above, as soon as a Vote has been agreed to by the House and without waiting for the approaching Appropriation Act. Way and Means granted by the latter Act are appropriated to individual Votes and hence are not available to cover any Supplementary Votes granted later in the session.

Finally, the Treasury issues Supply Votes not direct to the spending departments but to the Paymaster-General, who is, in effect, the departments' banker.[1] He keeps an account at the Bank of England

---

[1] Originally a high officer of state, and now often a Minister with non-financial duties also, the Paymaster-General operates in these Exchequer matters through a deputy—the Assistant Paymaster-General—who is a permanent civil servant.

and, as and when departments need money, he applies to the Treasury for issues from the Exchequer to that account. From that account all departmental payments are met, the Paymaster-General keeping subsidiary accounts showing the amounts of the votes the departments are entitled to spend and the payments he has made for them out of those votes.

CHAPTER XII

Spending and Accounting

WHEN under the procedure described at the end of Chapter XI a department has available the grant which Parliament has voted for it, the spending of the grant and the accounting for it are the responsibility of the department and of it alone. Once Treasury sanction has been given for a service and Parliament has voted the money demanded for it in the relevant Estimate, the Treasury does not attempt to exercise any check on the day-to-day spending of it—except, of course, in any special case where the Treasury may have asked for periodical reports on the expenditure; and subject to the possibility, referred to in Chapter X, that in connection with subsequent years' Estimates the Treasury may raise a question about the continuation of any particular item of expenditure. As we shall see, the Treasury has functions in connection with the form and procedure of departmental accounting; but it has no responsibility for what goes into the accounts. Even when a department may have sought its advice on some point of doubt or difficulty, the final responsibility is that of the department.

The Act which governs the system of accounting for parliamentary grants is the Exchequer and Audit Departments Act, 1866, as amended by an Act of 1921 with a similar title. Section 22 provides that, on or before specified days, 'accounts of the appropriation of the several supply grants comprised in the Appropriation Act of each year shall be prepared by the several departments'. These are to be called the 'appropriation accounts'. It is also provided that 'the Treasury shall direct that the department charged with the expenditure of any vote under the authority of the Treasury shall prepare the appropriation account thereof'. But the section adds the very important proviso that 'the term "department", when used in this Act in connection with the duty of preparing the said appropriation accounts, shall be construed as including any public officer or officers to whom that duty may be assigned by the Treasury'.

THE 'ACCOUNTING OFFICER'

The Treasury (subject to the personal approval of the Prime Minister) exercises its powers under the last-mentioned proviso in the case of every vote account. For some time after the passing of the Act there was much discussion as to who should normally be the person to prepare and sign the account; but for the last thirty years or so the general rule—strongly supported by successive Public Accounts Committees—has been that the Permanent Head of the department— as distinct from the Ministerial Head—should do so. In this capacity he is called the 'Accounting Officer'.[1] The title itsef shows that his duties are much wider than those of a mere 'accountant', which usually denotes someone whose duties are of a technical character in connection with actual book-keeping and accountancy. Whenever the Treasury appoints a new Accounting Officer it sends him a very full statement of his responsibilities and, since the 'Accounting Officer' practice is so basic to our system of control of public expenditure and interesting in itself, it is worth while noting what the letter of appointment says. The Accounting Officer's responsibilities start with the fact that he 'signs the Appropriation Account and thereby makes himself responsible for its correctness'. This responsibility cannot be delegated to subordinate officers. Accounting Officers must of course satisfy themselves, by means of statements from their subordinates, as to the correctness and propriety of payments; but 'if they can show that they have not acted except on such statements, that they have not failed in a due exercise of their own common sense and administrative experience, and that in case of serious doubt and difficulty they have consulted the officers deputed by [the Treasury] for the purpose,[2] they will be considered to have discharged themselves of their responsibilities'. The letter points out that, whatever the internal organization of a department for safeguarding public funds, it should invariably include, without regard to personal considerations, independent and effective checks of cash balances in the hands of any officer.

An Accounting Officer's responsibilities go further. He must ensure that the funds entrusted to him are applied only for the purpose

[1] He is at the same time appointed 'Accounting Officer' for any other statutory funds for which his Department is responsible.

[2] These Treasury Officers, two in number, are the 'Treasury Officers of Accounts', of whom the senior is usually the Head of the Home Finance Division of the Treasury. Their duties, in short, are, firstly, to assist and advise Accounting Officers when called upon to do so, and, secondly, to advise the Staff of the Treasury itself on technical accounting questions and on all aspects of Parliament's control of expenditure.

intended by Parliament, and that specific Treasury sanction has been obtained for the expenditure when necessary; and he is answerable to the Public Accounts Committee of the House of Commons on such points. 'Any dereliction of duty in this respect may lead to a recommendation by the Public Accounts Committee that expenditure already incurred may be disallowed. If this should happen, the doctrine of personal accountability means in theory—and it has been know to happen in practice—that the Accounting Officer is liable, unless Parliament is prepared, at the request of the Treasury, to make good the deficiency by voting the money, to have to defray the expenditure from his own purse.' The possibility is recognized that the Accounting Officer may himself object to a given item of proposed expenditure as being irregular or improper but may be over-ruled by his Minister. In such a case he is required to set out his objection in writing, with the ground for it, and to make the payment only on a written instruction from his Minister over-ruling his objection. After making the payment he should inform the Treasury and send the papers to the Comptroller and Auditor-General. 'Provided that this procedure has been faithfully followed—but only on this condition—the Public Accounts Committee will no doubt acquit him of any personal responsibility for the expenditure.' (A proposed expenditure may not be irregular or improper and yet may be objected to by an Accounting Officer on grounds of efficiency or economy. He will then, in the normal course of his duties, state his views to his Minister and if he over-ruled he can quote the policy decision of the Minister in his defence before the Public Accounts Committee.)

The Treasury letter of appointment then goes to show how an Accounting Officer's responsibilities stretch wider than questions of regularity and propriety. Its words here are worth quoting in full because they put on record the importance of financial control in any administration and justify the policy of appointing the Permanent Head of a department as its Accounting Officer.

'The traditional duties are now, and for many years past have been, embraced in a much wider conception of an Accounting Officer's responsibilities, which springs from the basic conception underlying British Government financial procedure and organization. This is that due regard can never be paid to financial considerations if finance and administration are divorced and finance is kept separate from other factors which enter into policy decisions. Finance is thus regarded as an essential element in the consideration of all policy questions from the outset; and the administrative Head of the Department must make sure, as a prerequisite of efficient and economical administration, that financial considerations are taken into account at all stages by his Department in framing and reaching decisions of policy and in their execution. It is for this reason that it is the general rule that the Permanent Head of the Department is the Accounting Officer: the Accounting Officer must be prepared to answer for the efficient and economical conduct of the Department as a whole, and the only Officer who is in a position to do that is its Permanent Head.'

Finally, the letter points out that an Accounting Officer cannot carry out responsibilities of such a wide range unless he is supported by a sound organization which permits of proper delegation of duties. Special attention must be paid to the Finance and Establishment branches and the closest liaison between them must be encouraged. It has always been regarded as an important part of the Treasury's responsibility for the general control of expenditure that it should see that the organization of each department is such that the Accounting Officer can exercise the degree of control which his letter of appointment demands.

DEPARTMENTAL ORGANIZATIONS

The organization and functions of Finance Branches vary somewhat between departments, but broadly they are of two types. The first type is that of a branch of which the technical functions of keeping books and preparing accounts is but one par of its duties and which also has the equally important duty of giving advice on the financial aspects of proposals for expenditure put forward by administrative branches before they become the accepted policy of the department. In such cases the branch will be in charge of a Principal Finance Officer whose appointment or removal is, like that of the Permanent Secretary himself, reserved for the consent of the Prime Minister. He is graded among the most important Officers of the department, and is entitled and expected to put forward his views on all matters of finance to his Minister and his Accounting Officer before decisions are reached. It is also generally the practice that correspondence with the Treasury on the proposals—as when Treasury sanction for them is first being sought—should be carried on by the Finance Branch. In the second type of case finance and administration are so closely interwoven that a department prefers not to give such a right of independent criticism to the Finance Branch but formally to emphasize the duty of administrative branches themselves to weigh fully the financial aspects of any proposals before putting them forward. They would be given varying degrees of encouragement to consult the Finance Branch where the special experience of the latter might enable them to give useful advice on special points. The decision between these two types is the responsibility of the department concerned, though it would nearly always be a matter for discussion with the Treasury. Much may depend on the grading and calibre of the officers whom the department is prepared to appoint to the more senior posts in the Finance Branch. On the whole it would seem that the interests of financial control are likely to be better served by Finance Branches of the first type, which is, in fact, the one more widely adopted. But there need be little doubt that Accounting Officers generally are fully aware, as a result of their own and their predecessors' experiences in answering to Parliament for their departments' financial transactions, that the same close correlation of financial and administrative policies is expected of them whichever type of organization is chosen.

FORM OF APPROPRIATION ACCOUNTS

We must now return to the Appropriation Accounts. Section 23 of the Act of 1866 provides that 'the Treasury may prescribe the manner in which each department of the public service shall keep its accounts'. The manner will naturally vary between one service and another; but the above provision has important public and parliamentary consequences. The form of a department's accounts is necessarily determined in its general outline by the form of the Estimate on which Parliament grants the money involved: so the Act implies an anterior responsibility on the part of the Treasury for the form of the Estimate. An Estimate is in fact, to quote the Treasury of long ago, 'the precursor and foundation of the account'. For any given service, therefore, the Estimate, the department's internal accounts, and the Appropriation Account follow broadly the same lines; but the internal accounts will, of course, be in very much more detail. It may be added that, though not legally necessary, it has long been the practice of the Treasury to submit important changes in the form of Estimates and accounts to the Public Accounts Committee and the Select Committee on Estimates before approving them; but this might not be done if a change resulted from major policy decisions affecting the responsibilities of particular Ministers, which might in turn affect the form of the Estimates. An Appropriation Account follows closely Part II of the relevant Estimate and compares subhead by subhead the provision in the Estimate and the actual outturn of the year. To the Account are appended a number of notes on various points. The most important of these notes are the explanations of the reasons for variations between provisions in the Estimate and the out-turn; and short descriptions of cases of extra-statutory or unusual payments, especially where the Treasury has stipulated, in giving sanction for a transaction, that it shall be 'noted in the Appropriation Account'.

A specimen Appropriation Account is given in Appendix I: it is that of the Vote of the National Maritime Museum, 1956–7, which may be compared with the Estimate for the same service in Appendix H.

DATES OF SUBMISSION

The Act of 1866 lays down the dates, after the end of the financial year, by which departments must submit their Appropriation Accounts. The dates vary as between the Defence and Civil departments and are as follows:

	Defence	Civil
(a) Departments must send their accounts to the Comptroller and Auditor-General by	December 31st	November 30th[1]
(b) The Comptroller and Auditor-General must send them on to the Treasury, with his Report on them, by	January 31st	January 15th
(c) The Treasury must submit the Accounts and Reports to the House of Commons by	March 15th	January 31st

The periods allowed to departments, after the end of the financial year, in which to send in their accounts may seem rather long; but allowances must be made in some cases for the great volume of transactions involved and for the fact that they take place at distant stations overseas. There are also two other special factors. First, it is the normal rule that if an order issued by a department is not presented for payment within three months it must be cancelled; and that if a claim for payment is subsequently made, a new order must be issued which is charged to the account for the year in which it is issued. This effectively delays the preparation of the Appropriation Accounts for the latter year by the waiting period of three months. Secondly, accounts are kept open for a period to complete adjustments with sub-accountants and on agency transactions. The general

[1] In fact the Civil and Revenue Departments now aim to render their Appropriation Accounts to the Comptroller and Auditor-General by September 30th. (See the *Epitome of the Reports from the Committees of Public Accounts, 1938–50*, page 164.)

rule is that the Civil and Revenue Departments close their accounts by July 31st.

The relatively short time allowed above for the preparation of the Comptroller and Auditor-General's Reports is due to the fact that, as we shall see below, a large part of his audit of the accounts and of the supporting vouchers will have taken place during the financial year itself. Finally, it will be noted that the Treasury can retain the Defence accounts for a much longer period than in the case of the Civil accounts before submitting them to the House of Commons. The reason for this is that time must be allowed for the process of authorizing the transfer of surpluses to meet deficits which has already been described on page 236.

CASH BASIS OF THE ACCOUNTS

Just as the Estimates provide only for the payments expected to be made during the financial year,[1] so the Appropriation Accounts show only the sums which have actually been paid during the year, including any orders for payment issued by March 31st but not cashed by then. The Accounts are thus made up on a strictly cash basis. (The only exception to this rule are of a technical character but still relate to matters arising during the financial year in question—such as transactions with other departments and the correction of improper charges. If such cases arise after March 31st and before the Account is closed, charges can be 'thrown back' into the Accounts.) In discussing the cash basis of the Estimates we noted its advantages as compared with the 'income-and-expenditure' basis of commercial accounts. Here, in connection with the Appropriation Accounts, we must note that the cash basis might appear to open up theoretical possibilities of abuses. Suppose that a department has been over-committing itself and realizes, towards the end of the year, that it has been spending faster than its vote would justify and that it cannot meet all its due liabilities by the end of the year and keep within its vote. On the cash basis, it could postpone payment of them until the following year and charge the payments to the Accounts for that year. Or suppose, on the other hand, that towards the end of the current year the department is faced with the prospects of an unspent balance of its vote. It could anticipate payments not due until the following year by meeting them in the current year, and count on having a free margin to that extent in the vote which it is seeking for the following year. Both the Treasury and the Public Accounts Committee are alive to these possibilities and have for long insisted on a

[1] See page 225.

strict rule that a liability must be met in the year in which it has matured and is due, and that a department must not postpone payment of a liability which has matured, even for the purpose of avoiding an excess on its vote. This rule prevents a department from exploiting either of the possibilities mentioned above. If it involves the department in expenditure in excess of its vote for any year, it will have to make a full confession when it applies for an Excess Vote under the procedure described on page 238. Checks on whether departments are keeping to the straight and narrow path in these matters are provided to some extent by three administrative arrangements. First, in some of the larger departments the books are examined by officers of the Comptroller and the Auditor-General who sit in the departments and conduct their audit currently. Secondly, departments to which that does not apply are normally required to render monthly accounts of their transactions, and supporting vouchers, to the Comptroller and Auditor-General. Thirdly, every department is required each year by Treasury Circular to provide the Treasury by the end of December with an estimate of the probable out-turn of its vote account, showing subhead by subhead how far the provision made in the Estimate is expected to be underspent or exceeded. The primary object of this is to inform the Treasury of the possibilities of supplementaries being required before the end of March; but the information automatically throws up any cases where departments are obviously spending faster than their votes justify. These departmental estimates, in cases where savings are foreseen, also give guidance to the Treasury on the extent to which Supply issues from the Exchequer can be restricted.

DIFFERENCES BETWEEN EXCHEQUER ISSUES AND DEPARTMENTAL EXPENDITURE

The size and complexity of the services carried out by many departments, however, make it very difficult, if not impossible, for their central accounting branches to estimate accurately the exact total of the liabilities they are going to have to meet by the end of the financial year and to charge in their Appropriate Accounts, or to gauge precisely when all the orders issued during the year, and especially near the end of the year, are going to be presented for payment. This applies particularly to departments which have large payments to make abroad through branches which are fed from time to time by 'imprests' in round sums. A department does the best it can in such circumstances in estimating, for instance, how much cash it should draw from the Exchequer against the vote. If it is pretty certain that it will underspend its vote the issues from the Exchequer will be restricted accordingly; otherwise the whole vote is issued to the Paymaster-General by March 31st and is thus available to the department. But when the department comes to make up its Appropriation Account it may find that the total charge to the Account differs not only from the parliamentary vote but also from the amount issued to it from the Exchequer. There are two consequences of this. First, if we add up the totals of all the Appropriation Accounts we shall find that the total Supply expenditure of the year as shown in those Accounts is different from the total Supply issues shown in the Exchequer Accounts for the year. Secondly, there must be some final settlement, between each department and Parliament and the Exchequer, of the differences which have arisen.

That settlement takes one or other of the following forms. We can assume that the department has not charged more to its Account than the parliamentary vote, because that would mean that it must seek an Excess Vote, the procedure for which we have already described. The other possibilities and the corresponding settlements can best be explained by concrete examples.

		£
(a)	Parliamentary Vote	500,000
	Exchequer Issues	500,000
	Appropriation Account	475,000

In this case the department has saved £25,000 of its vote; but it has drawn the whole vote from the Exchequer and has therefore drawn £25,000 more than it has spent. Unless the vote has come to an end, the department is not required to repay the £25,000 from the Exchequer in cash but the Treasury recovers the over-issue by reducing by that figure the amount it would otherwise issue in respect of the same vote during the year following the year of the Account.

		£
(b)	Parliamentary Vote	500,000
	Exchequer Issues	460,000
	Appropriation Account	475,000

In this case the department has again saved £25,000 of its vote; but it actually cut down its drawings by £40,000 and has therefore spent £15,000 more than it drew. (It would finance this excess temporarily by using other moneys in its hands.) It forgoes the right to draw more than· £475,000 and the Treasury makes the issues up to that figure by issuing a further £15,000 from the Exchequer. This further issue is, of course, made in the year following that of the Account, but it is covered by the original Parliamentary authority to make issues for the year of the Account. In this case the Exchequer issues in respect of the Supply granted for the following year are unaffected.

		£
(c)	Parliamentary Vote	500,000
	Exchequer Issues	460,000
	Appropriation Account	450,000

In this case the department has saved £50,000 of its vote and has underspent the Exchequer Issues by £10,000. It has already under-drawn its vote by £40,000 and the recovery of the £10,000 is effected by the same method as under (a).

In all these cases the department in effect 'surrenders' out of its vote the amount by which its spending falls below the vote. Under (a) the whole surrender takes the form of (in effect) surrendering cash to the Exchequer by abatement of issues in the following year. Under (b) it takes the form of an under-drawing in the year of account partly corrected by an adjusting issue in the following year. Under (c) it takes the form partly of an under-drawing in the year of account and partly of an abatement of issues in the following year.

These settlements naturally take many months to achieve and at any given point of time the position of the Supply grants for the current and preceding year is complex. The Treasury renders an account of it in a table which is published in the annual 'Finance Accounts' and which gives figures not only of Supply grants and issues in respect of them for the current year but also of the grants for previous years which have been surrendered or been drawn upon —under arrangements like those at (a), (b) and (c) above—during the year. The table for 1957–8 is reproduced in summary form, with comments, in Appendix J. The whole subject is somewhat recondite and probably receives very little, if any, public attention; but it is part and parcel of the detailed control exercised by Parliament over the funds which, year by year, it puts at the disposal of the Government.

We have seen above that all the actual Supply issues made out of the Exchequer during any year do not necessarily represent issues in respect of that year's Supply. It might be thought that this must falsify the Exchequer figures for the year on which the Chancellor bases his Budget. In theory that is so; but in fact any such falsification is, almost always, relatively very small. Thus in 1957–8 the total Supply grants for the year were £4,554 million and the total of the actual Exchequer issues were £4,473 million. Of the latter figure further issues in respect of 1956–7 accounted for only £3 million; and only £27 million was withheld to recover over-issues in 1956–7.

CHAPTER XIII

Audit

WE must now follow the Appropriation Accounts on the first stage of their journey from the departments to the House of Commons, which is their ultimate destination. That stage ends, as we have seen, with the Comptroller and Auditor-General. This high officer is independent of any Government department and, indeed, of the Government altogether. He is essentially Parliament's watch-dog in all that pertains to the collection, handling and disposal of public moneys. He is appointed by the Crown but can only be removed from office on an address from the two Houses of Parliament. His salary is borne directly on the Consolidated Fund, so he can continue in office independently of any effect which current relations between the Government and the House of Commons may have on annual Supply grants. His full title is 'Comptroller-General of the Receipt and Issue of Her Majesty's Exchequer and Auditor-General of Public Accounts'. In the dual role which his title displays he has a very ancient official ancestry. As Comptroller-General on the Exchequer side he succeeds to functions which can be traced back to the fourteenth century; and as Auditor-General to offices existing in the sixteenth century. The two roles continued, in fact, to be performed by separate officers until they were amalgamated in the present office by the Exchequer and Audit Departments Act, 1866, which lays down his status and duties.

We have already noticed the functions of the Comptroller-General in relation to issues from the Exchequer.[1] Those functions, important as they are, occupy little of his time and attention: most of his duties arise in his capacity as Auditor-General. To carry out his duties, he has a staff of over 500 whose salaries and expenses, unlike the salary of their chief, are provided on an annual Supply vote. They are divided into eight divisions each of which, under a Director of Audit, deals with the accounts of a group of departments; together with a central administrative division which also performs the Exchequer functions of the Comptroller-General.

[1] See Introductory Note, page 13; and page 244.

I

OBJECTIVES OF THE AUDIT OF APPROPRIATION ACCOUNTS

Under the Exchequer and Audit Department Act, 1921—which amended the Act of 1866 in certain particulars—the Auditor-General, in his examination of the Appropriation Accounts 'on behalf of the House of Commons', is required to satisfy himself 'that the money expended has been applied to the purpose or purposes for which the grants made by Parliament were intended to provide and that the expenditure conforms to the authority which governs it'. These words define the primary purpose of the audit and set the seal on Parliament's determination to control the way in which the Government of the day disposes of the grants made to it. A word should be added about the phrase 'intended to provide'. We have already seen that although the details in Parts II and III of an Estimate are not strictly binding on a department, Parliament is entitled to assume, when voting a grant, that the subheads in Part II indicate more or less how the spending of the total vote is going to be divided between different purposes, and that the details in Part III, if any, indicate the terms and conditions on which money will be spent under any given subhead. Parliament consequently expects that when the accounts of the actual expenditure are available, the Auditor-General will draw their attention to any material divergence between the department's express intention and its actual performance.

As regards the words 'the authority which governs it' in the statute quoted above, this may include not only any Act of Parliament relating to the expenditure in question—which Act will, in fact, usually be quoted in the Estimate—but also any conditions which the Treasury may have laid down in originally sanctioning the expenditure but which were not referred to in the Estimate. Indeed the Act of 1921 expressly provides that if in any given case the Auditor-General carries out only a partial audit (see below), the Treasury can nevertheless ask him to audit any particular field in greater detail—the object of this being to enable the Treasury, through the Auditor-General, to check whether the expenditure conforms to the precise terms of the relevant Treasury authority. (The Act of 1866 contained an explicit reference to Treasury authority; but in the Act of 1921 this was subsumed into the wider phrase—'the authority which governs it'.) This is, by the way, a significant sidelight on the close relations which must always exist between the Treasury and the Auditor-General. The functions of both of them are keystones in the whole structure of national finance. Although the Auditor-General is, in carrying out his primary functions, as independent of the

Treasury as of any other department, mutual support and harmonious relations between the two are essential. The Auditor-General can help the Treasury by reporting whether its instructions and intentions have been carried out; the Treasury can support the Auditor-General by exercising its financial control over departments in accordance with the rules which have been laid down over the years by his principals, the House of Commons. Sometimes, of course, there are genuine differences of opinion between the two. The Treasury may have to press the interest of the Executive against the Auditor-General who is bound equally to press the interest of Parliament. In such a case the matter will, as we shall see below, have to be argued out before the Public Accounts Committee.

EXTENT OF THE AUDIT

Under the Act of 1866 the Auditor-General was required to ascertain whether payments charged to a parliamentary grant were supported by voucher or proof of payment and this normally involved a detailed examination of 100 per cent of the payments. (There was an important statutory exemption for the Army and Navy in view of the great volume of payments at home and abroad and the existence of a system of internal audit within the War Office and Admiralty.) But with the increasing size and complexity of departmental transactions it became clear after the First World War that a complete, detailed audit could not be carried out except at a cost, in terms of money and manpower, which would be prohibitive. The amending Act of 1921 therefore allowed him, in his discretion, and having regard to the character of the departmental examination, to accept charges to the accounts without requiring supporting evidence, provided—a very important proviso—that he was satisfied that the vouchers had previously been examined and certified as correct within the department concerned. This change enabled the Auditor-General to substitute a partial or 'test' audit for a complete one throughout the whole field and that is the position today—subject, as we have seen, to cases where the Treasury asks him to carry out a complete audit in any particular part of the field. The extent of this test audit is extremely flexible: it varies from department to department according to circumstances, such as the degree of internal check and the state of the individual accounts. The Act of 1921 required the Auditor-General to report to the House of Commons any important change in the extent or character of any examination he makes; and he does this through the Public Accounts Committee. (Thus, there were discussions with the Committee about the extent of his audit during the Second World War when the field of audit greatly increased and he was at the same time asked to release staff for service in the Forces and for other important work. The proportion of transaction actually examined was, for those reasons, temporarily reduced.)[1]

NATURE OF THE AUDIT

The Auditor-General's audit, through his staff, is a continuous one. He does not wait for departments to send in a whole year's accounts and vouchers all at once: he could never do that and keep to his parliamentary time-table. It is possible for the audit to be continuous because, for the most part, it is conducted on the spot. Only a small part of the examining staff is situated at the headquarters of the Exchequer and Audit Department: most of it sits in groups in the various Government Departments in London and in the provinces. Some of them travel periodically about the country on the test of Revenue accounts as well as in connection with other accounts such as those of the Navy, Army, Pensions and National Insurance. Some go abroad to overseas stations: indeed, some are stationed abroad, as in Singapore, from which the staff examine accounts in the Far East. The auditors are, in fact, as ubiquitous as the spenders, and their work is thereby greatly facilitated. Under statute they have free access to all departmental books of account and to any documents relating to transactions they are examining. They can raise questions about any transaction within a very short time after it is carried out. If they are not satisfied about it from the books and documents they have seen, they address a formal 'audit query' to the department and on the nature of the reply to the query depends how far they report the matter to their superiors and, if the matter is serious enough, through them to the Auditor-General himself. The latter will then decide whether to report it to Parliament.

So far, we have been thinking of the original and primary purpose of the audit—to ascertain whether a department's financial transactions are covered by proper parliamentary and Treasury authority and whether they are correctly charged to the Account for the year in question. This aspect of the audit is generally known as the 'appropriation audit'. But the Auditor-General is now expected and encouraged to cast his net wider. When his staff have seen the books and other documents relating to a transaction, including discussions which have taken place about it within the spending department,

[1] In some cases the Auditor-General is authorized to accept other auditors' certificates.

they may be quite satisfied about its formal regularity and yet they may come to the conclusion that it was not handled very prudently or expeditiously or even that it definitely involved waste and inefficiency. If so, it is their duty to report it upwards and the Auditor-General may decide that their criticisms are sufficiently well-founded, and the matter is important enough in size or in principle, for him to report it to Parliament. This part of his audit—although, like all audits, it means barring the stable door after the horse has gone—is probably the most potent force making for prudent financial administration. What one department is publicly pilloried for today, all other departments will try to avoid tomorrow.

The Auditor-General is, in fact, openly critical of departments, on the score of either irregularity or imprudence or waste, in only a small proportion of the matters which he includes in his Report. Most of his comments are severely factual and he leaves the facts to speak for themselves. In some cases they are merely for the information of Parliament, whose interest he invites in some novel or unusual item or in the financial results of some service which is being wound up or in the financial outcome of recent legislation. In others he is no doubt pretty confident that the Public Accounts Committee will want to probe the reasons for many of the facts he has quoted and that the Committee will have its own comments to make on the transactions concerned.

If the Auditor-General considers that there is anything irregular or improper in any of the charges to an Appropriation Account he will not only report it but will also qualify his certificate to the Account. That is, instead of saying simply that 'In my opinion the above Account is correct' he will say that 'in my opinion the above Account is correct *subject to the observations in my Report*'. But in cases where he merely reports facts, or even when he comments on apparent waste or imprudence, he does not qualify his certificate in any way. It is interesting to note that, although he had a lot to report on the Civil Appropriation Accounts for 1955–6, he did not qualify his certificate in any single case. But his certificates to the Accounts of all three Defence Services were qualified, the reason in each case being the incompleteness of the department's records and checks of stores.

Before we leave these duties of the Auditor-General we must raise the age-old question: *Sed quis custodiet ipsos custodes?* Who is to guard the guards themselves? The Exchequer and Audit Department spends about half a million pounds a year, nearly all on salaries, for which the Comptroller and Auditor-General is himself the Accounting Officer. The answer to the question is that his Appropriation

Account—which has to be submitted to the House of Commons like all other such Accounts—is audited by one of the Joint Permanent Secretaries to the Treasury. (The same Treasury official is, incidentally, the auditor of the Queen's Civil List and so describes himself when certifying the Appropriation Account of the Exchequer and Audit Department.)

THE PUBLIC ACCOUNTS COMMITTEE

When the Comptroller and Auditor-General has completed his Report and certified the Appropriation Accounts—and in any case by January 15th for the Civil Accounts and January 31st for the Defence Accounts—he sends them, as we have seen, to the Treasury. The Treasury's only action on them at this stage is to submit the Accounts and the Report to the House of Commons which orders them to be printed and referred to the Public Accounts Committee.

We have already seen that the Committee of Supply, being a Committee of the whole House, is not really an effective instrument for ensuring either regularity or economy in public expenditure. Any assembly of six hundred members which tried to achieve such control would obviously set itself an impossible task. The first half of the nineteenth century therefore saw several efforts by the House to achieve stricter financial control by other means. These efforts culminated in a proposal by a committee of 1857—the proposal being suggested to them by the then Chancellor of the Exchequer—that there should be a Select Committee of Public Accounts on a regular sessional basis. Such a Committee was first appointed in 1861 and the following year the Standing Order of the House made permanent provision for it. Standing Order No. 90 now provides that 'there shall be a select committee, to be designated the Committee of Public Accounts, for the examination of the accounts showing the appropriation of the sums granted by Parliament to meet the public expenditure, and of such other accounts laid before Parliament as the committee may think fit, to consist of not more than fifteen members, who shall be nominated at the commencement of every session . . .' By a convention of long standing, the Chairman of the Committee is a member of the Opposition and has often, but by no means always, been an ex-Financial Secretary to the Treasury. The Financial Secretary to the Treasury in office for the time being is always a member of the Committee. This enables him to attend on special occasions when it is useful, in the Committee's or the Treasury's interest, to have a Treasury Minister there; but as a general rule he does not attend and this leaves the Committee a freer hand to pursue their inquiries unembarrassed by the presence of a Minister who might afterwards be closely involved in the Treasury's comments and actions on the Committee's Reports.

The Committee's work is based primarily on the Appropriation Accounts and the Comptroller and Auditor-General's Report thereon.[1] It meets normally on two afternoons a week from December to July when the House is sitting. The Comptroller and Auditor-General and officials of the Treasury[2] are present as witnesses when the Committee meets to examine an account. The Committee could not hope to take evidence on the details of every Appropriation Account every year. The larger Accounts are examined each year, but the smaller ones are taken at longer intervals. When the Committee is examining a particular Account the Accounting Officer for that Account is the principal witness and he is allowed to bring with him such of his subordinates as he thinks fit. Unlike the Select Committee on Estimates, the Committee does not normally call non-official witnesses, although it has power to do so. The Accounting Officer is first examined on any paragraph in the Comptroller and Auditor-General's Report which relates to his Account and this generally involves the most searching part of his examination. After that, members of the Committee can and do ask questions about any item in the Account itself; and he is a lucky Accounting Officer who does not have to satisfy some member of the Committee who has made a special study of, or has a special interest in, some part of his Accounts. The ordeal of an Accounting Officer of a large department is by no means a light one. He is readily allowed to refer to his subordinates for detailed facts; but woe betide him if he gives the Committee the least impression that he has not a full grasp of the broad financial controls required by the policies he is administering.

After taking evidence and deliberating thereon in private, the Committee publishes its Reports. Its First Report each session is on the Accounts which show Excess Votes to be required.[3] Its Second Report normally deals with the virement which the Treasury has temporarily authorized between the votes of the Defence Services.[4] Its subsequent Report or Reports deal with all the other points which it wishes to raise on the Appropriation Accounts. These subsequent Reports will for the most part consist of the Committee's views on

---

[1] The 'other accounts' they are free to examine are of great variety, but they do not attempt to examine all these in detail.

[2] Including one or both of the Treasury Officers of Accounts: see page 248, note 2.

[3] See page 238.

[4] See page 236.

matters raised in the Comptroller and Auditor-General's Report. The Committee may criticize the financial administration of a department in this or that respect, and may propose alterations of practices where they consider this to be necessary to avoid the repetition of the occurrences which have called for criticism. It is then the duty of the Treasury to consider the Committee's Reports. It sets out its views in a Treasury Minute and issues any necessary consequential instructions to departments. The above Minute is communicated to the Committee in the year following that in which the Report was made, and the Committee is thus enabled to see how far measures have been taken to give effect to its recommendations. Occasionally, the Treasury does not see eye to eye with the Committee on some questions. In that event it says so, and gives its reasons, in the Minute, and the Treasury and the department concerned will be examined by the Committee again. This further examination may or may not lead to a reconciliation of views or at least to a compromise, temporary or permanent. If no such agreement is reached, it is understood that the Treasury will arrange to bring the question before the House of Commons in a form that will place before the House unreservedly the arguments on both sides: the ultimate decision then rests with Parliament. We have already noticed that Reports from the Public Accounts Committee may be discussed on an 'allotted' Supply Day, and this affords an opportunity, if it is desired, for discussion of any such persistent difference of opinion.[1]

It is mainly through the work of the Public Accounts Committee over the last hundred years that there has been built up in public departments the code of financial practice that we know today. Lapses there may well be from year to year, though they concern but a tiny fraction of the whole field of public expenditure. The code itself need not fear comparison with either governmental or commercial standards anywhere in the world.[2]

[1] There has been no case of a discussion in the House of any such persistent difference of opinion. But on October 7, 1942, the House debated a special Report from the Committee on questions arising out of certain contracts for war supplies.

[2] Those who wish to pursue the work of the Committee in greater detail and see the types of questions raised, and principles laid down, by the Committee should refer to the 'Epitome of the Reports from the Committees of Public Accounts, 1857–1937, and of the Treasury Minutes thereon' (HC 154 of 1937–8), and the continuation volume for 1938–50 (HC 155 of 1952), supplemented, of course, by the Reports and Minutes for later years.

AUDIT OF OTHER ACCOUNTS RELATED TO THE
APPROPRIATION ACCOUNTS

It is convenient to refer here to certain other accounts which have
to be submitted for audit by the Comptroller and Auditor-General
and some of which are closely related to the Appropriation Accounts.
The Public Accounts Committee is free to examine all the accounts
mentioned in the rest of this chapter.

First, *Stock or Store Accounts* have to be kept in all cases where
(to quote the Act of 1921) 'in the opinion of the Treasury, the receipt,
expenditure, sale, transfer or delivery of any securities, stamps, provisions or stores the property of Her Majesty in any Government
department is of sufficient amount or character to require the keeping
of such accounts'. It is also provided that 'the Comptroller and
Auditor-General shall, on behalf of the House of Commons, examine
any such accounts so required to be kept in order to ascertain that
adequate regulations have been made for control and stocktaking,
and that the regulations are duly enforced, and that any requirements
of the Treasury have been complied with'. The need for such accounts,
for adequate control and for regular stocktaking is obvious for two
reasons. It would be odd if, when the most exact arrangements had
been made for the control and audit of expenditure of public
funds, no steps, or inadequate steps, were taken to control and audit
the stores (or other valuable assets) into which any part of those
funds had been converted. Again, if a department has stocks of stores
on hand on April 1st and runs them down during the financial year,
that is tantamount to increasing, by its own decision, the amount
which Parliament has voted for the services run by the department
during the year. The latter point is, of course, a matter of degree; but
there clearly should be some machinery for informing the House of
Commons if a department has supplemented its vote to any significant degree in such a way. It was, however, some time after the Act
of 1866 before departments were obliged to keep stock or store
accounts. The practice started in 1890 with the Navy and Army,
which required large amounts of stores in their dockyards, ordnance
factories and manufacturing establishments; it was extended after
the passing of the Act of 1921 to all departments where stores are
purchased and held of more than trivial value. Mere accounts of
stores are of little value unless checked by periodical stcoktakings
and it is an essential part of current practice that the stocktakings
shall be carried out by departmental officials other than those who
actually keep the stores and the accounts of them. Stocktaking in any
department is the responsibility of the department itself. But the

Auditor-General is concerned to see that adequate arrangements for it exist and are carried out; and if he is not satisfied on this he has power to call on the departments to carry out the stocktaking in the presence of his officers. He always includes in his Report on the Civil Appropriation Accounts a paragraph to the affect that test examinations of the store and stock accounts have been carried out and he is usually in a position to add 'with generally satisfactory results'; he reserves any comments on individual cases for the paragraphs of his Report which deal with the Appropriation Accounts concerned. Stock and store accounts are not published; but departments append to their respective Appropriation Accounts lists of losses or deficiencies of stores with a short note for such reasons as can be given for them. The store accounts of the Defence departments, owing to their very size, loom much larger and generally call for special comment, whether critical or not. After the Second World War, for instance, inventories of stores were greatly increased as a result of wartime accumulations, and there were manpower difficulties in coping with them, so the process of settling down to peacetime procedure was bound to take a long time. Also where military operations have to be conducted in peacetime—as in Malaya—accidents are bound to happen to store accounts, apart from the difficulty of maintaining them in such circumstances. Nevertheless, except in the smallest cases, the Defence departments, like the Civil departments, append details of their losses of stores to their Appropriation Accounts.

Next come what are known as *Trading Accounts*. In the course of the duties which have been given to them, a number of departments carry out services which are in the nature of trading or manufacturing operations. They are often similar in general character to operations carried out by ordinary business undertakings and, between the two world wars, there was a demand inside and outside Parliament for means of judging the financial results of these departmental activities by ordinary commerical standards. The Appropriation Accounts do not afford such means partly because they are purely cash accounts and partly because their form is not designed for the purpose. As cash accounts they are concerned only with the actual cash required from the Exchequer during the year, whether for capital expenditure on stocks of commodities or for current expenses like wages and salaries. Their form does not enable a complete picture to be given of a department's trading operations since that department's own vote does not cover 'allied services'[1] like accommodation and stationery and also since it makes no provision, for example, for the payment of interest on capital provided by the Exchequer or for

[1] See page 226.

setting aside sums for depreciation. So special forms of account, called 'Trading Accounts', were devised and made obligatory on the departments concerned. The Act of 1921 provided that 'there shall be prepared in each financial year, in such form and by such Government departments as the Treasury may from time to time direct or approve, statements of account showing the income and expenditure of any shipbuilding, manufacturing, trading, or commercial services conducted by the department, together with such balance sheets and statements of profit and loss and particulars of costs as the Treasury may require'. Such accounts are to be examined by the Comptroller and Auditor-General and 'in his examination he shall have regard to any programme of works, shipbuilding or manufacture which may have been laid before Parliament'. The trading accounts must normally be prepared and submitted by the same dates as the corresponding Appropriation Accounts except that rather more time is allowed for the Royal Ordnance Factories' accounts and the Navy Expense and Manufacturing accounts. There is also an arrangement that certain Civil departments (Food, Supply and Trade) shall submit their trading accounts to the Comptroller and Auditor-General by August 31st (instead of November 30th) after the year to which they relate, on the understanding that certain figures may be estimates rather than actual out-turn when that is unlikely to affect the accounts materially.

Every year a volume of 'Trading Accounts and Balance Sheets' is submitted to the House of Commons and published as a House of Commons Paper. This volume covers a great variety of services, including the trading services of the Ministry of Agriculture, Fisheries and Food by which it implements some of the Agricultural Price guarantees and the Welfare Food Schemes; the credit-insurance and other schemes of the Export Credits Guarantee Department; the Forestry Commission; the Royal Mint; the Stationery Office; the Royal Ordnance Factories; and some of the Board of Trade's trading operations in raw materials. The form of a trading account will naturally vary according to the service concerned and the reader who wishes to pursue the matter in detail should study the accounts themselves and the explanatory Foreword which precedes each group of accounts. Normally the trading account proper will include on the one side all actual outgoings and 'notional' charges for insurance (at commercial rates), depreciation (on commercial principles) and services provided free by other Government departments (like accommodation and stationery); and on the other side the proceeds of sales (or, where appropriate, the value at full cost of goods delivered to other departments) and any other receipts. The account is on an 'income and expenditure' basis and not on a cash basis: that is, it includes for any year income earned irrespective of when it is received and expenditure incurred irrespective of when it is paid. The balance on this account is carried forward to a profit-and-loss account, in which (apart from any other appropriate items) is made a notional charge for interest on funds which the Exchequer has provided and which are still outstanding. On Exchequer advances which have been used for capital expenditure the rate charged is in line with the yield in the market of longer-term Government securities. On advances used for working capital the rate is kept in line with the rate charged by the banks on the Government-guaranteed overdrafts of the nationalized industries. (At present this is the same as Bank Rate.) Finally, there is normally a Balance Sheet showing outstanding liabilities (including Exchequer advances, sundry creditors and balance of profit-and-loss) against assets (including fixed assets and stocks and other current assets). Most departments' forewords give a reconciliation between the out-turn of their trading accounts and the relevant parliamentary votes for the year of account, or, in some cases, between that out-turn and the net receipts shown in the Appropriation Account. The details of this reconciliation will vary from case to case; but broadly it must take account first of the notional charges for insurance, depreciation, allied services and interest, and, secondly, of any reductions of stocks—none of which are reflected in the Appropriation Accounts.

The Trading Accounts and related Balance Sheets are audited by the Auditor-General and certified by him, and he makes a report on anything in them which he thinks requires notice in the same way as he does for the Appropriation Accounts. One difference, however, is worth attention. Whereas his certificate to an Appropriation Account states that 'in my opinion the above Account is correct', his certificate to a set of Trading Accounts states that 'in my opinion these Accounts and Balance Sheet are properly drawn up so as to exhibit a true and fair view of the transactions and state of affairs of the services to which they relate'. The difference between the two certificates is not surprising in view of the notional and estimated character of some of the entries in the Trading Accounts.

Two other important sets of accounts are published separately. One is the volume of *Commercial Accounts* of the Post Office, which have already been described in Chapter IV (page 98). The other is the volume of *Navy Dockyard and Production Accounts*.[1] These latter

---

[1] Unlike the trading accounts referred to earlier, these Navy accounts do not include a balance sheet. They are more in the nature of a summary of cost accounts.

accounts comprise an account of Dockyard and contract production and supply and of other Dockyard services, and production accounts for Naval Establishments other than Dockyards, such as the RN Torpedo Factory. The Dockyard account covers not only ship-building and ship-repairing but also the activities of the Dockyards as naval bases and storage and distribution centres for the Fleet. To facilitate the control of expenditure the latter is (with some relatively small exceptions) costed under a uniform procedure at all the main Dockyards and recorded under three main headings—direct labour, direct materials and overhead expenses, the last-named being dis-tributed as on-cost on labour and materials and as service charges. No charge is made for interest but otherwise all items of expense (in-cluding maintenance and depreciation) are included. The production accounts for the non-Dockyard Establishments are drawn up on much the same basis as the Civil Trading Accounts, that is, they include all overhead expenses and depreciation.

AUDIT OF REVENUE AND MISCELLANEOUS OTHER ACCOUNTS

The residue of the accounts which are audited by the Auditor-General is a very mixed collection indeed, stretching over the activi-ties of a large number of departments and containing some very large accounts and some very small. They can be grouped as follows :

(*a*) The accounts of the receipt of revenue by the Customs and Excise and the Inland Revenue departments and by the Post Office. We have already noticed the audit of these in Chapter IV. It is re-quired to be made under Section 2 (1) of the Exchequer and Audit Departments Act, 1921.

(*b*) Certain individual statutes which set up Accounts or Funds required that they should be audited by the Auditor-General. In some cases the statutes add that the audit should be conducted in the manner provided for the examination of Appropriation Accounts; in others the scope of the audit is left to his discretion. There are about twenty of these accounts ranging from the Consolidated Fund downwards.

(*c*) Other individual statutes required audit of the accounts con-cerned by the Auditor-General but said that the audits should be carried out in such manner as the Treasury might direct. Having regard to the discretion given to the Auditor-General by the Act of 1921 as to the extent of his examination of the Appropriation Accounts the Treasury has agreed that he shall have the same dis-cretion in examining the accounts concerned under this paragraph.

There are about twelve of them, including the Local Loans Fund and the National Insurance Funds.

(d) The Act of 1921, Section 3 (1), provided that the Auditor-General should 'examine, if so required by the Treasury and in accordance with any regulations made by the Treasury in that behalf, the accounts of all principal accountants and any other accounts whether relating directly to the receipt or expenditure of public funds or not, which the Treasury may, by Minute to be laid before Parliament, direct'.

As to 'principal accountants', these are defined in Section 2 of the Act of 1866 to mean 'those who receive issues directly from the accounts of Her Majesty's Exchequer at the Banks of England and Ireland respectively'. In fact they are: the Paymaster-General (who receives Supply Issues for distribution to the spending departments); the Commissioners of Customs and Excise and the Commissioners of Inland Revenue (who receive Supply Issues, for their departmental expenses, direct under the special arrangement described on pages 86 and 70 instead of through the Paymaster-General); the Postmaster-General (for the same reason as the other two Revenue departments); the Chief Cashiers of the Bank of England and the Bank of Ireland (who receive direct the dividends and principal moneys of the National Debt and also the remuneration earned by those Banks for the management of the debt and other services); and the National Debt Commissioners (who receive various repayments of debt and Sinking Fund moneys).

The 'other accounts' which the Treasury have required to be audited by the Auditor-General under the above Section 3 (1) are again a very mixed bag. There are about forty of them, mostly small but including, for example, the Bankruptcy Estates and Companies Liquidation accounts of the Board of Trade and the accounts of the Official Trustees of Charitable Funds. Generally the Treasury has agreed that in these cases also the Auditor-General shall have the same discretion as to the extent of his audit that he has in regard to Appropriation Accounts.

As required by Section 3 (1) above, the Treasury presented a Minute to Parliament in 1923 which reviewed the various classes of accounts which were required to be audited by the Auditor-General and contained lists of the accounts concerned.[1] The lists of accounts then given have been replaced by lists in later Minutes. In Appendix K below is given a complete list of all accounts presented to Parliament and it may be assumed that, except where it is there stated to the

[1] Reproduced in the *Epitome of the Reports from the Committee of Public Accounts, 1857–1937*, page 672.

contrary, all of them are audited by the Auditor-General under one or other of the arrangements described above. In addition to the cases in Appendix K there are many accounts which are audited by the Auditor-General but which are not of sufficient public interest to be published at all.

THE END OF THE ROAD

In these last four chapters we have traced the Supply procedure from the time when the Government asks for money from Parliament until the money has been spent and accounted for, the accounts audited and the results examined on Parliament's behalf by the Public Accounts Committee. The incidents of long procedural history of any given Supply vote can vary greatly from case to case; but the details given in Appendix L may be of interest as showing what happened, over a period of more than three years, on one particular voted granted in 1954.

EPILOGUE

MOST of the chapters of this book, particularly the later ones, have necessarily been crowded with detail about the contents of the Budget or about the administrative and parliamentary processes by which it is prepared, launched and implemented. Before taking leave of the subject we ought briefly to look back over this detail and note the two main features which emerge from it all.

First, there is the acknowledged supremacy of Parliament. In a parliamentary democracy that supremacy is effective at all times and in every department of State activities. But in financial matter it is especially significant by reason of the long and sometimes bitter struggles which Parliament had to wage in this field and which have led to it insist on having control of financial detail to a degree which it is prepared to forgo in some other, purely administrative, directions. Such detailed control, as we have seen, extends not only to the imposition and administration of taxation but also—by an exact system of rules prescribed over a hundred years of parliamentary examination and criticism—to the accounting for, and audit of, the spending of the revenue so raised.

At the same time, such detailed parliamentary control has never, in practice, hindered the flexibility which is an inherent feature of the Budgetary system as a whole and by which the system can adopt itself to ever-changing current needs and conditions. It stood the test of adaptibility through the financial upheaval of the Second World War. More recently it has been a major arm of the forces deployed against inflation; and it would no doubt have a large part to play in any battle against deflation. Public policy has never been frustrated by Parliament's control, or indeed by any rigidity or limitations in the system. It is as well that it should be so; because, as we saw early in our survey, the annual Budget must now be looked on as an occasion not only for taking stock of the national economy as a whole but also for directing Budget policy in whatever courses current economic, as well as social, conditions require.

That has been brought about over the last twenty years by a notable change in informed public opinion, both inside and outside Government circles; and the result has been one of the most far-reaching reorientations of our financial system since the Exchequer was first established. It may be that, over the future, yet other conceptions of Budget policy will find favour, requiring new methods of financial technique to carry them out. We can be confident that, if that happens, the system can, subject to any necessary authorities from Parliament, offer or devise whatever means of Budgetary action the Government of the day requires to have at hand.

APPENDICES

———————

APPENDIX A

National Income and Expenditure
1957

INCOME

	£ million
Income from employment	12,920
Income from self-employment	1,782
Gross trading profits of companies	3,193
Gross trading surpluses of public corporations	324
Gross profits of other public enterprises	129
Rent	855
Residual error	—141
Total domestic income before providing for depreciation and stock appreciation	19,062
Less stock appreciation	—100
Gross domestic product	18,962
Net income from abroad	226
National income and depreciation	19,188

EXPENDITURE

	£ million
Consumers' expenditure	14,045
Public authorities' current expenditure on goods and services	3,558
Gross fixed capital formation at home	3,388
Value of physical increase in stocks and work in progress	425
Total domestic expenditure	21,416
Exports and income received from abroad	5,269
Less imports and income paid abroad	—4,955
Less taxes on expenditure	—2,953
Subsidies	411
Gross national expenditure	19,188

APPENDIX B

Personal Income and Expenditure
1957

INCOME BEFORE TAX	£ million	EXPENDITURE	£ million
Wages and salaries	11,760	Consumers' expenditure:	
Pay in cash and kind of the Forces	401	Food	4,563
Employers' contributions:		Drink and tobacco	1,909
National Insurance	309	Housing, fuel and light	1,807
Other[1]	450	Durable household goods	1,007
		Clothing	1,382
Total income from employment	12,920	Private motoring and cycling	548
		Other goods and services	2,829
Professional persons[2]	261		
Farmers[2]	435	Total	14,045
Other sole traders and partnerships[2]	1,086		
		Remittances abroad	36
Total income from self-employment[2]	1,782	Taxes on income	1,630
		National Insurance contributions	657
Rent, dividends and interest	2,031		
National Insurance benefits and other current grants from public authorities	1,254	Total current expenditure	16,368
		Balance: Saving[2]	1,619
Total personal income	17,987	Total	17,987

[1] E.g. to pension schemes.
[2] Before providing for depreciation and stock appreciation.

APPENDIX C

Customs and Excise Duties

ESTIMATED YIELD IN 1958–9

Head of Duty	Customs (£'000)	Excise (£'000)	Total (£'000)
Spirits	30,000	110,000	140,000
Beer	16,000	249,000	265,000
Wine	19,440	—	19,440
British Wine	—	3,310	3,310
Tea	300	—	300
Cocoa	1,300	—	1,300
Coffee and Chicory	300	—	300
Sugar, Molasses, Glucose and Saccharin	8,000	4,500	12,500
Dried Fruits[1]	400	—	400
Tobacco	740,000[2]	—	740,000
Matches and Mechanical Lighters	4,500	8,250	12,750
Silk and Artificial Silk[1]	6,000	—	6,000
Oil, etc.	336,000	9,000	345,000
Entertainments	—	12,000	12,000
Television	—	9,000	9,000
Liquor Licences: Duties	—	5,600	5,600
Monopoly Values	—	850	850
Other Licences	—	250	250
Playing Cards	—	50	50
Key Industry Duty[1]	3,500	—	3,500
Duties under Import Duties Act, 1932[1]	82,000	—	82,000
Ottawa Duties[1]	5,500	—	5,500
Beef and Veal[1]	3,500	—	3,500
Purchase Tax	—	490,000	490,000
Betting	—	30,250	30,250
Other Articles and Deposits	200	250	450
	1,256,940	932,310	2,189,250

[1] These heads of duty will lapse after December 31, 1958. The estimates for 1958–9 include the estimated yield from similar duties which may be imposed under the Import Duties Act, 1958. (See Chapter IV, page 90.)

[2] Includes a negligible amount of Excise.

APPENDIX D

The National Insurance Fund

1. The finances of the National Insurance system do not form part of the Budget: they are contained in a separate Fund, the National Insurance Fund, into which all contributions are paid and out of which all claims for benefits are met.[1]

2. The regular income of the National Insurance Fund arises mainly from two sources—contributions (including an Exchequer supplement thereto) and income from investments. To these may be added a third source, an additional Exchequer contribution in respect of any excess of current expenditure over current income.

(*a*) The weekly rates of contributions are laid down from time to time by statute. Different rates are prescribed for employed persons, self-employed persons and non-employed persons. Within each category there are different rates for men, women and juveniles; and in respect of employed persons there are separate and different contributions from the insured person and from his or her employer. In respect of all insured persons the Exchequer pays into the Fund a 'supplement' which, for employed persons, is one-sixth of the combined National Insurance contributions of employers and employees, and, for self-employed and non-employed persons, is one-third of their National Insurance contributions. These Exchequer supplements are provided on the annual Supply Vote for National Insurance and Family Allowances (Class X, Vote 4).

(*b*) The Investment income of the Fund arises from two sources—first the investment of the balance of the Fund itself; and secondly, the investment of the National Insurance (Reserve) Fund. The former balance, which at March 31, 1958, was about £350 million, is invested in short- and medium-length Government securities. The Reserve Fund, standing at over £1,100 million, is the result of the accumulation of surpluses on the Funds and Accounts connected with earlier State schemes of insurance for unemployment, health and pensions and on the National Insurance Fund. This Reserve Fund is invested in British Government securities and securities guaranteed by the British Government, with some Local Authority stocks and mortgages. The investments include a fair proportion of long-dated securities. Under statute, the annual income from these investments is paid into the National Insurance Fund; but any other payment

---

[1] For the purposes of the Blue Book on National Income and Expenditure, the National Insurance system is treated statistically as part of the Central Government sector. The reasons for this are that the system—unlike private insurance arrangements—is under the control of the Central Government, which is responsible for paying benefits, and that contributions are compulsory. But the latter are shown separately from taxes in the Blue Book, and benefits are shown separately from other Government expenditure.

out of the Reserve Fund requires to be authorized by a resolution of the House of Commons.

(c) The additional Exchequer contribution is governed by the National Insurance Act, 1954. This Act provides that during the period of five years beginning April 1, 1955, the Exchequer may contribute such sums as the Treasury may determine not exceeding £325 million in all, and for any subsequent period such sums as Parliament might later determine. The first Exchequer contribution under this authority was included in the Estimates for 1958-9 at a figure of £14 million, the Government Actuary's estimate of the excess of current expenditure over current income in that year. (See paragraph 7 below.) This contribution also was provided in the Estimate for National Insurance and Family Allowances.

3. On the expenditure side of the Fund the main items are:

(a) Benefit: of the total of £622 million in 1956-7, the main items were retirement pensions (£448 million), sickness benefit (£97 million), widows' benefit (£38 million), unemployment benefit (£21 million) and maternity benefit (£15 million). As regards the figure for retirement pensions, see paragraph 7 below.

(b) Administration expenses of the National Insurance Scheme: these are repaid to the Government departments which incur the expenses and which appropriate the payments from the Fund in aid of the Votes bearing the expenses. These include not only the expenses of the Ministry of Pensions and National Insurance but also those, for example, of the Post Office (for selling stamps and paying pensions at the counters), the Ministry of Labour (in connection with unemployment) and the Ministry of Works (for accommodation).

(c) Occasionally, when the balance of the Fund is judged to be more than adequate for current purposes part of the balance may be transferred to the Reserve Fund.

4. As an illustration of the form which the annual accounts take, the following is a shortened version of the account for 1956-7. The figures will vary a good deal from year to year—partly because rates of contributions and benefits are changed from time to time and partly because of the growing cost of pensions referred to in paragraph 7 below.

YEAR ENDED MARCH 31, 1957

RECEIPTS		£ million	PAYMENTS		£ million
Balance at April 1, 1956 ..		318	Benefits	..	622
Contributions:			National Health Service[1]	..	41
Employers and insured			Administration Expenses	..	31
persons	588		Miscellaneous	..	6
Exchequer supplement ..	96				
		684			
Income from Investments:					
National Insurance Fund	9				
Reserve Fund	40				
		49	Balance March 31, 1957	..	351
		1,051			1,051

[2] See note at end of this Appendix.

5. Accounts of the National Insurance Fund and of the Reserve Fund are presented annually and published as a House of Commons Paper, together with a report thereon by the Comptroller and Auditor-General. These accounts should be referred to for further details. Much further statistical and other information about benefits and contributions is contained in the annual Report of the Ministry of Pensions and National Insurance, which is presented to Parliament as a Command Paper.

6. The original, and still the principal, statute governing the National Insurance scheme—the National Insurance Act, 1946—provided in Section 39 for periodical reviews of the scheme by the Government Actuary. At the end of each five years from the commencement of the scheme, he is to report to the Treasury on the financial condition of the National Insurance Fund and on the adequacy or otherwise of contributions to support the benefits payable out of the Fund and its other liabilities. He is also to make annual interim reports except in years covered by quinquennial reviews or when the Treasury dispense with such annual report: in fact he has always made such Interim Reports. All reports made to the Treasury are published as House of Commons Papers. The Government Actuary also normally makes a report to the Minister on the financial provisions of any Bill laid before Parliament to alter the rates of contributions or benefits and such a report is presented to Parliament as a Command Paper and at the same time as the Bill.[1]

7. Such reports by the Government Actuary are invaluable guides to the current and prospective states of the finances of the scheme from time to time. Thus the report on the National Insurance Bill (now Act), 1957, not only examined in detail the effects of the increase of benefits and contributions proposed in the Bill but gave a table showing the estimated income and expenditure of the Fund, after allowing for those increases, at intervals up to 1979–80. This table shows that, whereas in 1958–9 there would be only a relatively small excess of expenditure over income, estimated at £14 million, this excess was expected to grow to £322 million by 1969–70 and to £475 million by 1979–80. Of the increase to the latter date, no less than £356 million is attributed to a rise of nearly 60 per cent in the cost of retirement pensions and is due to the expected growth in the number of pensioners. (For the purpose of the estimates it is assumed that the level of unemployment will rise from $1\frac{1}{2}$ per cent to 4 per cent for 1961–2 and later years; but, as the resulting increase in the estimated total of unemployment benefit is only some £60 million, this conservative assumption does not significantly alter the main trend of the figures.) Under the present law, and in the absence of any new remedial measures, the whole of the growing annual deficit will, in so far as it is not met by running down the balance on the Fund, have to be met by the Exchequer.

8. A final point of general interest in the National Insurance scheme is Section 3 of the Act of 1946, which allows the rates of contribution to be

---

[1] The first Quinquennial Review was completed in November 1954 (House of Commons Paper No. 1 of 1954–5). The latest report on a Bill was that on the National Insurance Bill, 1957 (Cmnd 294).

varied in order to help to stabilize the level of employment. Since one of the factors affecting the demand for goods and services, and therefore the level of employment, is the volume of personal income available for spending, an increase or reduction of weekly insurance contributions might be expected to reduce or increase that demand.[1]

Under the Act the variation of contributions may be made by Treasury order; but the contributions of employers and employed persons must be increased or reduced by the same amount; and the Exchequer supplement can only be varied if those contributions are varied and the proportion which it bears to them must not be altered. A draft order must be approved by resolution of each House of Parliament; and when it is laid before Parliament it must be accompanied by a report from the Government Actuary on the estimated consequences to the National Insurance Fund.

In fact, the power to vary contributions in this manner has never been used. Since 1946 other measures have been adopted to check excessive demand; and, having regard to the steady increase in contributions to provide for increases in benefits, it is doubtful whether it would ever have been politically practicable to increase them further on general economic grounds. There have rarely, if ever, been times when it would have been justifiable to reduce contributions on such grounds. Moreover, when there is a deficit on the Fund, a reduction of contributions would merely relieve the contributors at the expense of the taxpayers and it would be doubtful, to say the least, how far there would be any net reflationary effect.

9. Structurally similar to the general National Insurance Scheme, but on a much smaller scale financially, is the *Industrial Injuries Scheme*. This provides benefit for disablement or death arising out of industrial accidents and for certain diseases due to the nature of employment. Contributions are paid by the insured person and his employer, in combination with contributions under the main National Insurance scheme, and the Exchequer pays a corresponding supplement; but Industrial Injuries benefits are not dependent on any contribution conditions. There is a separate Industrial Injuries Fund. In 1956–7 total contributions amounted to £42 million, Exchequer supplement to £8 million, and benefit to £34 million. The Government Actuary reported on the scheme in his report on the National Insurance Bill, 1957 (Cmnd 294) and advised that the increases of contributions then proposed should be sufficient to ensure the solvency of the Industrial Injuries Fund. The annual accounts of the Fund are included in the same House of Commons Paper as those of the National Insurance Fund.

NOTE ON THE NATIONAL HEALTH SERVICE

The cost of the National Health Service is not, and never has been, borne on the National Insurance Fund. It is borne wholly on annual Supply Votes. Until September 1957, a sum towards the cost of the Service was

[1] Such a scheme for varying contributions was first officially proposed in the White Paper on Employment Policy published in 1944 (Cmnd 6527), paragraphs 69–71.

included in the contributions paid by, or in respect of, insured persons, and this was paid in the first instance into the National Insurance Fund; it was then paid out of the Fund to the Government Departments (the Ministry of Health and the Department of Health for Scotland) which incurred the costs of the National Health Service and which appropriated the receipts in aid of the Votes bearing the costs. The National Health Service Contributions Act, 1957, provided for a separate National Health Service contribution, although as a matter of convenience this is still collected with the National Insurance contribution by means of a single stamp. The receipts from the separate National Health Service contribution are paid over to the Health Departments. No Exchequer supplement is payable in respect of these contributions since the Exchequer, through the two Supply Votes, is already bearing the whole net cost of the National Health Service.

APPENDIX E

Loans to Local Authorities for Capital Expenditure

PUBLISHED STATISTICS

THE Budget estimates contained in the annual Financial Statement include the amount expected to be issued below-the-line for loans to Local Authorities during the coming year, as well as the amount actually issued during the year just ended. These issues are made in the first instance to the Local Loans Fund, from which, in turn, issues are made to the Public Works Loan Board for loan by the latter to the Local Authorities. An account of the Local Loans Fund is presented annually to Parliament. The Public Works Loan Board publishes an annual Report on its operations which normally includes details of the purposes for which, and the terms on which, loans have been made. This Report also contains figures showing the proportion of the total loans raised by Local Authorities which has been raised from the Board—although, since these figures depend on information to be obtained from all Local Authorities through other channels, they are not so up to date as the figures for the Board's own operations.

The Paper *Local Government Financial Statistics* gives figures for loans as a whole, but is not concerned to distinguish between loans from the Central Government and those from other sources. A Research Study, *Local Authority Borrowing*, published by the Institute of Municipal Treasurers and Accountants in January 1957, gives useful statistical and other information in this field.

The annual Blue Books on National Income and Expenditure (but not the Preliminary Estimates) contain a capital account for Local Authorities, showing borrowing from the Central Government separately, but this is on the basis of calendar, not financial, years.

LOCAL AUTHORITIES' CAPITAL RESOURCES GENERALLY

Over 90 per cent of Local Authorities' capital expenditure is financed by borrowing from one source or another. To finance the small balance not borrowed, they use in varying degrees a number of alternatives. First, the expenditure can be charged to revenue subject to the approval of the appropriate Central Government departments, who, however, mostly put limits to the amounts which can be so charged. This form of finance has never been extensively used and its use is decreasing. It seems unlikely to increase while the growing pressure of expenditure on the rates continues. Secondly, in the case of a very few services, the Central Government makes capital grants out of Budget revenue; but the Central Government itself is also unlikely to charge its annual revenue with any significant increase in such grants. Thirdly, many Local Authorities have capital funds derived from capital receipts of one kind or another and, possibly, limited transfers from revenue; and these funds may be used either to lend money to their spending departments or to make outright capital grants to them. Others have repairs and renewal funds of limited amounts, provided by contributions from revenue, which can be used for capital expenditure.

As to borrowing, certain rules and practices apply whatever the source of the borrowing. Subject to certain exceptions, a Local Authority desiring to borrow to finance capital expenditure on a given service must get a 'loan sanction' from the appropriate Government Department.[1] (The Ministry of Housing and Local Government is responsible for the issue of all but a very small amount of these sanctions.) The exceptions to the general rule are the London County Council, whose capital budget is directly controlled by Parliament; the Corporation of the City of London, whose borrowing powers are controlled by Local Acts of Parliament; and specified borrowing by Local Authorities who have obtained powers for particular purposes under Local Acts. This sanction is not concerned with the source of borrowing, but it lays down a maximum period for the borrowing—for example, eighty years for land purchase, sixty years for houses, twenty years for roads. The loan may then be raised specifically for the service involved and ear-marked for that service throughout; or, in some cases, where Local Authorities operate loan pools or consolidated loan funds, the expenditure may be met from those sources, which are then replenished by money borrowed for amounts and periods not directly related to particular sanctions. In the latter case, however, the total borrowings at any time outstanding must conform in amounts and periods to the total sanctions available. Further, the sanctioned periods are maxima and there is nothing to prevent a Local Authority from borrowing for shorter periods. This involves, of course, an increase in the annual loan charges payable out of revenue and a Local Authority must consider not only whether it is prepared to meet such increased charges but also whether they will be within the limits of capital charges to revenue authorized by the appropriate Central Government departments.

As will be seen below, a large, though varying, proportion of Local Authorities' total borrowing take place from the Central Government. But before describing the latter we must notice what the other sources of borrowing are. First, the larger Authorities—mainly the County Boroughs and Boroughs—raise money from time to time by issues of stock which is negotiable on the Stock Exchange and the terms of which are generally slightly more favourable to the subscribers than the terms on which the Central Government itself could borrow. Stock may be issued to the public in the ordinary way or, within limits, placed privately. Secondly, a great many Local Authorities raise money by mortgage loans. Before the Second World War a lot of money was raised by this means from local investors with small sums available who were unaccustomed to dealing on the Stock Exchange and liked to invest their money, for quite short periods,

---

[1] It must also get the consent of the Treasury under the Control of Borrowing Orders. Arrangements are made to co-ordinate the examination of applications and the issues of approvals by the sanctioning department and the Treasury.

over the counter at the local Town Hall. For a number of reasons this form of local investment is not now so widespread. On the other hand, Local Authorities have, to an increasing extent, turned to the money market, where they have been able to issue mortgages for larger sums and longer periods to financial institutions, commercial and industrial superannuation funds and Trustee Savings Banks. These two kinds of borrowings—stock issues and mortgages—account for most of the borrowing from sources other than the Central Government. A third and less important source consists of the internal funds of the Authorities— mainly their superannuation funds, but also including reserve funds, sinking funds and others.

LOANS THROUGH THE PUBLIC WORKS LOAN BOARD

Loans from the Central Government to Local Authorities are made through the Public Works Loan Board. This Board is an independent, statutory body of twelve unpaid Commissioners, several of whom have in the past had first-hand experience of Local Authority finance and others of whom have had general financial experience. Their powers derived originally from the Public Works Loans Act, 1875,[1] and their duties are broadly to consider applications by Local Authorities and, where loans are made, to collect the repayments. The funds so lent are now made available to the Board from the Local Loans Fund, which will be described later. Under the Act of 1875 the total amounts to be lent are restricted to the amounts authorized from time to time by Public Works Loans Act, which Parliament has been asked to pass at broadly annual intervals. The amounts laid down in such Acts are based on estimates of the amounts likely to be borrowed from the Central Government having regard on the one hand to current policies governing capital expenditure by Local Authorities on the various public services involved and on the other hand to current policies governing the lending of money through the Public Works Loan Board.

Prior to the Second World War, loans through the Board, except for certain specified purposes, were confined to the smaller authorities—those with a total rateable value not exceeding £200,000—and the larger Authorities were expected to finance their capital programmes by borrowing from other sources. During the war special arrangements were made, with which we need not concern ourselves. A major change took place after the war. In order to co-ordinate the borrowing demands of the Local Authorities and the Central Government's own borrowings, in what seemed likely to be a difficult market, the Local Authorities Loans Act, 1945, which operated from August 1, 1945, compelled all Local Authorities to borrow only from the Public Works Loan Board. Exceptions were

---

[1] Prior to 1875, Exchequer loans for public works—which began to be made about the end of the eighteenth century—were made first by the Treasury, then through Exchequer Loan Commissioners, and later through the National Debt Commissioners.

allowed for borrowing from internal sources and for borrowing up to limited amounts by mortgages and bonds. This policy, superimposed on the post-war increase in capital expenditure, naturally led to a considerable increase in the loans approved by the Board—as distinct from the amounts actually advanced—from £294 million in 1946–7 to £573 million in 1952–3. By the end of 1952, however, the Government judged that conditions in the stock and money markets had settled down sufficiently to enable freedom of borrowing to be restored to Local Authorities and, as from January 1, 1953, the obligation on them to borrow from the Public Works Loan Board was allowed to lapse. Thenceforward they were free to choose their sources of capital finance, and the total of approvals by the Board decreased. The amounts to be found by the Exchequer to finance the Local Loans Fund continued, however, on a high level and, in the original Budget for 1955–6, represented more than half the net charge below-the-line which had to be met from borrowing or the Budget surplus. As a means or reducing this call on the Exchequer, a new kind of limitation was imposed on Local Authorities' borrowings from the Public Works Loan Board. On October 26, 1955, the Chancellor of the Exchequer announced[1] that he had asked the Board, before it granted any advances in future, to put all applications on inquiry as to their ability to raise the finance on their own credit, either in the stock market or in the mortgage market. Up-to-date figures are not available to isolate the effect of this limitation from the decline, which set in shortly afterwards, in Local Authorities' programmes of capital expenditure; but the limitations must clearly have been an important contributory factor in reducing the Exchequer loans from £331 million in 1955–6 to the Budget estimate of £65 million for 1958–9.

The result of these changes in policy has been that in recent years the proportion of the total loans raised by Local Authorities which represents loans raised through the Public Works Loan Board has varied appreciably. From 1947–8 to 1952–3 the proportion varied between 75 and 85 per cent; for 1953–4, 1954–5 and 1955–6 it was 55, 69 and 61 per cent respectively; later figures are not available. But, whatever that proportion has been, the bulk of the Exchequer loans—something of the order of three-quarters—has always been made for housing purposes.

THE ROLE OF THE PUBLIC WORKS LOAN BOARD

In the past, questions have often been raised whether it was really necessary that Local Authorities wishing to borrow from the Central Government should have to submit their applications to the Board for a further scrutiny in addition to their application for a 'loan sanction' by the Government Department concerned with the purpose of the borrowing. Only very rarely indeed would the Board challenge the necessity for, or the wisdom of, borrowing which had received that sanction: in such in-stances the Board might, for example, suggest that, in the light of its

[1] In the House of Commons: *Hansard*, Col. 215.

financial resources, an Authority might be over-borrowing. Rare as such cases may have been, there is still a good general case for saying that where the Exchequer is advancing such large sums it should have some special agency to which it can look to ensure that, from a financial point of view, applications for, and grants of, such advances are strictly in order. The policies governing Exchequer loans to Local Authorities may be changed at any time and may be of a kind—as in 1955—which cannot be left to the non-financial departments to administer. It was fortunate that in 1955 the improvization of new machinery was not necessary and that the Board was then at hand to implement the new policy. It is now perhaps the Board's most important function to satisfy themselves that applicants for loans cannot borrow in the market.

INTEREST RATES

Loans granted by the Public Works Loan Board must be repaid either by the annuity method (that is, equal annual amounts combining interest and principal) or by equal annual instalments of principal with interest on the amounts outstanding. Much the greater part of the loans is, in fact, repaid by annuities. The Board is precluded by the terms of the Public Works Loans Act, 1875 (Section 11), from making 'maturity' loans, that is, loans repayable wholly on some fixed future dates. The reason for this is that either of the two methods of repayment allowed provide the Exchequer with a steady source of receipts which help to finance new loans.

The rates of interest charged on the loans vary according to the periods of the loans: that is, normally there may be different rates according as the loans are for not more than five years, for more than five years but not more than fifteen years or for more than fifteen years. (The rates do not in any way purport to reflect the 'credit-worthiness' of a Local Authority.) When, in 1945, Local Authorities were compelled to borrow from the Public Works Loan Board, they were assured that the Board's rates would reflect the rates at which the Central Government itself would expect to borrow in the market for comparable periods. This rule was not followed exactly, day by day, but lending rates were altered, broadly, whenever market rates showed that an appreciable change in Government credit had been established one way or the other. The rule itself, however, was altered in 1955. When the Chancellor of the Exchequer announced the new policy of requiring Local Authorities to borrow, if they were able to do so, in the stock or mortgage market, he also announced that in future an authority which made its case for borrowing from the Public Works Loan Board would pay a rate reflecting, not the Central Government's credit, but the credit of authorities of good standing in the market for loans of comparable periods. There was obvious justification for this change, since it was ilogical that if a Local Authority borrowed on the market it should pay a rate of interest based on its own credit whereas if the same Authority borrowed from the Board it paid a rate based on the Central Government's credit.

K

THE LOCAL LOANS FUND

The Local Loans Fund, from which the Public Works Loan Board draws the funds which it lends to Local Authorities, was established under the National Debt and Local Loans Act, 1887, and placed under the control of the National Debt Commissioners. Before that date local loans had been financed in different ways—partly from Exchequer balances and partly from a variety of borrowings—and it was impossible to tell how the Central Government stood on its loan business with the Local Authorities. So Mr Goschen, who was responsible for the Act, proposed to 'take it entirely out of the Budget'. The new Fund was financed from the outset by a new security—3 per cent Local Loans Stock, which was irredeemable except at the option of the Government. Although the Treasury was responsible for the interest, the latter was covered by the Fund's receipts from the Local Authorities to whom loans were made and for this reason the Stock was never included in the National Debt. The Fund continued to be financed by the issue of such Stock—sometimes privately to the National Debt Commissioners, sometimes publicly—until 1931. Over most of the period ruling long-term rates of interest exceeded 3 per cent and most of the Stock was therefore issued at a discount. To cover the eventual possibility of redemption of the Stock at par, the rates of interest charged to borrowers from time to time included a margin calculated to make good the discounts in the prices of issue. The effect of these arrangements has been, shortly, to produce in the Fund a surplus of income which is capitalized annually and is gradually reducing the deficiency in the Fund's Balance Sheet due to the cash loans outstanding being less than the nominal amount of the Stock created.[1]

By the Finance Act, 1935, the Treasury received authority to finance the Fund by 'new Local Loans securities' on any other terms desired, instead of by 3 per cent Local Loans Stock. This authority was never, in fact, used and, during the Second World War the much restricted capital requirements of Local Authorities (mainly in connection with redemptions and conversions) were financed through Votes of Credit. The present method of financing the Local Loans Fund began after the war with the passing of the Local Authorities Loans Act, 1945, already referred to above, under Section 3 (1) of which the Fund has, since the end of 1946, been financed by direct issues from the Exchequer below-the-line. The Fund repays the Exchequer by terminable annuities on terms corresponding as closely as possible to those on which loans are currently made to Local Authorities. In view of these new arrangements the Government exercised its option in January 1947 to repay, at par, the whole amount (£429 million) of Local Loans Stock then outstanding. Under an old authority in the Finance Act, 1935, the redemption moneys were found by the Exchequer; but the Fund remains liable to repay those moneys to the Exchequer and, until it is in a position to do so, is paying interest on them to the Exchequer at $2\frac{1}{2}$ per cent per annum.

[1] For more details see the Foreword to the annual accounts of the Local Loans Fund.

The state of the Local Loans Fund is broadly as follows. On Income Account the interest received by the Board (rather over £100 million a year) on loans it has made normally exceeds by four or five millions the interest which the Fund has to pay on the Exchequer's advances. This surplus income is capitalized by being used for new loans. The Balance Sheet for March 31, 1957, showed liabilities to the Exchequer of £429 million for the redemption moneys of Local Loans Stock and of £2,808 million for advances since 1946; and assets of £3,178 for loans outstanding and cash and investments of £24 million; leaving a deficiency of £35 million. This deficiency was originally as much as £140 million, due to the discount on issues of Local Loans Stock; but it has been reduced to its present figure by successive capitalizations of surplus income and should continue to be steadily, if slowly, reduced year by year in the future.

APPENDIX F

BANK OF ENGLAND

AN ACCOUNT for the Week ending on Wednesday, the 16th day of July 1958.

ISSUE DEPARTMENT

			£				£
Notes Issued:				Government Debt	..	..	11,015,100
In Circulation	..	..	2,078,892,497	Other Government Securities	..	..	2,085,225,261
In Banking Department	..	..	21,468,402	Other Securities	..	..	747,814
				Coin other than Gold Coin	..	..	3,011,825
				Amount of Fiduciary Issue	..	..	£2,100,000,000
				Gold Coin and Bullion (at 250s 10d per oz. fine)	..		360,899
			£2,100,360,899				£2,100,360,899

Dated the 17th day of July 1958

L. K. O'BRIEN, *Chief Cashier*

BANKING DEPARTMENT

			£				£
Capital	..	..	14,553,000	Government Securities	..	..	258,499,550
Rest	..	..	3,666,805	Other Securities:			
Public Deposits (including Exchequer, Savings Banks, Commissioner of National Debt and Dividend Accounts)	..	..	10,718,459	Discount and Advances	..	12,695,000	
				Securities	..	18,950,481	31,645,481
Other Deposits:				Notes	..	..	21,468,401
Bankers	..	..	212,107,517	Coin	..	..	2,324,048
Other Accounts	..	..	72,891,700				
			284,999,217				
			£313,937,481				£313,937,481

Dated the 17th day of July 1958

L. K. O'BRIEN, *Chief Cashier*

APPENDIX G

Power of the Bank of England to make Advances to the Government

1. The Statute of 1694 (5 and 6 William and Mary, cap. 20), under which the Bank received its Charter from the Crown, imposed penalties on all Members of the Corporation who agreed to advance or lend to the Soveriegn, upon the account of the Corporation, any sum by way of loan or anticipation upon any Funds other than those Funds on which a Credit of Loan was granted by Parliament. This governed all advances made by the Bank down to 1819, such advances being mostly temporary loans secured on Exchequer Bills and expressly permitted by the Statutes authorizing the issue of the Bills.[1] The Act of 1694 was superseded by the Act of 1819 referred to below, but was not formally repealed until the Statute Law Revision Act of 1948.

2. The power of the Bank to make advances to the Government is still regulated by the Bank of England Act, 1819. The Act prohibits the Bank from advancing to the Sovereign 'any sum or sums of money whatever upon the credit of any Exchequer Bills or Treasury Bills [i.e. certain Irish Treasury Bills then in existence], or other Government securities, or in any other manner whatever, without the express and distinct authority of Parliament for that purpose first had and obtained'. But nothing in the Act was to extend to prevent the Bank from purchasing any Exchequer Bills or Treasury Bills or other Government Securities, which by law they were then authorized to purchase; and there was a similar saving for the quarterly 'Deficiency Advances' by the Bank.

Under the same Act, whenever application has to be made to the Bank for any advances authorized by Parliament, such application has to be made in writing by the First Lord of the Treasury or the Chancellor of the Exchequer; and copies of such applications with the answers thereto and the relevant Minutes of the Court of the Bank are to be laid annually before Parliament. An account showing the amounts of all Exchequer Bills, Treasury Bills, etc., purchased by the Bank, or upon which any sums have been advanced, was also to be laid before Parliament annually by the Bank; but, under the Currency and Bank Notes Act, 1928, the Bank is not required to include in this account the securities in the Issue Department. Papers are still laid before Parliament under both these heads, but are not printed.

3. Since the Act of 1819 specific authority has been given to the Bank to make advances in the following cases:

(a) *'Deficiency Advances'* to cover quarterly deficiencies of the Consolidated Fund under Section 12 of the Exchequer and Audit Departments

[1] See page 196.

Act, 1866. These are referred to on page 197; and, as there stated, this power was repealed by the Finance Act, 1954.

(b) *Ways and Means Advances* under the annual Consolidated Fund Acts and Appropriation Act. The provisions of these Acts are explained on pages 170 and 240–1; and the limited use of Bank Advances under these authorities is referred to on page 171. Correspondence relating to them is laid before Parliament each quarter under the provision of the Act of 1819 referred to above.

(c) The Bank are empowered to lend on the credit of *Exchequer Bills or Bonds* issued under the Exchequer Bills and Bonds Act, 1866. This Act merely authorized the machinery for issuing such Bills and Bonds; the actual issue of either security on any given occasion would require specific statutory authority. Although the Act is still in force it is not used. Exchequer Bills ceased to be issued, as already stated, in 1892. Exchequer Bonds were issued during and after the First World War, not under the Act of 1866 but under the the then operative War Loan Acts; one reason for this was the need in some cases to offer interest exceeding the maximum of $5\frac{1}{2}$ per cent permitted under the Act of 1866.

(d) The power of the Bank to lend on the credit of *Treasury Bills* is conferred by the Treasury Bills Act, 1877, and is referred to on page 194.

(e) When the Finance Act, 1932, authorized the Treasury to borrow any sums to be issued as capital to the *Exchange Equalization Account* it also authorized the Bank to advance any such sums. No use has been made of this authority: issues to the Account from the Exchequer have been financed out of the funds (including borrowed moneys) available for issues below-the-line generally.

4. When the Bank of England Act, 1946, transferred the ownership of the Capital Stock of the Bank to the Treasury, no change was made in any of the statutory provisions referred to above.

APPENDIX H

Estimate for the National Maritime Museum 1956-7

I. ESTIMATE of the amount required in the year ending March 31, 1957, for the salaries and expenses of the National Maritime Museum including a grant-in-aid.

Fifty-one thousand two hundred and ninety-four pounds
(£51,294)

II. Subheads under which this Vote will be accounted for by the Trustees of the National Maritime Museum.

	ESTIMATES		IN-CREASE	DE-CREASE
	1956–7	1955–6		
NATIONAL MARITIME MUSEUM ACT, 1934	£	£	£	£
A.—SALARIES, ETC	49,419	49,914	—	495
B.—TRAVELLING EXPENSES, ETC. ..	1,030	700	330	—
C.—PREPARATION AND CARE OF EX-HIBITS	550	550	—	—
D.—PURCHASES AND ACQUISITIONS (GRANTS-IN-AID)	380	380	—	—
GROSS TOTAL	51,379	51,544	330	495
Deduct—				
Z.—APPROPRIATIONS-IN-AID ..	85	152	67	—
NET TOTAL	51,294	15,392	397	495

NET DECREASE .. £98

Continued overleaf

III.	Details of the foregoing

NATIONAL MARITIME MUSEUM ACT, 1934 (24 & 25 GEO. 5, C. 43)

A.—SALARIES, ETC.

NUMBERS			ESTIMATES	
1955–6	1956–7		1956–7	1955–6
			£	£
1	1	Director .. .. (£1,650–1,925)	2,025	1,925
1	1	Deputy Director .. (£995–1,530)	1,270	1,206
3	3	Assistant Keepers	3,550	3,225
		[Here follow further details of numbers, grading and salary costs]		
74	75	TOTAL ..	49,419	49,914

B.—TRAVELLING EXPENSES, ETC.:

Travelling and subsistence allowances, etc. (£250); entertainment (£30); uniforms (£300); other miscellaneous expenses (£100); telephones, etc. (£350)	1,030	700

C.—PREPARATION AND CARE OF EXHIBITS:

(1) Restoration of paintings	350	350
(2) Binding, mounting, framing, labelling, etc. ..	100	100
(3) Workshop tools and materials, etc.	100	100
TOTAL ..	550	550

D.—PURCHASES AND ACQUISITIONS (GRANTS-IN-AID):

Expenditure out of this grant-in-aid will be accounted for in detail to the Comptroller and Auditor-General. Any balance of the sum issued which may remain unexpended at March 31, 1957, will not be liable to surrender to the Exchequer	380	380

Z.—APPROPRIATIONS-IN-AID:

Receipts from reproduction fees	60	108
Miscellaneous receipts	25	44
TOTAL ..	85	152

Notes: (*a*) Certain unimportant footnotes have been omitted.
   (*b*) The table of 'allied services' has also been omitted. This appears at the end of Part II and shows the amounts borne on other Votes for this service in respect of buildings, stationery and printing, superannuation, etc. (See text, page 226.)

APPENDIX I

Appropriation Account of the National Maritime Museum, 1956-7

ACCOUNT of the sum expended, in the year ended March 31, 1957, compared with the sum granted, for the salaries and expenses of the National Maritime Museum, including a grant-in-aid.

Service	Grant	Expenditure	Expenditure compared with Grant	
			Less than Granted	More than Granted
	£	£ s d	£ s d	£ s d
A.—Salaries, etc. *Original* .. £49,419 *Supplementary* .. £3,692	53,111	53,075 14 9	35 5 3	—
B.—Travelling Expenses, etc.	1,030	954 3 1	75 16 11	—
C.—Preparation and Care of Exhibits *Original* .. £550 *Less Supplementary* .. £117	433	422 1 3	10 18 9	—
D.—Purchase and Acquisitions (Grant-in-Aid)	380	380 0 0	—	—
GROSS TOTAL *Original* .. £51,379 *Supplementary* .. £3,575	54,954	54,831 19 1	122 0 11	—
	Estimated	Applied		
Deduct— Z.—Appropriations-in-Aid *Original* .. .. £85 *Supplementary* .. £36	121	121 0 0	—	—
NET TOTAL *Original* .. £51,294 *Supplementary* .. £3,539	54,833	54,710 19 1	Surplus to be surrendered £122 0 11	

Receipts payable to Exchequer	Estimated	Realized
	£	£ s d
Receipts authorized to be used as Appropriations-in-Aid	121	132 10 7
Appropriated-in-Aid (Subhead Z)		121 0 0
Payable separately to Exchequer		£11 10 7

EXPLANATION of the Causes of Variation between Expenditure and Grant

B.—Saving on travelling (£77), entertainment (£23) and telephones (£5) offset by increases on uniforms (£12) and miscellaneous expenses (£18).

GRANT-IN-AID ACCOUNT (PURCHASES AND ACQUISITIONS)

Receipts	£ s d	Payments	£ s d
Balance, April 1, 1956 ..	588 0 10	Purchases	713 12 8
Grant-in-Aid, 1956–7 (Sub-head D)	380 0 0	Balance, March 31, 1957	504 8 2
Donations	250 0 0		
	£1,218 0 10		£1,218 0 10

September 16, 1957

Frank G. G. Carr,
Accounting Officer

I have examined the foregoing Accounts in accordance with the provisions of the Exchequer and Audit Departments Act, 1921. I have obtained all the information and explanations that I have required, and I certify, as the result of my audit, that in my opinion these Accounts are correct.

F. N. Tribe,
Comptroller and Auditor-General

APPENDIX J

Supply Services—Grants and Issues

THE Finance Accounts for 1957–8 give a Statement of 'the Amount Issued from the Exchequer in the year ended March 31, 1958, for SUPPLY SERVICES: showing also the amounts of the several grants for those SERVICES (including the balance of grants for former years), the surplus balances written off in the year and the balances remaining unissued at the end of the year'.

This should be read in conjunction with the next Statement of 'the application of the Balances of the Grants of Ways and Means remaining unissued on April 1, 1957, and of the Grants for the year 1957–8'.

In summary form the facts recorded in the Statements were as follows:

	£ million	£ million
(*a*) Balance of former years' Grants unissued from the Exchequer at April 1, 1957		31
(*b*) Grants for 1957–8		4,554
(*c*) TOTAL GRANTS		4,585
(*d*) Issues during the year—		
In respect of 1956–7	3	
In respect of 1957–8	4,470	
		4,473
(*e*) Surplus balances written off during the year in respect of grants for 1956–7—		
Undrawn in 1956–7	28	
Issued in 1956–7 and adjusted in 1957–8 ..	27	
		55
(*f*) Balances of Grants unissued from the Exchequer at March 31, 1958 (that is (*c*) *less* (*d*) and *less* (*e*))		57

Note on some of the above items:

(*a*) Although this uses the phrase 'former years' grants', the balances relate to 1956–7. They are the amounts by which departments under-drew their votes for that year and which were awaiting settlement until the Appropriation Accounts of the year were completed and audited. (See Chapter XII, page 254.)

(*b*) The grants for 1957–8 are those voted in the Consolidated Fund and Appropriation Acts in respect of that year together with the Excess Votes passed during 1957–8 in respect of 1956–7 (amounting to £469,985 15s 0d).

(*d*) The issues made during the year 1957–8 in respect of 1956–7 were further issues of the kind under example (*b*) on page 255. The issues in respect of 1957–8 were in fact £27 million less than they would otherwise have been because that amount was thereby recovered from departments in respect of over-issues in 1956–7. (See examples (a) and (c) in the text, pages 255–6.)

(e) The balances written off are those for 1956–7 of which £28 million had been undrawn by departments, and £27 million drawn but not needed. The total of £55 million was finally surrendered by them during 1957–8 when the Appropriation Accounts for 1956–7 were completed and audited.

(f) These balances related entirely to grants for 1957–8. It will be seen that the balances of £31 million brought forward from 1956–7 under (a) above had been entirely disposed of—as to £3 million by being issued in 1957–8 under (d) and as to £28 million by being written off (that is, surrendered) under (e).

APPENDIX K

List of Funds and Accounts

OF which annual statements are presented to Parliament or published as non-parliamentary publications (excluding the Appropriation Accounts and accounts appended thereto).

Agricultural Land Commission Accounts
American Aid and European Payments Accounts
Atomic Energy Act, 1954, Balance Sheet
Bankruptcy and Companies (Winding Up) Proceedings Account
British Phosphate Commission Report and Account
Royal Hospital Chelsea Accounts
Cinematograph Film Production (Special Loans) Acts, 1949–54, Account
Cinematograph Fund
Civil Contingencies Fund
Coal Industry Nationalization Act, 1946, Account
Consolidated Fund Abstract Account
Cotton (Centralized Buying) Act, 1947, Account
County Courts Fund
Crown Estates Account
Czechoslovak Refugee Fund Account
Development Fund
Development of Inventions Acts, 1948 and 1954, Account
Distribution of German Enemy Property Acts, 1949 and 1952, Account
Finance Accounts[1]
Finance Act, 1934, Account[1] [guarantees of certain foreign loans]
Foreign Compensation Act, 1950, Accounts
General Lighthouse Fund Accounts
Greek Loan of 1898 Account
Greenwich Hospital Accounts
Herring Industry Acts, 1935–53, Accounts
Receipts and Expenditure of the High Court and Court of Appeal Account
Hospital Endowments Fund Account
House of Commons Members' Pension Fund
Housing Act, 1914, Account
Housing (Temporary Accommodation) Act, 1944, Account
Industrial Organization and Development Act, 1947:
    Lace Furnishings Industry (Export Promotion Levy) Account
    Lace Industry (Levy) Account
    Wool Textile Industry (Export Promotion Levy) Account
    Wool Textile Industry (Scientific Research Levy) Account
Irish Land Purchase Fund
Irish Sailors and Soldiers Land Trust Accounts

[1] Not audited by the Comptroller and Auditor-General.

Iron and Steel Realization Account
Japanese Treaty of Peace Act, 1951, Account
Land Purchase Account
Legal Aid and Advice Act, 1949, Account
Legal Aid (Scotland) Act, 1949, Account
Local Loans Fund
Malta (Reconstruction) Act, 1947, Account
Marshall Aid Commemoration Commission Account
Mineral Workings Act, 1951, Account (Ironstone Restoration Fund)
Miscellaneous Financial Provisions Act, 1955, Account
National Debt Reduction Funds
National Debt Return[1]
National Health Service Acts, 1946–52:
  Accounts of Regional Hospital Boards, Executive Councils, Hospital
    Management Committees and Boards of Governors of Teaching
    Hospitals
  Ditto for Scotland
National Insurance Acts, 1946–55, Accounts:
  National Insurance Fund
  National Insurance (Reserve) Fund
  Industrial Injuries Fund
  National Insurance (Existing Pensioners) Fund
National Land Fund
Navy Dockyard and Production Accounts
Overseas Resources Development Act, 1948–56
Post Office Commercial Accounts
Post Office Savings Bank Account[1] [deposits received and paid and
  balance due to depositors]
Public Income and Expenditure Account
Royal Air Force Prize Fund Account
Royal Navy Prize Fund Account
Savings Banks Funds Account [disposal of interest received on in-
  vestments]
Sugar Industry (Research and Education) Fund Account
Supreme Court of Judicature Accounts
Television Act, 1954, Account
Tithe Redemption Annuities Account
Town and Country Planning Act, 1954, and Scotalnd Act, Accounts
Town and Country Planning (The Planning Payments (War Damage)
  Schemes, 1949) Account
Trade Facilities Acts, 1921–6, Account[1]
Trading Accounts (one volume)
Transport Fund Account
Treasury Chest Fund [wound up on March 31, 1958]
Trustee Savings Banks Account[1] [deposits in Ordinary Departments in-
  vested with National Debt Commissioners]

[1] Not audited by the Comptroller and Auditor-General.

War Damage (Business and Private Chattels Schemes) Account
War Damage (Land and Buildings) Account
Wheat Fund Account
White Fish Authority Account

APPENDIX L

Proceedings, in Chronological Order, on the Vote for Ministry of Food, 1954-7

February 23, 1954. *Original Estimate* for Ministry of Food presented (Class VIII, Vote 10). Its total of £255·9 million included (Subhead I.1) £38·7 million for payments under guarantees of prices of home-grown cereals. It also included appropriations-in-aid of £69,500.

February 23, 1954. *Estimate for Civil Vote on Account* for 1954–5 presented, which included £50 million on account for the Ministry of Food. (This Estimate went through its own separate stages until Ways and Means to cover the money voted on account was made available by the Consolidated Fund Act, 1954.)

March 31, 1954. *Revised Estimate* for Ministry of Food presented, to take account of the results of the 1954 Farm Price Review. They enabled the total Estimate to be reduced to £228·6 million; but the provisions for home-grown cereals and appropriations-in-aid remained unchanged.

June 3, 1954. In *Committee of Supply* a general debate on Agriculture took place. The formal basis for this was a resolution proposing a further (token) sum of £10 on each of the Agricultural Estimates and on that for the Ministry of Food. The debate was adjourned and the resolution lapsed.

July 22, 1954. *Committee of Supply* voted (under the guillotine, with many other items) £178·6 million for the Ministry of Food, that is, £228·6 million (the Revised Estimate) less the £50 million already provided on account.

July 22, 1954. *Committee of Ways and Means* voted Ways and Means covering the Supply voted that day.

July 26, 1954. *House* (on Report) agreed to the Supply and Ways and Means voted in Committee on July 22nd.

July 30, 1954. *Appropriation Act*, 1954, received Royal Assent. It included, in Schedule B (Part 16) £228·6 million for the Ministry of Food, together with the appropriations-in-aid (£69,500).

February 7, 1955. *Supplementary Estimate* for token £10 presented. Extra gross expenditure of £18·5 million on some subheads was offset by savings on others (including savings of £13·2 million on cereals) and by an increase of about £0·5 million in appropriations-in-aid.

March 16, 1955. *Committee of Supply* voted the Supplementary £10 (under the guillotine) and *Committee of Ways and Means* voted the corresponding Ways and Means.

March 17, 1955. *House* (on Report) agreed to the Supply (under the guillotine) and Ways and Means voted in Committee on previous day.

March 29, 1955. *Consolidated Fund Act*, 1955, received Royal Assent making the Supplementary vote available.

May 6, 1955.[1] *Appropriation Act*, 1955, received Royal Assent. It included, in Schedule B (Part 2), the Supplementary £10 and authorized the additional Appropriations-in-aid (£492,990).

February 1955. *Appropriation Account* published, with the *Comptroller and Auditor-General's Report* thereon. The Report included comments on the arrangements for verifying claims to payments in respect of home-grown cereals.

May 10, 1956. *The Public Accounts Committee* of Session 1955–6 took evidence on the subject. (The Accounting Officer, being ill, was represented by his Deputy.)

July 26, 1956. (*Sixth*) *Report of the Public Accounts Committee* presented, which included their comments on the subject.

January 31, 1957. *Treasury Minute* drawn up, which contained observations on the Committee's Report. (This Minute was published with the First Report of the Committee of Session 1956–7 on February 7, 1957.)

March 7, 1957. The *Public Accounts Committee* of Session 1956–7 took evidence from the Accounting Officer and Treasury representatives on the Treasury Minute.

July 25, 1957. The Committee presented their (Third) Report, but made no further comments on the subject of home-grown cereals.

[1] This Act was passed at an abnormally early date in order that all Supply should be appropriated before the impending General Election.

APPENDIX M

Parliamentary and Non-Parliamentary Papers

VERY broadly the difference between these two classes of publications is as follows. 'Parliamentary' papers are those which are prepared primarily for the use of Members of both Houses in carrying out their duties. They include most 'Act' papers (that is, papers—such as the accounts of particular Funds—which are required by statute to be laid before Parliament and which are published as House of Commons Papers); Command Papers (which are presented at the discretion of Ministers and include, e.g., statemnts of Government policy, reports on the activities of Government departments, and information on particular subjects asked for, or promised, in Parliament); and Acts of Parliament. All other publications of the Stationery Office—in fact the great majority—are 'non-parliamentary' publications. They include 'Act' papers of less general interest, reports of departmental committees, and papers of a technical or advisory character issued by departments as much for the use of the general public as for that of Members of either House.

INDEX